French Colonialism Unmasked

France Overseas:
Studies in Empire
and Decolonization

SERIES EDITORS

Philip Boucher

A. J. B. Johnston

James D. Le Sueur

Tyler Stovall

RUTH GINIO

French Colonialism Unmasked

The Vichy Years in French West Africa

University of Nebraska Press
Lincoln and London

Library of Congress
Cataloging-in-Publication Data
Ginio, Ruth, 1966–
French colonialism unmasked: the
Vichy years in French West Africa
/ Ruth Ginio.
p.   cm.—(France overseas)
Includes bibliographical
references and index.
ISBN-13: 978-0-8032-2212-0
(cloth: alk. paper)
ISBN-10: 0-8032-2212-2
(cloth: alk. paper)
1. Africa, French-speaking West—
History—1884–1960. 2. Africa,
French-speaking West—Colonial
influence. 3. World War, 1939–
1945—Africa, French-speaking
West. I. Title. II. Series.
DT532.5.G56   2006
966'.0097541—dc22
2005017224

In loving memory of my mother, Aviva Lipstein,
who was persecuted by the Vichy regime and saved
by noble-hearted French men and women

Contents

Illustrations

Map

Photographs

Tables

Acknowledgments

This book is the culmination of a long research project that started as a Ph.D. dissertation presented to the Hebrew University of Jerusalem. It all began in a conversation I had with Michel Abitbol, my advisor, who understood my deep and personal interest in the Vichy period and suggested that I dedicate my thesis to this period in French West Africa, which was fascinating but emotionally easier than delving into wartime Europe. During the years in which I wrote my dissertation and later, when he was no longer formally responsible for my work, Michel never ceased to provide professional guidance and practical help and advice. He read every chapter promptly but carefully, and although he was occupied with many other responsibilities and duties at the time, he always had time to resolve an unexpected difficulty. I wish to thank him with all my heart for his patience, his caring, and most of all his trust and encouragement. I would also like to thank the members of my dissertation committee, Naomi Chazan, Richard I. Cohen, and Robert Wistrich, for their useful advice. To Naomi I owe special thanks for teaching me some basic rules of academic writing and for "inflicting" on me her love for Africa.

The Harry S. Truman Research Institute for the Advancement of Peace provided me with an intellectually and socially vibrant environment, first as a Ph.D. candidate and later as a Research Fellow. The corridor conversations I had with some of my colleagues and friends there often proved very useful, as well as pleasant, and opened my mind in new directions. Efrat Ben Ze'ev never ceased to encourage me to think further about every statement I made, Louise Bethlehem opened up for me a whole new world of academic thinking, with Lynn Schler I could always discuss African history, and Asher Kaufman shared with me his perspective on French colonialism in Lebanon. I would like to thank the former director Amnon Cohen and the present one, Eyal Ben-Ari, for their encouragement and, no less important, for the institute's invaluable financial assistance over the years. The research scholarships I received from the institute during the preparation of my thesis, particularly the Young Truman Scholar post-doctoral fellowship, allowed me to dedicate most of my time to research and travel to archives abroad. A special grant from the Truman Institute's publications committee enabled me to complete the process of turning my dissertation into a book. Also from the Truman Institute, I would like to thank my friend and English editor, Lisa Perlman, who is probably a

Vichy-in-FWA expert by now. Her sharp eye and professional skills helped cover the weaknesses of a text written by a nonnative English speaker. Tirza Margalioth and the library staff at the institute were friendly and helpful in ordering microfilms and journals.

I would like to thank the heads of the Institute for Asian and African Studies at the Hebrew University, Reuven Amitai, Steven Kaplan, and Arye Levin, who offered me a place to teach and work, as well as financial support. I received additional help from a Centre Désmarais de recherche sur la culture française research award, a Hebrew University scholarship for fieldwork in Senegal, and a French government scholarship for research in France.

The members of the Department of Middle Eastern and African History at Tel-Aviv University, Yekutiel Gershoni, Mordechai Tamarkin, Galia Sabar, and Irit Back, invited me to present my research, offered interesting insights, and made me feel at home.

During my research in France and Senegal and a postdoctoral year in England, many people, some of whom became good friends, assisted me in many ways. In France the cheerful and professional staff of the Centre des archives d'outre-mer in Aix-en-Provence were always helpful. In these archives I also met Eric Jennings, with whom I had the pleasure to work and collaborate, and although we did not have many chances to meet personally in later years, our common interest in French colonialism and our frequent e-mails reinforced our friendship. Marc Michel and Charles-Robert Ageron provided useful tips when I embarked on my research in Paris and Aix. I would also like to thank Catherine Atlan, now a close friend, for her hospitality and the help she was prepared to offer me through her great knowledge of Senegal and her personal acquaintances there.

In Senegal the director of the Archives nationales du Sénégal, Saliou M'baye, gave me guidance and excellent advice, and Mamadou N'diaye responded to my endless requests for documents during the difficult days of the Ramadan fast. At Cheick Anta Diop University in Dakar Ousseynou Faye from the Department of History provided invaluable help in arranging interviews and supplied me with an enthusiastic research assistant from the Department of English, Saliou Dione. The staff of the Israeli embassy in Dakar, especially Ambassador Doron Grossman and Noa Furman, were most helpful in providing contacts. Noa's hospitality made my first encounter with this city smooth, pleasant, and friendly.

In England Richard Rathbone, my host at the School of Oriental and African Studies in London, deserves my special thanks for reading drafts and encouraging me to publish this book, even stating that he needed it desperately for his course. Tony Chafer, from Portsmouth University, invited me to present my research in his department, where I benefited from helpful comments. Martin Thomas provided useful advice. In Oxford I was happy to make the acquaintance of Owen White and to exchange ideas about France and Africa.

I would also like to thank Myron Echenberg for his interest in my research since its embryonic stages and his willingness to help in any possible way.

I presented parts of this research at the meetings of the French Colonial Historical Society, where I found a second home. The pleasant intellectual yet friendly atmosphere that reigns at these meetings and the constructive comments I received encouraged me and eventually led to the publication of this book. At the Yale meeting in 2002 I had the pleasure and honor of meeting the late William B. Cohen; indeed, it was he who suggested that I publish this book in a special series he was planning with James Le Sueur. His warm encouragement and suggestions for improvement gave me the necessary energy to complete this project.

At the University of Nebraska Press I owe special thanks to Elizabeth Demers, who guided me patiently through the complex process of publishing a book; to the series editors; to my project editor, Joeth Zucco; to Terence Smyre; and to the anonymous readers whose comments contributed to the improvement of the original text. I would also like to thank Carol Sickman-Garner, the press-assigned copy editor, who painstakingly and prudently polished the final text of the manuscript.

Finally, on a more personal note, I would like to thank my parents. My late mother, Aviva, to whom this book is dedicated, always believed in me and shaped my optimistic view of life. Her love for France—in spite of the Vichy shadow—inspired me to learn its beautiful language and study its fascinating history. My father, Zwi, who has promised to stick around at least until the book is out, passed on to me his love for history and made sure I did not become a lawyer like him—for this I am grateful.

I would also like to thank my parents-in-law, Alisa and Gabriel Ginio, who supported me and never tired of hearing about Vichy and Africa. Alisa, who is well acquainted with the special difficulties of being a mother and an academic, never ceased to encourage me to pursue my research and always lent a sympathetic ear when needed.

And last but certainly not least I would like to thank my children—my son, Nitai, who was born when I began to write my dissertation, and my daughter, Ophir, who was born shortly after I submitted it. They were both patient and understanding about the long hours I spent in front of the computer and my travels around the world. Their smiling faces helped me overcome all the obstacles and complications in the process of writing. Eyal, my husband, best friend, and best critic ever, read innumerable drafts of this book and provided me with his endless academic knowledge and a loving companionship without which this book would have never been written.

When the news of Germany's conquest of France in June 1940 reached Dakar, the capital of the federation of French West Africa (FWA), many Africans, especially from the Western-educated elite, shed tears. Decades later Bara Diouf, then a young boy of eleven, tried to explain this reaction, which in retrospect seemed to him rather ridiculous: "You know, the sentiment we felt for France was beautiful, noble. What was it based on? I do not know, perhaps on a myth. Because we were all, more or less, prisoners of a myth of an admired republican France toward which we all felt great esteem."[1]

The explanation Diouf gave for the African elite's response to the news from France well summarizes the essence of the Vichy period in FWA. Soon after the debacle this federation fell into Vichy hands when, after he declared his support for Vichy, the new regime appointed Pierre Boisson as its governor-general there; until then Boisson had served as governor-general of the smaller and much less significant federation of French Equatorial Africa (FEA).

World War II in general and Vichy rule specifically shattered many myths for Africans, as well as for colonial subjects in other parts of the empire. This period paved the way for the challenging of colonial rule and the subsequent dissolution of the European empires in Africa and Asia.

It is widely accepted that World War II was a watershed in the decolonization process in Africa and elsewhere. But was this related only to the colonial powers' loss of prestige or to the dramatic changes in the international arena after the war—notably the rise of two new powers, which were, at least in their rhetoric, anticolonial? To establish the claim that World War II was a decisive point in the history of colonialism, this period in the colonies themselves must be examined. In the French case the division of the empire between the Vichy regime and the Free French had a special significance. Although the British, like the French, experienced humiliating defeats during the war, some from non-Western peoples (e.g., the Japanese in Burma), their wartime situation did not even come close to that of the rival colonial power, France. Britain did not surrender to Germany, and its territory, although threatened, remained free. The colonial subjects of France witnessed their ruling nation being humiliatingly defeated and then occupied by another European power. And that was not all. Out of this defeat two Frances emerged—each claiming to be the

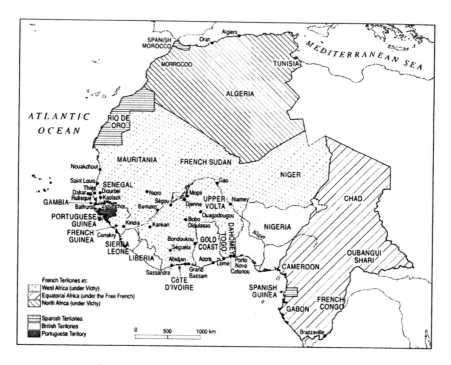

Northwestern Africa (1940–42). Designer: Tamar Soffer.

"true" France, and both appealing to colonial subjects for their loyalty and trying to prove their legitimacy. In "normal" colonial circumstances no empire had ever pleaded for its subjects' loyalty, and legitimacy was quite irrelevant. Now, suddenly, France's colonial subjects were no longer taken for granted.

But it was not only weakness and the colonial power's loss of prestige that made the Vichy period important in the history of FWA. It was also the nature of the regime and its colonial policy. The complex and sometimes ambivalent encounter between the Vichy government and the African population of FWA had significant repercussions for this territory after the war.

Only a decade ago the story of Vichy in the empire was still virtually untold. Eric Jennings filled this lacuna with regard to three regions of the empire: Guadeloupe, Madagascar, and Indochina.[2] Jacques Cantier addressed the Vichy regime in Algeria, Christine Levisse-Touzé wrote about World War II in French North Africa in general, and Catherine Akpo wrote about World War II in FWA.[3] While Akpo's book gives a basis for the study of the Vichy experience in the region by presenting the major political processes during the war, it does not provide a full picture of the Vichy years in FWA. Vital aspects such as Vichy economic visions and policies are not included, and the examination of the Vichy encounter with African society is based too extensively on metropolitan notions of "collaboration" and "resistance" that are, in my view, irrelevant in the African context. Since Akpo examines the Vichy period as part of the history of the region from 1939 to late 1945, its special significance cannot be fully appreciated. Finally, the events in FWA are not explored in the context of the reality in France, and thus an artificial separation between the history of France and that of its colonies is created.[4]

The idea that France's colonial history should be fused with its metropolitan history has been developed in recent years. The social and political problems that France faces today with regard to its vast population of immigrants, most hailing from its ex-colonies, emphasize the necessity of viewing colonial and metropolitan history as one research area. The story of the Vichy period in the colonies in general, and in FWA specifically, proves the impossibility and futileness of separating these "two" histories. On the one hand Vichy colonial policy in FWA cannot be understood without relating it to the nature of this regime in France. Moreover, the striking resemblance of some aspects of Vichy ideology to colonial ideas and policies that existed in FWA well before Vichy presents the colonial arena as an experimental ground for ideologies that could not have flourished in republican France and thus might point to the existence of "Vichy before Vichy" in the colonies. On the other hand the Vichy period in France cannot be completely understood without examining the colonial facet of this regime. Although some political leaders of the Third Republic, notably Jules Ferry, France's prime minister in the years 1880–81 and 1883–85, were certainly empire-minded, it was the Vichy government, more than any earlier French regime, that embraced the empire and treated it as part of France. Its colonial visions and policies are a vital element in the study of this period that still haunts French collective memory.

This book focuses on three dramatic years in the history of FWA, years in which the Vichy regime tried to impose the ideology of the National Revolution in the region. The Vichy period in FWA came to its official end following the signing of the Boisson-Eisenhower agreements on 7 December 1942, by which time Boisson had agreed to cooperate with the Americans but not with Free French leader Charles De Gaulle.[5] Nevertheless, I have chosen to define the end of the Vichy period as the departure of Boisson from FWA on 7 July 1943, which left the territory in the hands of the Free French forces. The importance of the Vichy period, rather than the entire war period, is further reinforced by the testimony of Africans who lived in FWA at the time and attribute all the hardships and traumatic

events of the war, including those that occurred in the Gaullist era, to
Vichy. In the memory of these Africans all that was evil was Vichy, and
the end of the war did, in fact, mark the end of Vichy rule in FWA.

My aim is to examine in depth Vichy colonial visions and practices in
FWA and to present a narrative of the intriguing encounters between this
colonial regime and African society and the responses of different sectors
of the African population to Vichy policy. Examining the nature of the
Vichy colonial regime in FWA and the way it was perceived by Africans,
and relating this to the various political processes of the postwar era, will
both enhance our understanding of the significance of the Vichy period
in FWA to the colonial history of this part of the French empire and point
to the specific elements of this period that made it a watershed.

The examination of this short yet eventful period in FWA has additional
relevance, related to the republican myth with which I opened. The republican ideals of Liberty, Equality, and Fraternity, and the theory of
assimilation that stemmed from these notions, made French colonialism
appealing for those Africans who belonged to the Western-educated elite.
Some of them held French citizenship and therefore were not exposed
to the injustices and repression of colonial rule. Those who were not
citizens still felt themselves privileged and believed that France wished
to assimilate them and that eventually they too might become French
citizens. Before the change of regime in France there was already a certain
disturbing contradiction between the essence of the republican ideology
and the practice of colonialism. Alice Conklin shows how the colonial
administration in FWA constantly and unsuccessfully tried to resolve this
contradiction.[6] The establishment of the Vichy regime in France put an
end to this impossible burden. The colonial administrators could now
implement a policy that coincided perfectly with the official ideology
of the "new" France. The members of the Western-educated elite saw
the shift from republican assimilationist discourse as an exposure of the
"true" nature of French colonialism. The fall of this ostensible "republican mask" from the face of French colonialism turned the Vichy period
into an excellent prism through which the entire colonial history of the
region, until World War II, can be viewed with great clarity.

Although this book focuses on one region within the French empire, it
also has relevance to French colonial history in general. FWA is, in fact,
the last region of the French empire in which the Vichy years have not
yet been deeply studied. This book thus provides the missing pieces in
the jigsaw puzzle of Vichy in the empire. A comparison of the findings of
the present investigation with those of studies on other parts of the Vichy

empire will contribute to a fuller understanding of the colonial facet of the Vichy regime.

This study is based on archival documents from the Archive nationales in Paris, the Centre des archives d'outre-mer in Aix-en-Provence, and the archives of FWA in the Archives nationales du Sénégal, Dakar, as well as newspapers from France and West Africa, intercepted letters, memoirs written by Africans after the war, and contemporary interviews conducted in Senegal.

The oral sources used here represent only a small fragment of the primary material on which this study is based; nevertheless, their contribution to our understanding of the significance for Africans of the Vichy period in FWA is important. During a relatively short period of time I managed to talk with ten Africans (all males) who resided in Senegal during World War II. Most of them lived in Dakar and therefore could only reflect on the urban experiences of the period. Most were also Western educated. Only one lived in a rural area, and two did not study in the colonial educational system, while one other served in the colonial army. The interviews, then, mainly provide a glimpse into the experience of urban, Western-educated African men. Although I realize that these interviews do not offer a vast picture of African experiences under Vichy, and that wide conclusions about the African "side of the picture" cannot be drawn from them, I believe that the insights they offer are invaluable and can make the story of FWA under Vichy more vivid. Such oral information also emphasizes the need for scholars to be critical about some of the information found in written documents, especially those produced by colonial officials. Colonial documents usually tend to focus only on radical responses, revolts, or actions that endangered colonial stability, such as migration to British colonies, smuggling, or espionage. A whole range of possible reactions and strategies of survival thus remains shrouded. The use of oral sources, even if limited, can contribute to exposing Africans' feelings about and reactions to the Vichy regime. A better understanding of the colonized is vital if we wish to evaluate the weight of the Vichy episode in the postwar political developments in FWA.[7]

French Colonialism Unmasked comprises four parts. The first presents the political and social circumstances of FWA on the eve of World War II, focusing on the reforms of the Popular Front government, which made the Vichy blow even harder. This section includes a discussion of the role of FWA in particular and the French empire in general in metropolitan Vichy ideology.

The second part discusses the implementation of the Vichy ideology—

the National Revolution—in FWA. It examines three aspects of this implementation: political—the administrative changes introduced in FWA and
the acts of repression against potential real or imagined enemies of the
new regime; social—the attempts of Vichy colonial authorities to rally
African society to the National Revolution using propaganda, education,
and social organizations; and economic—the visions of the Vichy colonial
regime, such as the revival of the presumptuous Trans-Saharan railway
project, as well as policies regarding the use of forced labor, industrialization, and European agricultural settlement.

The book's third part depicts encounters between the Vichy regime
and different sectors of African society and the diversified responses of
Africans to the Vichy regime. The first chapter here discusses various
African groups that the colonial regime saw as "products" of assimilation: the *originaires* of the four communes, who held French citizenship; the Western-educated Africans referred to as *évolués*; and Africans
converted to Christianity. The second chapter addresses three segments
that the colonial regime saw as "traditional" in their orientation: real
and "invented" chiefs; leaders of the maraboutic Muslim orders; and
soldiers, who in spite of being a clear product of colonial rule were mostly
Muslim and rural and therefore seen as traditional elements. Within the
framework of these two chapters the various responses of Africans from
different sectors to Vichy policy are discussed, without falling into the
dichotomy of "resistance" and "collaboration." There is an emphasis
throughout on a wide range of African responses that were usually nonviolent, subtle, and cultural.

Finally, the fourth part places this study in a wider perspective. Its
first chapter compares the Vichy impact on FWA to other parts of the
empire, while considering the differences among various colonial realities.
The last chapter explores the impact of the Vichy period on the political
processes in FWA during the postwar years, revealing the ways in which
African politicians used Vichy in their dialogue with the colonial power
to attain their political goals, now reshaped following the shattering of
the myth of republican France.

French Colonialism Unmasked

PART I

French West Africa and Its Place in the Vichy Colonial Idea

On 25 June 1940, immediately after signing the armistice with Germany, the new leader of France, Marshal Henri Philippe Pétain, made a speech to the nation in which he referred to the French empire: "I was no less concerned about our colonies than about metropolitan France. The armistice maintains the bonds that unite us with them. France has the right to rely upon their loyalty."[1]

Pétain made it clear that he had fought to keep the French empire intact during the negotiations over the armistice, and indeed Vichy France was allowed to keep its colonies so long as they remained neutral and the armies stationed in them were reduced in size. Within the empire the African colonies—geographically the closest to Europe—had special significance for a regime that now controlled only one-third of its metropolitan territory, the Germans having taken over the remainder. The following chapters address the circumstances in the federation of FWA on the eve of World War II and the Vichy period and the special place this federation and the entire French empire had in Vichy discourse.

1.

Setting the Stage for Vichy

French West Africa on the Eve of World War II

The federation of FWA was officially established in 1895. However, French presence and some form of governance, at least in certain regions, had existed since the seventeenth century. The federation was composed of seven territories—Senegal, Côte d'Ivoire, Niger, Dahomey (now Benin), French Sudan (now Mali), French Guinea, and Mauritania—as well as one territory under French mandate since it was wrested from German control during World War I—Togo. The overall territory of the federation was 4,700,000 square kilometers, and on the eve of World War II its population stood at over fifteen million, including many diverse ethnic groups.[1] A governor-general ruled the federation from its capital, Dakar, assisted by a secretary-general; a cabinet director; and a director of political, administrative, and social affairs. The governor-general was also directly responsible for the governor of each territory, and these governors in turn ruled with the aid of a colonial council.[2] Under the governor a highly hierarchical system was created, beginning with the *commandant de cercle* and ending with the village chief—usually an African appointed by the French. Although the French colonial method of governing clearly favored direct rule down to the lowest level, in some areas, based on administrative and economic considerations, the precolonial ruler was kept in place, though he was divested of most of his power. An example is the Mossi kingdom in Upper Volta, which remained under the rule of its king, the Moro Naba.[3]

The establishment of the federation marked the transition from military to civilian rule, although military officials continued to govern problematic areas such as Niger and Mauritania.[4] The first region in FWA that was exposed to French influence already in the seventeenth century was the coast of Senegal. The towns Dakar, Rufisque, Gorée, and Saint Louis became in 1848 an experimental ground for the theory of assimilation, and their inhabitants, referred to as *originaires*, were granted the right to send a representative to the National Assembly in Paris. Until 1914 all the candidates for the National Assembly, the city councils, and the colonial council were either French or *métis*. In 1914, however, Blaise Diagne became the first African to be sent to the French parliament.[5] At this time Africans also began to form their own political parties in Senegal.[6]

This political activity among the colonized was rare in the French empire and had no equivalent in other colonial systems either. However, it is important to bear in mind that the *originaires* represented only a tiny portion of the Africans of FWA. The rest of this vast population was under harsh colonial rule and subjected to forced labor and to the *indigénat*, a legal system that enabled any French official to inflict limited punishments on Africans without trying them (see chapter 3). Most Africans were considered subjects (*sujets*) and had no political rights whatsoever.

Before examining the political situation in FWA, it is important to consider the period that preceded the war and that brought certain winds of change to French colonial rule in FWA—namely, the period of the Popular Front.

The 1936 electoral victory of the Popular Front in France raised hopes for improvements in the empire, as two of the parties of which it was composed, the Communist and the Socialist, were anticolonial in their views.[7] However, it soon became apparent that the Popular Front had no coherent colonial program. Colonial affairs did not interest the French public and therefore remained marginalized. The new minister of the colonies, Marius Moutet, had claimed to support autonomy and eventual self-governance for the colonies, but once in power he stopped referring to these notions. Instead, he firmly upheld the principle of the civilizing mission.[8] In fact, the Popular Front government had come to power in a context in which colonialism was universally accepted, with the exception of a very small minority on the radical Left. Therefore, it could not have been anticolonial. Nevertheless, its proclaimed aim was to establish a maximum of social justice within the context of colonialism. While in Algeria, due to settlers' opposition, this remained mainly rhetoric, in FWA some reforms were indeed implemented.[9]

The first step the Popular Front government took was to establish research commissions to study economic and social conditions in the colonies. In the economic sphere Moutet did not believe in grand-scale projects such as port and railway construction.[10] He specifically objected to the agricultural project of the Office du Niger as being expensive, inefficient, and having negative repercussions in French Sudan.[11] He was also opposed to its despotic management and use of forced labor. He was in favor of reducing taxes, downsizing the colonial administration, and encouraging local production. He also curtailed the power of trading companies, whose activities crippled local economies.[12]

The newly appointed governor-general of FWA, Marcel De Coppet, had a radically different approach to colonial rule than his predecessors. He had served in Africa for over thirty years and seemed to be motivated by a genuine commitment to social justice. One of his greatest achievements was the formation of the Inspection du travail—an organ that was to examine work conditions in both the public and the private sectors and to regulate labor recruitment.[13] The most dramatic measure the Popular Front's government took was the 1936 promulgation of a law authorizing trade unions. As a result FWA became the only territory on the continent to allow Africans to join a union (trade union rights were not extended to FEA). By the end of 1937 there were in Dakar nearly eight thousand union members grouped into forty-two trade unions and sixteen professional associations. Following a wave of strikes the colonial government published social decrees implementing an eight-hour working day in Senegal and a nine-hour day in the rest of FWA and covering such issues as accidents at work and the working conditions of women and children.[14] De Coppet's "soft" response to the strikers' demands was soon criticized in the French press, and the 1938 railway strike in Thiès (Senegal), which was severely repressed, led to the end of his colonial career in FWA. He was fired by Minister of the Colonies George Mandel, who had replaced Moutet.[15] De Coppet's removal put an end to the wave of strikes. The benefits won by these strikes soon disappeared because of the rise in prices of imported products and the devaluation of the franc.[16]

The reforms of the Popular Front were limited and only affected some of the colonies in the federation, mainly Senegal, Côte d'Ivoire, and Dahomey. The most impressive reform, the authorization of trade unions, had its own limitations. To join a union one had to be literate in French, and Africans living outside the four communes had to present a school diploma. People who had been imprisoned for more than a month could not join a union. In addition to these limitations, union heads had to present a yearly report on their activities to the colonial authorities.[17] Nevertheless, in the context of prewar colonialism these were not reforms to be easily dismissed. Some scholars even present them as a prelude to the postwar decolonization process and to the reforms formulated at the Brazzaville congress in 1944.[18] But, of course, something happened between the end of the Popular Front in 1938 and the Brazzaville congress six years later. World War II and the political upheavals it spawned in FWA created a bridge between an era of high hopes for massive colonial reforms and the beginning of an unconscious decolonization process. It is possible, though, that the hopes raised by the Popular Front, while not completely fulfilled, made the period of the war, especially the Vichy years, look even more thorny and repressive.

By the time World War II had broken out, all of the Popular Front's reforms had been abolished, including the right to organize in trade unions. The federation entered an emergency situation, and the French began a program of massive compulsory recruitment to the army. The African leadership usually assisted the colonial administration in this recruitment. Between September 1939 and June 1940 around one hundred thousand Africans enlisted to fight the Germans.[19]

At the outset of the war France and Britain decided on tight cooperation all over the world. This cooperation was clearly seen in FWA.[20] For the combating parties in Europe Sub-Saharan French Africa was strategically important for two reasons, apart from the human and material resources it provided. First, the port of Dakar was the largest French harbor after Marseille and Le Havre. Second, Niger and Chad (in FEA) had common boundaries with the Italian colony of Libya (Tripolitania), and Chad also allowed access to Anglo-Egyptian Sudan and the British colonies in East Africa.[21]

With France's defeat by Germany in June 1940 the colonial administration in FWA, like those in other parts of the French empire, found itself in a quandary. The colonial administrators had to decide whether to answer the Free French leader Charles De Gaulle's call in his 18 June speech from London to continue the struggle against Germany from the land of the empire or to accept the authority of Marshal Pétain—the legitimate leader of France. It is important to bear in mind that while Pétain's credentials as the hero of Verdun were extremely strong, De Gaulle at that time was a relatively unknown and marginal figure. During that June, when events in the *métropole* were not yet clear, the tendency of most administrators was to continue the war as a united African body, with FEA. But when Marshal Pétain declared his intention to sign an armistice with Germany, the situation dramatically shifted. On 25 June 1940, the day of the signing of the armistice, FEA governor-general Boisson declared his support for Pétain and was swiftly promoted to high commissioner of French (Sub-

Saharan) Africa (*haut-commissaire de l'Afrique française*) and transferred to Dakar.[22]

In his trial after the war the prosecution claimed that Boisson opted for Vichy because he knew that Pétain intended to promote him to the more desirable position of governor-general of FWA. If we take a brief look at Boisson's biography, however, we can see that the motives for his choice in 1940 were far more complex. His biography can also help clarify his policy of fiercely opposing the Free French and their British allies, on the one hand, and rejecting outright collaboration with the Germans on the other.

As it was for many of his generation, the main formative event in Boisson's life was World War I. He was born in 1894 in the Breton town of Saint-Lauseuc. In 1914 he enlisted in the Forty-eighth Infantry Division and served under Pétain, who was then a general. He was severely wounded in February 1915, and his left leg had to be amputated below the knee. Boisson was captured by the Germans but was soon released after being declared *grand blessé* (severely wounded). In 1917 he was discharged and in the same year was made a chevalier of the Legion of Honor. After the war Boisson entered the *école coloniale* (colonial school). He was promoted rapidly and in 1934 received his first important job overseas as the secretary-general of FWA. Two years later he was appointed as the high commissioner of Cameroon, where he served under the Popular Front and pursued its colonial reforms. His success in fending off German demands for restitution of Cameroon won him the title of commander in the Legion of Honor. The following year Mandel, minister of the colonies, appointed him as the governor-general of FEA.[23] As a wounded veteran of World War I who had served under the war's French hero Pétain, Boisson had an obvious inclination to respond again to his ex-commander's call. His hatred for the Germans, though, made him reject their interference in his colonial territory as much as he could.

FWA's support for Vichy ruptured Anglo-French relations. Boisson's declaration upon his arrival in Dakar that he intended to protect the territory entrusted to him against the Germans and the Italians, as well as against the British and the Gaullists, did little to improve the atmosphere. The British were concerned that FWA would now easily fall to German troops. The relations between Vichy France and Britain further deteriorated following the British attack on Mers el-Kebir on 3–4 July 1940. This attack followed a British ultimatum to the French to surrender their fleet or destroy it so that the Germans would not be able to use it. When the French refused, the British sank the entire fleet, causing over twelve hundred French sailors to meet their deaths at sea.[24] According to William Hitchcock, this attack completely changed the atmosphere in FWA to support of the Vichy regime even before the arrival of Boisson.[25] At the same time Chad's governor, Félix Eboué, pledged his allegiance to De Gaulle and was promptly appointed governor-general of FEA, which turned officially to De Gaulle's side on 26 August.[26] Encouraged by this support, the British and the Gaullists launched an unsuccessful attempt to win over FWA on 23–25 September 1940, which caused the final break in the Anglo-French bond. The British and the Gaullists dispatched a delegation to Boisson before the attack, asking him to join them voluntarily. His response was to imprison the members of the delegation and shoot its commander. The British retaliated by bombing Dakar for three days, injuring two hundred people, most of them Africans.[27] The French in Dakar used their battleships to defend the port, and the old Portuguese canon that stands at the island of Goreé to this day was activated for the second time in history.

According to a number of testimonies of Africans who recounted their wartime experiences to me, this attack left a remarkable impression on Africans living in Dakar at the time, as it was their first real encounter with modern warfare. For the children among them it was both a terrifying and an exciting experience that was engraved in their memories. Diouf remembered that he was taken to his uncle's office that morning and went reluctantly. He was watching the sea, contemplating his boredom, when he saw four or five bombs falling into the water and the old Portuguese cannon in Goreé firing back. He was then evacuated with his aunt and other women and children to Tivaouane and remained there until the attack was over.[28] The youngest informant, who was only four in 1940, also vividly remembered the bombardment of Dakar despite his age at the time. In fact, he claimed, this was his first memory. He was in the yard with the cleaning lady when he saw an airplane in the sky throwing little white sheets of paper, which he believed were birds. These were in fact Gaullist tracts explaining the aim of the attack. He heard bombing and cannon fire all day, and in the evening the whole family went to the main square to see an airplane that had been shot down by the Vichy army. Some, he recalled, took pieces of it as souvenirs.[29]

In October–November 1940 fighting erupted between pro-Vichy forces in Gabon (FEA) and the Gaullists, but within a few weeks Gabon joined the rest of FEA in its support for the Free French.[30] With these events Sub-Saharan French Africa was divided in two, and FWA found itself isolated between British and Gaullist colonies. The Vichy government planned a military attack to retake the colonies of FEA, but Boisson opposed any military ventures. He was supported by General Maxime Weygand, Vichy minister of defense for the first three months of the regime, who was at the time the delegate-general to North Africa.[31] Thus the failure of the attack on Dakar and the Free French victory over Gabon ended the military phase in FWA, and the new governor-general of the federation could now focus on the difficult mission ahead of him—ruling the vast area in his hands while a major part of his own country was being ruled by others.

2.

"A Source of Pride and Greatness"

The Place of the Empire in Vichy Ideology

Although the Vichy regime gradually lost its grip over most of the French empire, especially after the Allied landing in North Africa in November 1942, its place within the regime's ideology and discourse was firm and central. While the loss to Prussia in 1871 and the consequent loss of Alsace and Lorraine encouraged some French politicians to seek compensation overseas, the debacle of 1940, which left France with control over only one-third of its territory, turned the empire into a real lifesaver. It became the last opportunity to restore lost French honor. For the Vichy regime the empire was both a diplomatic and political playing card and a myth that was to compensate France for its defeat. The empire enabled France to prove to the world that it was still an independent state with resources, territory, and enormous manpower in its service.[1]

It is no wonder, then, that Pétain did his best to keep the empire out of German control in the negotiations over the armistice. Another worry the regime had stemmed from a British attempt to encroach on French colonies, and efforts were made in the colonies to resist such attempts. After all, on the colonial scene Britain—not Germany—was France's major rival.

One of the multiple publications dealing with the empire, produced under Vichy, described to its readers how much worse their country's destiny would have been without the empire:

> Thanks to this empire, France, though defeated and reduced in Europe, is not a people without space, not a nation without men, not a state without resources. . . . The French should only consider how their country would have been wiped out if it was limited in 1940 to its metropolitan

territory and its scant 39 million inhabitants! Deprived of all communication with the outside world, erased from the rank of the sovereign
nations for an undetermined period, condemned to wait in the future
for only the pity and generosity of others, France would have been, for
years, just another Poland or a slightly larger Belgium.[2]

The empire, then, is presented as the supplier of the three necessities
France had lost in the defeat to Germany—territory, manpower, and
resources—as well as a way in which the humiliated French nation might
regain at least some of its lost honor. Only the empire's resources had
enabled France to tackle the war's difficult economic circumstances. The
empire, in short, is pictured as a ship battling stormy seas, seriously
damaged but eventually rescued by the wisdom of an experienced leader
and thus able to aid, comfort, support, and feed France.[3]

But the importance of the empire was not limited to the present. It also
had a major role to play in the rehabilitation of France as a great nation in
the world that would arise after the war. The Vichy regime perceived this
world as an arena in which Germany, after defeating Britain or reaching
some sort of agreement with it, would be the dominant power. However, a
hope was expressed that France would be able to find for itself a respected
status in this new world. Only the empire could secure such a status for
France, and this would happen only if France invested efforts in nurturing
it. As René Viard explains in *L'Empire et nos destins* (The Empire and Our
Destiny):

> Thanks to its Empire that reassures notions of demonstrated force and
> permanent influence, it is on the world map, a piece that still has a
> proper value that no one can ignore. Through the Empire, it retains
> its chance to be counted among the great nations; through it, it can
> safeguard the possibility of offering the most productive contribution for
> the rehabilitation of a Europe destroyed by the war. When the moment
> of decisive peace negotiations arrives, our action will justify the rights
> of an "imperial" power. It will be able to show that it is determined and
> capable of accomplishing all of its duties.

Later Viard appeals to his readers not to limit their vision to the borders
of France, not to see only a defeated country divided in two, but to look
across the sea to the vast territories of the empire, its economic wealth
and the crowds of people connected to the fatherland by strong bonds of
love. Only then will they be able to feel a sense of pride and greatness and
help the empire fulfill its great role in Europe and the new world about

to rise.[4] A recurring idea in publications such as Viard's is the notion of Euro-Africa: the creation of a union between the two continents with France as the connecting element.[5]

Any discussion of the Vichy colonial discourse has to take into account the regime's overall ideology. Only in this light can we understand a certain dilemma the Vichy regime had in extolling the empire: its theoreticians had to confront the embarrassing fact that most of this extremely useful empire had been built under the "detested" Third Republic, the same "corrupt" regime that was blamed for all of France's ailments and eventually for its defeat by Germany. This problem was tackled in several ways. Some of the writers who addressed colonial issues during the Vichy period attributed the formation of the empire to earlier periods, the era of Charles X, the eighteenth century, or even the time of the Crusades.[6] Others admitted that most of the empire's territory had been conquered under the Third Republic. However, they maintained that this did not necessarily mean that the achievement should be attributed to the republican regime. The credit for the formation of the empire was usually given to the "men on the ground." One of the books that discusses the creation of the empire examines soldiers, settlers, missionaries, and doctors, but not politicians.[7] Occasionally, the former regime was accused not only of not contributing anything to the establishment of the empire but also of limiting the steps of those heroes who aspired to establish it.[8]

The assumption here is, then, that the empire was not established by the Third Republic but in spite of it. The "men on the ground" presented to the regime established facts, and although many parliamentarians objected, the empire survived these objections.[9] French politicians wasted the energies of the empire builders on limited goals and demonstrated their inability to plan long-range projects.[10] One writer even went so far as to claim that the politicians of the Third Republic had not accepted the idea of the empire because of the fear and ambivalence the word evoked in the hearts of republicans.[11] The only exception was Jules Ferry, who was praised by some of the writers and even noted as one of the pillars of France's colonial fame.[12] Indeed, his responsibility for the colonial annexation of Tunisia and Tonkin won him considerable credit.[13]

But it was not only the politicians of the Third Republic who were found guilty of neglecting the colonial mission. Vichy-era writers also pointed a finger at the French public. Here again their criticism of French society under the republican regime must be viewed in relation to the general Vichy ideology, which maintained that the former regime had encouraged such false values as unresponsiveness to the fate of the fatherland, individualism, and even hedonism. The French public's indifference toward the colonial mission overseas was seen as an integral part of this general tendency. Vichy theoreticians saw colonial indifference as one of the major obstacles to the development of the empire. This indifference of the masses, they claimed, damaged colonization: "no colonization without a conscious *métropole*," maintained colonial administrator Robert Delavignette.[14] He went on to explain that it was not enough for elites to have colonial consciousness. The people of France had to take part in the colonial "game" as well. All French people must have basic ideas about colonization. Obviously not everyone could reach the colonies, but they were responsible for what occurred in overseas France. This responsibility should be reflected in their everyday behavior. That meant, according to Delavignette, that the moral conduct of the French people directly affected the motivation of colonial administrators. He cited some examples to support his claim. A *métropole* of dances and cafés, for example, could not support the administrators of Islamic countries; a *métropole* deprived of family spirit could not guide administrators in Annam; a *métropole* that had suffered a drop in its birthrate and lost its confidence in life would leave its colonial administrators, talented as they may be, with no hope regarding their mission abroad.[15]

Beyond the dangers of metropolitan indifference, Delavignette raises an interesting assertion here. He calls upon the French people to adopt values promoted by Vichy propaganda, such as the importance of the family, parsimony, and an increased birthrate. However, he relates these values not to "good old France" but to the inhabitants of the empire. It can be deduced from his claims, although he does not say this explicitly, that the French should learn from the values of their empire's subjects to improve their own moral conduct. Only then will the administrators of the colonies be encouraged to fulfill their overseas mission. Given the background of the French colonial discourse of the civilizing mission, this view seems extremely odd. However, Delavignette indeed believed, even before the war, that the technological superiority of Europe over Africa did not necessarily entail cultural superiority. He believed in cultural exchange and thought that the French had a great deal to learn from the inhabitants of their colonies: respect for nature, the capacity to live in harmony with it, and spiritual values. In his book *Soudan Paris Bourgonge*, published in 1935, he maintains that the Soudan was a French province just like his own beloved Bourgonge. According to him, a symbiosis existed between the two provinces and Paris. They both accorded a human dimension to the city: both incarnated the historic values of man, his old connection to the earth, and the traditions of his ancestors. Paris turned to the future, but to maintain its equilibrium the city had to be inspired by its provinces.[16]

In *L'empire et nos destines* Viard claims that the French public's lack of interest also damaged the empire in a more concrete way. It entailed a derogative view toward coffee from Côte d'Ivoire, rice from Indochina, bananas from Guinea, and other products from the colonies. The French preferred to purchase products imported from America or the Canary Islands.[17] For this ignorant approach he holds both Third Republic politicians and colonial settlers responsible. The latter, he claims, in spite of their numerous organizations—perhaps too numerous—never succeeded in sounding their voice in France or glorifying the empire in the eyes of the French public. Just like the politicians they were unable to reach an agreed-upon plan of action due to their narrow particular interests.[18]

The solution Vichy theoreticians proposed for struggling against this indifference toward the French colonial mission, which had actually saved France from a much worse destiny, was to spread propaganda and embed the colonial idea in the education system. In fact, propaganda and educational reforms were generally the main tools the new regime used in its attempt to transform French society, destroy its republican values, and replace them with a new set. These new values, based on the trinity "Travail, Famille, Patrie" (Work, Family, Fatherland), were destined to create a "new" France free of the ailments inherited from the Third Republic that had led it to disaster.

In the educational sphere the Vichy regime introduced new textbooks that were substantially dedicated to colonial issues. For example, two new geography books published during the Vichy period devoted the last quarter of their text to a detailed description of the colonies.[19] Neither book mentions the fact that the Free French forces controlled part of the French empire. The idea here, as in the general Vichy philosophy, was that children were the best means of transmitting the new desired values to general French society. To create a colonial consciousness, one had to start in early childhood.[20]

The colonial idea, as the Vichy regime saw it, would also be well promoted through propaganda. The new government had to justify the armistice with Germany and prove to the French public that it was strong enough to pull the fatherland out of the deep mire into which it had sunk.[21] The empire could play a vital role in persuading the French people that France was still strong and that its government still had power. The Vichy regime did not, of course, invent imperial propaganda. General public indifference to the importance of the empire for France was evident even when colonization was at its peak in Africa and Asia, in the late nineteenth century. Thus films, newspapers, exhibitions, fairs, and advertisements had propagated the idea of the empire well before Vichy in an attempt to jog the people out of this indifference. However, never before, not even after the 1871 loss to Prussia, had the empire been so vital to France's existence. Its centrality to Vichy political discourse is equally well reflected in the scope of the regime's imperial propaganda as in its contents. Indeed, the large number of empire-related publications—books, published lectures, newspaper articles—that appeared during the relatively short period of Vichy rule, combined with references to the empire in other media such as radio, cinema, and expositions, demonstrates the importance the regime accorded it, its past and its future.

At the outset of the Vichy period the Ministry of Information established a special service for imperial propaganda. The purpose of this service was to evoke the sensitivity of French public opinion to traditional issues developed by supporters of colonialism at the turn of the twentieth century, as well as to the imperial slogans of the regime. Short and beguiling slogans attempted to transmit the message of the significance of the empire to France. Some of the most popular were "The empire guarantees the French future" (L'Empire garant de l'avenir français), "The empire will not let the *métropole* down" (L'Empire ne décevra pas la métropole), and "The empire is the secret to the nation's survival" (L'Empire, secret de la survivance de la nation).[22]

In addition to the emphasis on the empire as the savior of France, Vichy propaganda also presented to the French public the regime's extravagant projects throughout the empire in order to stress both its sovereignty and its efficiency. For instance, the Trans-Saharan railway was advertised in a poster showing the train passing against the background of a French Sudan mosque under the words "La France continue."[23]

An important part of the propaganda was aimed at the British, France's most significant rival in the imperial arena. One poster showed a map of the French colonies being devoured by a bulldog that greatly resembled Winston Churchill; in the background was the Union Jack. The text that accompanied this image described the history of wars between France and Britain and the events at Mers el-Kebir and Dakar in 1940 and concluded with the question, "Where else will Britain spill French blood?"[24]

Naturally, the mass media were also recruited to promote public interests in the empire. During 1942 a weekly fifteen-minute radio broadcast was entitled *La France colonial*. Each edition focused on an issue related to the empire. Some addressed its strategic and economic importance, and others discussed planned projects, such as the Trans-Saharan railway.[25] The "dismal" issue of the fall of part of the empire to the Gaullists was not ignored in these broadcasts, as it was in the geography books. Two programs, one dedicated to the one-hundredth anniversary of the French conquest of Gabon and another to FEA in general, discussed the severe ramifications of the loss of this region to the "Anglo-Gaullists."[26]

The French press, even papers without a specific colonial bent, almost constantly addressed issues related to the empire and to French colonialism. Articles reported not only on war events in the empire, such as the British attack on Mers el-Kebir and the British-Gaullist bombing of Dakar, but also on everyday life in the colonies, the customs of their native inhabitants, their economies, educational policy, and so on.[27] The weekly *L'illustration* ran an article on 22 March 1941, for example, on how funerals were conducted in black Africa and, on 21 November 1942, described in detail a ship's voyage from Gao to Mopti.[28] The monthly *La Légion* dedicated its third issue, of August 1941, to the empire and regularly ran articles that discussed various aspects of the French colonial mission: the Catholic mission in the colonies, education, economic policy, and medicine.[29] *La Légion* also published articles about the history of French colonization and the loyalty of African soldiers to France and the affectionate and warm treatment they received from their commanders, who regarded them as brothers. In this latter article the writer described the broad smiles on the soldiers' faces that exposed their bright teeth, a smile that attested, according to him, to their excellent mental and physical health.[30] An article a month later also focused on the loyalty of African soldiers. This one told the story of an African who was told that France had lost the war but that his two sons who took part in the battles in Europe were still alive. Contrary to what the reader might expect, this African father did not rejoice at his sons' survival but cried out in rage: "Can it be that France was defeated and my two sons are still alive?"[31] The journal dedicated a few articles to the arts in the colonies and to the empire's influence on the exoticism and romanticism found in French literature; it also highlighted the heroic deeds of the empire's builders.[32] The newspaper *Gringoire* also dealt frequently with the empire, reporting on news events and emphasizing the dangers posed to the empire by the Anglo-Gaullists. In addition, it published fiction depicting events and characters from the empire's past.[33]

Marius Leblond, a Réunionais of Greek origin, gave a public lecture in which he discussed literature as an effective tool for attracting the

French public to the idea of the empire. He protested that French literature did not deal sufficiently with this subject. Familiarity with the suffering and nobility of the empire's seventy million inhabitants, he declared, was much more important than the love stories of Montmartre. He called upon French writers to exploit their writing skills to arouse the awareness of the French public to the empire and to the creation of an imperial elite so that the empire would be saved and France would become more beloved by the French people.[34]

Fairs and exhibitions provided another forum for promoting the idea of the empire. This mode of imperial propaganda also existed well before Vichy. Beginning in the late nineteenth century colonial exhibitions had aimed to expose the French public to the empire by offering it a chance to "tour" without leaving the *métropole*. One of the most successful expositions was that of 1931. This exposition and others like it attempted to create a unified identity for "greater France." Yet the differences between metropolitan France and its overseas territories were equally emphasized. The representations of the empire in these exhibitions highlighted both its difference and its domestication. The most popular exhibits in these colonial fairs featured humans. Many people were brought from the colonies and placed behind ropes to perform so-called everyday activities and thus create the atmosphere of a "real" native village.[35]

During the Vichy period, however, when the empire became much more vital than before, the use of this tool became more excessive. The Agence economique des colonies (Economic Agency of the Colonies), established on 22 January 1941, was responsible for ensuring the representation of the colonies at fairs and exhibitions inside and outside France. Throughout 1942 the agency organized a number of displays whose declared purpose was to praise the idea of empire, to remind the public about its relevance to the life of the nation, and to excite French youth. During the annual fair in Grenoble, for example, the agency decided that due to the large concentration of students in the city the colonial exposition should be directed especially at young people. In one of the exhibition's five halls leaflets were distributed among young people to encourage them to pursue a colonial career.[36] The agency also helped organize an exhibition of colonial paintings in the town of Vichy in January 1942 by supplying artifacts made by inhabitants of the empire.

Finally, the agency was responsible for the French colonies' stands at international fairs around Europe and at French fairs and for the organization of the Imperial Fortnight train exhibition that traveled all over France. The exhibition train traveled from south to north and east

FIGURE I. A map of Africa presented at the colonies' exposition in Paris, October 1942. Photo by Lapi/Roger-Viollet.

to west from 1 May until 31 July 1941. One of its main aims was to pass through university towns and enable young people to inquire about career prospects in the colonies. The train included five wagons, each containing an exhibition, as well as a dining and sleeping wagon for the crew. The first wagon was dedicated to the colonial army, the navy, and important figures from the colonial past. The second represented the students of the *école coloniale* and administrative careers in the colonies. The third contained an exhibition about commerce and agriculture, the fourth concerned the economic value of the empire, and the fifth was dedicated to the Ligue maritime et coloniale (Maritime and Colonial League). In addition, the agency organized charity sales for the benefit of prisoners of war from the empire.[37]

The cinema was also a popular means of propaganda in France during the war. The Vichy regime saw it as one of the most efficient tools for shaping public opinion. Feature films and documentaries aimed to inspire the French imagination with the adventures of the empire. One such film screened in France in 1941 was *L'homme sans nom* (The Nameless Man). The main character is a scientist who decides, following some dramatic events in his life, to move to the colonies in order to test a vaccination against leprosy that he has invented. Another film from 1942, *Malaria*, tells the story of a "native" who is so loyal to his master that he is willing to kill anyone who does not respect him. This was, in fact, an allegory for the loyalty of the empire's inhabitants to Pétain. The film *Le pavillon brûle* (The Pavilion Burns) transmitted the message that self-satisfied capitalists from Paris had destroyed the remarkable work other Frenchmen had performed in the empire. Some documentary films also concerned the empire, such as *Français, voici votre empire* (Frenchman, Here Is Your Empire), which was screened during the Imperial Fortnight of 1942, along with two short films directed against the British, *La tragédy de Mers el-Kebir* (The Tragedy of Mers el-Kebir) and *Dakar*.[38] A successful documentary series of sixty-six parts, *La France en marche*, was filmed in the unoccupied zone and the colonies from late 1940 to late 1944. This series offered extensive coverage of life in the empire and dramatized the continued success of the "civilizing mission." French officials were shown curing sleeping sickness in the jungles of central Africa (episode 52, *Les chasseurs du sommeil*), converting natives to Christianity (episode 54, *Avant-garde blanche*), and teaching modern agricultural techniques (episode 62, *Paysan noir*). These episodes also presented France's colonial subjects as absolutely loyal to France in its difficult hour.[39]

The Vichy period demonstrates extremely well the important role the French empire played in French history. Never before had the empire been more central in the political discourse of the French government. The Vichy attitude to the empire was expressed in a practical way as well. The regime saw it as an integral part of nonoccupied France, and all the decrees published during the Vichy period were immediately implemented throughout the empire. The resilient protection of French sovereignty that guided the regime's actions in France thus also prevailed in the empire. This defense was two-pronged: against the Germans and against the British-Gaullists.[40]

The regime also tried to act on the constitutional level. Pétain instructed General Weygand to prepare the future constitution of the empire. This constitution, which was never completely drafted and remained mostly unknown, attempted to institutionalize the empire as an integral part of the French nation and to create an imperial citizenship and parliament.[41]

The Vichy vision of the empire as a territorial continuation of metropolitan France led the regime to implement its official ideology, known as the National Revolution, in the colonies under its rule, despite the problem of using both concepts in a colonial environment. This marked a major change from republican colonial philosophy, which encountered difficulties and dilemmas whenever it attempted to implement republican ideology in the colonies. However, the colonial ground proved more difficult to work on than the metropolitan one. Convincing the people of France of the significance of the empire was one thing. Convincing the people of the empire of the persisting legitimacy and "greatness" of France in its new awkward circumstances was a totally different matter. Part II addresses the implementation of Vichy's National Revolution in FWA and the means that the regime used to make colonial subjects adhere to Pétain's ideology, thereby gaining their loyalty.

PART II

The National Revolution in French West Africa

The place the Vichy regime accorded in its ideology to the empire in general and to FWA specifically was manifested in its treatment of the colonies as an integral part of France. Every decree and law that was published in France was immediately valid in the colonies as well.[1] Another aspect of this view of the colonies as simple extensions of the *métropole* was the attempt to implement the ideology of the National Revolution in the colonies and propagate its messages to the local populations. As Eric Jennings shows, this was no easy move. Metropolitan ideologies had never been "imported" to the colonies before Vichy, and the two words *national* and *revolution* carried connotations that no colonial power would have been happy to encourage locally.[2] Indeed, in the West African case we cannot speak of the importation of the National Revolution but rather of its adjustment to suit the colonial reality. On the one hand Vichy ideas were far more suitable for governing colonial subjects than were the republican values of Liberty, Equality, and Fraternity; therefore their implementation in FWA went rather smoothly and was welcomed by the colonial administration. On the other hand, as we shall see, Boisson refused to copy in the colonies the National Revolution as it was. Occasionally he tried to protect the autonomy of the colonial administration from the Vichy center by blocking Vichy's more radical elements. He did this, for example, by preventing certain metropolitan organizations from opening branches in FWA. Not everything that was considered good for France was also perceived as good for the colonized populations, and a certain process of selection informed the implementation of the National Revolution on African soil.

This section of the book examines three aspects of this implementation: the initial political and administrative moves of the new regime, its attempts to promote the National Revolution in the social sphere, and its economic plans and visions in FWA.

3.

Vichy Settles In: Administrative
Changes and Continuity

With the end of the battles in Africa between the Anglo-Gaullists and the pro-Vichy French it was time for Governor-General Boisson to enhance his grip on the vast territory that was now under Vichy rule. His aims were well defined. First, he vowed to keep the federation free of German or Italian influence and presence and to protect it from the British and the Gaullists. Second, and this was no simple task either, he intended to keep the African population calm and to forestall the eruption of revolts in the new and delicate situation that had been created.

As to the first aim, Boisson indeed refused to allow Germans to enter FWA. His insistence was motivated by his apparent dislike for Germans, by his wish to assert his autonomy, and by his fear that if Germans became too visible in FWA the already damaged colonial prestige would further diminish in the eyes of the Africans. The Germans, for their part, resented this attitude, and after long negotiations it was agreed that a German delegate would visit Dakar disguised as a French official; he even changed his name from Eitel Friedrich Mulhausen to René Martin for the occasion. This was the only official German visit to FWA during the war.[1]

Boisson saw in the British and Gaullists no less significant a threat. The attacks on Mers el-Kebir and Dakar did nothing to allay his Anglophobia, and he was highly suspicious of British intentions regarding the French colonies, especially since, in the colonial arena, Britain had always been a fiercer opponent of France than Germany had been. Boisson exploited the Anglo-Gaullist attack on Dakar and his own fierce resistance to demand that the Germans allow an increase in the size of both the Armée d'Afrique and the colonial army in West Africa. The Germans agreed to raise the troop level to thirty-three thousand men; by mid-1942 it actually approached one hundred thousand men.[2] This increase helped Boisson to better protect FWA from a potential invasion, but it did not seal the federation off from British and Gaullist propaganda. Thus the new regime established a propaganda machine of its own that was designed both to create counterpropaganda and to spread the messages of the new regime among the African population. But first, in order to be sure that the National Revolution would not be thwarted by unwanted elements, some administrative changes both in personnel and in laws and regulations had to be made.

During the period between June 1940 and March 1943 four ministers of the colonies served under the Vichy government. On 12 July 1940 Henri Lemery replaced Albert Rivière, the first minister, in a cabinet reshuffle.[3] Lemery was a senator from Martinique and was very close to Pétain. He kept his position for less than two months as his appointment enraged the Germans, who could not accept a *métis* serving as a minister in a country occupied by the Third Reich.[4] Admiral Réné Charles Platon, appointed as his successor, remained minister for most of Vichy rule in FWA. Jules Brevié replaced him when Pierre Laval returned to government as prime minister in April 1942.[5] Brevié knew the region of FWA well because he had served as governor of Niger and governor-general of FWA (1930–36).[6]

In FWA the same Vichy-appointed governor-general—Pierre Boisson—served throughout the whole period. He remained in his position well after the Allied landing in North Africa, managing to cooperate with the Americans while refusing to acknowledge De Gaulle. He was dismissed only on 7 July 1943, some three years after his appointment.[7] The Americans did not wish him to be dismissed, but the atmosphere in Dakar was against him. The decision to discharge him came after a demonstration against him that took place in Dakar on 18 June 1943 (the anniversary of De Gaulle's call from London).[8] While in office Boisson loyally implemented all the Vichy decrees that ordered the dismissal from public service of all foreigners, Communists, Freemasons, and Jews.[9] In fact, Boisson arrested so many people that by the end of November 1940 he wrote to his superiors in Vichy that the prison in Dakar was full to capacity.[10] At the level of territorial governors a few changes were introduced. In Senegal George Rey replaced G. Parisot on 1 January 1941; in Côte d'Ivoire Horace Crocicchia, who had met with a British major of the Gold Coast regiment on 23 June 1940, was dismissed at the end of the year and replaced by Hubert Deschamps; in Niger L. Soloniac replaced Rapenne; and in Togo L. J. Delpech replaced M.-L. Montagne, who was later replaced by J. St. Alari.[11] All these changes took place early in 1941. In Mauritania, Guinea, Dahomey, and Sudan the pre-Vichy governors retained their positions.[12]

All the governors were dismissed for political reasons—Parisot, Montagne, and Delpech for being Freemasons and Crocicchia for his British sympathies.[13] Nevertheless, their replacements were not new people parachuted in by Vichy authorities. Just as in France, where some Vichy politicians, such as Prime Minister Laval, had served under the Third Republic, in FWA republican and Socialist administrators now served as governors in the Vichy regime. Most had no problem with continuing to serve in the colonies after the war. In fact there is no clear relation to be made between individuals' serving under Vichy in the colonies and their political views toward decolonization after the war. Rey, for example, who served under Vichy rule, was in favor of reforms, while, as Nancy Lawler shows, Edmond Louveau, the lieutenant-governor of Côte d'Ivoire, who was sent to a concentration camp in France for his resistance to the Vichy regime, became after the war, as the governor of French Sudan, one of the most repressive administrators in FWA.[14]

At the lower levels of the colonial administration Boisson fired thirty-one administrators out of four hundred for "political" reasons, which meant that they were Jews, Communists, or Freemasons.[15] A relatively well-known example of such an administrator is Léon Geismar, the secretary-general of the governor of Senegal, who was demoted because he was Jewish.[16] Another example is Louveau, who declared his support for De Gaulle and was subsequently imprisoned. On 14 August 1940 the governor of Guinea, P. Giacobbi, demanded that his secretary-general, Martin, and two subaltern colonial officers be dismissed for inciting the African population against the Vichy regime and declaring their support for De Gaulle. The governor clarified that as Martin was supposed to serve as his replacement when he was away, he could not trust him.[17] William Cohen suggests that Boisson also took advantage of the ease with which he was able to dismiss administrators to get rid of those who were too old or too lazy or who suffered from mental disturbances.[18]

The personnel changes affected several dozen French administrators. However, on the whole a large degree of administrative continuity was maintained. Even in cases where administrators had to leave their posts, their replacements came from the ranks of the same administration that had been in place at the time of the Third Republic. These officials had to abandon their republican convictions and spread the new ideology of France in their colonies. As we shall see, in one sense this was easier to do in the colonial arena than in the *métropole* because republican values were not so useful for colonial regimes.

In addition to shuffling personnel, the new governor-general introduced some structural changes to the colonial administration. Their common aim was to alleviate the colonial task of keeping order in the new complex circumstances. In the spring of 1941 Boisson established the Antinational Activities Agency (Service menées antinationales), which was supposed to coordinate all activities against dissidents. This agency was in close contact with the North African police and reported to the Vichy Ministry of the Colonies. By November 1941 it had investigated 568 civilians in FWA. [19] To enhance the colonial ability to control the African population and prevent Africans from cooperating with the British and Gaullists in neighboring colonies, Boisson enhanced the powers of the Directorate of Political and Administrative Affairs (Direction des affaires politiques et administratives), which had been established at the beginning of the war. This body was responsible for gathering information from all colonies and circles and following the "mood" of the African population and their activities in neighboring colonies. In addition Boisson established the General Security Service, which was responsible for the Dakar police and for a network of security services in each colony. The Vichy administration also created the Youth and Sports Agency (Service du jeunesse et du sport) on 11 August 1940. This was encouraged by the Vichy ideology in France, which viewed youth as the healthiest element of society, one that would lead it to a better future. Youth were encouraged to engage in sports so as to create a population of young French people healthy in body and spirit. The aim of the new agency was to promote, organize, and direct the activities of various European and African youth institutions. [20] Beyond the idea of promoting the "healthiest segment of society" in the colonial context, there was also a concern with supervising African youngsters and directing their energies into channels that would not disrupt colonial order.

Boisson also made use of already existing colonial devices in order to enhance his control over the African population. One such tool, which existed well before Vichy, was the *indigénat*. Formulated on 30 September 1887, the *indigénat* gave all administrators the right to enforce disciplinary sanctions (imprisonment of up to fifteen days or a fine of up to one hundred francs) without trial on any African who was not a French citizen. These sanctions could be applied for a variety of offenses, mostly political or administrative ones. The *indigénat* was essentially a device that enabled the administration to recruit manpower for forced labor and the army and to ensure regular payment of taxes.[21]

After the publication of the first decree in 1887 successive decrees introduced amendments, including the addition of more punishable offenses. By July 1918 the *indigénat* covered fifty-three offenses. Another amendment exempted certain elements of the African population from the law. At the end of World War I, for example, all African war veterans were exempted from the *indigénat*. In 1924 the list of exemptions increased to include African administrative employees, École primaire supérieur (EPS) diploma holders, council members, and property-owning businessmen.[22] Ten years later all African women were also exempted.[23]

During the Vichy period the need to resort to the *indigénat* was raised more frequently, as it was considered a first-rate measure to punish some Africans quickly and deter others. In February 1942 Boisson suggested to the minister of the colonies that he enforce the first and harshest version of the law in two "problematic" circles in Côte d'Ivoire: Bobo-Dioulasso (later Burkina-Faso), where a group of Africans had murdered several Europeans, and Bondoukou, where the superior chief of the Abron people had crossed the border to join the Gaullists in the Gold Coast. These two incidents, discussed in detail later, were perceived as the most threatening to the stability of colonial order in the Vichy period. This is why Boisson was keen to enforce the *indigénat* more vigorously in these regions.[24] Nevertheless, the Vichy administration hesitated to introduce major changes in the *indigénat*. A suggestion of far-reaching changes raised by the governor of Senegal was only partially accepted. The governor asked to add to the list of offenses one regarding damage to a public utility, which had once existed but was revoked in 1935, and another regarding refusal to send chiefs' sons to school. He also asked to revoke the exemption of African women from the law, bringing as an example the difficulties in fighting diseases if women could not be forced to receive guidance regarding hygiene habits. The Directorate of Political and Administrative Affairs discussed these suggestions and decided not to accept them, hoping to avoid undesired upheavals. It approved only minor amendments to some of the law's articles. For example, instead of annulling women's exemption in general, it did so only with regard to agricultural production and public health.[25]

While aiming not to change the law, the Vichy administration did attempt to minimize the number of exemptions from it. The director of political affairs suggested limiting exemptions only to Africans who had made extraordinary achievements. Exemptions were indeed limited, as the numbers show. In 1941 eighty-six Africans were exempted from the *indigénat* in all of FWA. Most of them had been born in the 1870s or 1880s, and none was younger than forty; they all had families. The motives for according exemptions were: proven loyalty to the colonial regime, a "positive" influence on African society, assistance in recruitment of soldiers, and filling an administrative position dedicatedly and efficiently.[26] Unlike in previous years these motives were all related to one main goal—maintaining order. The exemptions were cautiously given only to older people with families who did not seem to pose a real threat to colonial stability.

An important tool that the Vichy administration tried to encourage, though not always successfully, was the administrative tour. While the *indigénat* was only effective following a breach of order, the administrative tour was meant to prevent a breach from happening in the first place. Most of the African population in FWA lived in rural areas away from main roads. The only way for the *commandant de cercle* to maintain some sort of relations with them was through periodic touring. Governor-General William Ponty (1907–11) had already emphasized the importance of this tool for keeping in direct touch with the "masses."[27] But due to travel difficulties and manpower shortages such tours were not performed regularly. This was especially true for the post–World War I period, when administrators began to bring their wives to the colonies and thus preferred not to leave their residences for long periods to conduct the tours.[28]

The importance of maintaining close contacts with the rural population increased during the Vichy period, when the colonial administration was not alone in searching for these contacts. The fear of Anglo-Gaullist influence on the "mood" of the African population, in addition to the difficult economic condition that burdened the African farmer, made such tours vital. Boisson regularly sent circulars to remind his governors to ensure that their commandants perform the tours and write detailed reports afterward. Deschamps, Côte d'Ivoire's governor, set an example for his commandants by conducting his own tours in the colony. During tours administrators were supposed to be present at village discussions (*palabres*) and to conduct population censuses themselves instead of relying on chiefs' reports. In a circular to his administrators the governor of Senegal insisted that they stay in the villages for several weeks, talking with the people, learning their traditions, observing their way of life, and even helping them prepare their meals.[29] It is difficult to assess whether such tours did indeed take place. From the many reminders that Boisson issued we can assume that a great amount of real contact with the African villagers remained an unfulfilled wish. Still, it is obvious that the Vichy administration was aware of the need to maintain close contacts with the African population and to monitor the atmosphere so as to prevent trouble.

A significant administrative change that affected a small but important fragment of the African population was the abolition of all representative institutions to which Africans holding French citizenship could be elected. During September and October 1940 all municipal councils of the four communes were suspended and replaced by representatives chosen by the regime.[30] These steps were similar to those taken in France: after the National Assembly voted for its own suspension on 10 July 1940, the Vichy regime began to "suffocate" all local political life.[31] It was only natural, then, that the representative institutions in the colonial environment would be suspended as well. And yet it seems that the Vichy colonial administration did not take this step lightly. Correspondence from the time indicates there were concerns about the resentment this might cause among the African elites. Concerns were also raised about possible Gaullist exploitation of this move and subsequent propaganda that might claim that the Vichy government wished to curtail Africans' rights. This fear did not make the Vichy administration revoke the decision, but the administration did attempt to follow closely the reactions of African citizens to the suspension.[32]

Vichy historiography ever since Robert Paxton has shown that the Vichy period in France was not a parenthesis in French history. In spite of the drastic change of regime, a great deal of continuity was preserved.[33] In FWA the continuity was emphasized even more, as here the change of regime was much less drastic than in the *métropole*. There was no democracy to abolish except for the small minority of the four communes. Continuity was manifested both in the administrators, most of whom remained in power, and in the policy and goals of the regime. The introduction of administrative changes and tools of repression pertained more to the unprecedented dangers that were created following the establishment of the Vichy regime in FWA than to the character of the new regime itself. Nevertheless, the Vichy colonial regime was different from its predecessor. One major difference was in the way it attempted to socially mobilize the African population to support the metropolitan cause—that is, the National Revolution.

4.

Spreading the National Revolution in FWA

Propaganda, Education, and Social Organizations

The first part of this book addressed the important place held by the French empire, including FWA, in Vichy propaganda aimed at the French public. Propaganda in the colonies was no less important, and sometimes even more so. The defeat of the French colonial power by another European power and the emergence of two "Frances," each fighting for the loyalty of colonial subjects, created an unprecedented and extremely hazardous situation for the French colonial administrations. The presence of Gaullists just across the border of French West African colonies, in Gambia and the Gold Coast, made the situation even more delicate.

Indeed, the Vichy regime wasted no time in dealing with the issue of propaganda in the colonies. The Ministry of the Colonies issued a circular on 31 August 1940 calling for the modification of propaganda and information services due to the new circumstances. It explained that whereas previously these services had provided information to France from the colonies, it was time for the information (read: propaganda) to emanate *from* France *to* its colonies.[1] The aim of Vichy propaganda in FWA was twofold. First, it was meant to ensure the African population's obeisance in spite of the upheavals in France. This was to be achieved by blocking alternative channels of information, mainly through censorship; suspending all newspapers in FWA, except for a few that were made administrative mouthpieces; and providing an official interpretation of news events. Second, and no less important, the regime wished to transmit to Africans the crux of Pétain's National Revolution ideology, stressing this because the values it promoted, administrators believed, would help enhance Africans' loyalty to France and eradicate the negative influence, as the regime saw it, of republican values.

Vichy propaganda in FWA included both general themes, such as veneration of Pétain, love of the fatherland, "morality," the importance of the
family, and the negation of secularism and democracy, and themes that
were specifically relevant to the empire, such as French colonial heroes,
the benefits France had brought to the colonies, and the integration of the
empire in the new world that was to arise from the ashes of the war.

To disseminate this propaganda the Vichy colonial administration exploited the gamut of available media—radio, press, cinema, books, bro-
chures, lectures, photographs, and ceremonies. Just like in France the
education system, as well as old and new social organizations, also served
as an important channel. At the same time the regime had to counter the
Anglo-Gaullist propaganda diffused in FWA. The British, concerned about
the risk of FWA falling into German hands, tried to persuade the Africans
under Vichy rule to support the Anglo-Gaullist cause. [2] The embarrass-
ment and consternation caused to the French by this move can be well
imagined. This British-Gaullist propaganda is typified by a text that was
diffused in FWA in several African languages:

> One hundred thousand black gunmen fought for France. Today, the
> French who stayed in France are like women, like slaves, dependent on
> the Germans. Moreover, they discuss the transfer of the Blacks to the
> Germans. By selling the Blacks they will be able to buy back the regions
> in which they live. This is the way France wishes to reward the thousands
> of Blacks who died for her. The Germans have no regard for the Blacks.
> They see in them nothing but slaves. As if we were destined to suffer for
> them. Hitler, the leader of the Germans, wrote in one of his books: "The
> black man is worth only half a chimpanzee." If we accept this man's rule
> he will use us like monkeys. . . . Encourage all your peers to cooperate
> to weaken the defeated Frenchmen. Refuse to pay taxes, do not use their
> money; it is worthless, and soon it will be used as toilet paper. Let the
> native gunmen revolt against their white masters. [3]

The British and Gaullists also deliberately spread rumors in the colonies
of FWA using African agents as their prime means of dissemination. This
was called the "whispering campaign." The agents said things—often
untruths—in the company of waiters, hairdressers, or others who were
liable to pass them on. These rumors were aimed to cause unrest among
Africans and thus destabilize the Vichy colonial regime. Among the rumors was the threat that Germans were making war on the entire Nas
el Kitab: they had dealt with the Jews, they were dealing with the Christians, and next would come the Mohammedans. [4] Another claimed that

three pilgrims on their return from Mecca had a vision near Timbuktu of the Archangel Gabriel sharpening his sword.[5] This whispering campaign was indeed effective, as a Vichy intelligence report from 3 January 1941 shows; it notes restlessness among the inhabitants of Dakar following rumors that France intended to join Britain in its war with Germany and that for this purpose Pétain had sent "his nephew" De Gaulle to London.[6]

Leaflets that spread "dangerous" ideas of revolt and rumors that aimed to unsettle the African population encouraged the Vichy colonial administration to communicate with the Africans. The French were aware that they could not be regarded as a homogenous group, but they tried to reach all the different African sectors. While part III will discuss the numerous ways the Vichy regime treated these sectors, we will now focus on the means of propaganda and the ways they were used to spread the messages of the Vichy regime.

Vichy Propaganda in FWA

The press was the main conduit of printed propaganda aimed at literate Africans. While it was possible to make information accessible and palatable to illiterate Africans by adding pictures or asking schoolchildren to read the newspapers to their parents, the press was mainly used to transmit more complex ideas to educated Africans. Of the newspapers the Vichy colonial authorities exploited as their mouthpieces, the most important was the daily *Paris Dakar*. In 1942 a supplement was added, entitled *Dakar-jeunes* (Dakar youth).[7] Launching the supplement, the Vichy regime addressed its potential readers thus:

> From now on you will have your own journal. Don't forget that every Thursday *Dakar-jeunes* appears. *Dakar-jeunes*, six pages written, edited, and illustrated for you. Here you can read articles, reports, and accounts of issues that are close to your heart: sports, games, life in the open air, choosing a profession, the future. You'll find advice, either from your elders still close to you by age and affection, or even from young people with a certain experience. You'll find spiritual and moral directions, rules of conduct. . . . This is the pure air of France circulating in the six pages of *Dakar-jeunes*, every week—Breathe it.[8]

Paris-Dakar and other newspapers, such as *La Côte d'Ivoire française* and *Sénégal*, focused on issues related to Vichy ideology. They attempted to explain the meaning of the National Revolution and to examine the ways in which it should be implemented in FWA. The activities of the Legion of Black Africa (Légion de l'Afrique noire) were also regularly reported, as were ceremonies and celebrations in which Africans took part. [9] Propaganda, of course, also took the form of interpretation of news events, especially the more embarrassing ones. The armistice, for instance, was explained as being instigated by the British, who did not invest enough in their ground forces and only defended Britain with their naval and air forces. [10]

One example that typifies such printed propaganda can be found in a 1942 booklet describing Pétain's 1925 visit to French West Africa. A chief accountant in the railway company, Maurice Montrat, who had served as the Marshal's interpreter on that tour, wrote a short text in 1942 entitled, "When the Marshal Spoke to the Natives." In the introduction Montrat explains his motives in writing this booklet: "I would like to tell my brothers what I know about the hero of Verdun who, twenty-four years later, for the second time, saved the Fatherland and bound his fate with that of France and the empire. I hope that these lines provide the natives with further proof of the affectionate solicitude that our great and venerable leader feels toward them, a solicitude that I myself have often witnessed." [11]

In the text he describes Pétain's meetings with African soldiers and his long and fatherly conversations with them. Pétain inquired about their military service, whether they had been wounded and who their commanders were. Then he patiently answered their questions and forgave them for mistaking him for a Corporal Pétain from Madagascar, noting gently that he himself had never been a corporal. [12]

The paternal side of Vichy colonial propaganda was much stronger in the colonies than in France. As can be seen from the conversations quoted in this booklet, the Vichy colonial regime regarded the "children of the Marshal" in Africa as much younger than their French "brothers." The presentation of Pétain as a loving father who forgives his African children for being a little "slow" would be repeated in other forms of Vichy colonial propaganda.

Another example, a booklet entitled *Mémorial d'Empire*, was distributed among African notables and *évolués*. The text describes acts of courage and devotion performed by African soldiers during the battles of 1940. The *commandant* of the circle of Diourbel in Senegal noted to the governor of this colony the positive influence the book had had over local Africans. To make his point he attached several responses that, he claimed, were written without any encouragement or pressure from his side. For example, Amadou Diouf, a principal clerk in the financial section in Diourbel, wrote that he was impressed more by the publication of this booklet than by the acts of courage described therein, which he did not think exceeded the call of duty, considering the great advantages that France had brought to its colonies: "By giving these acts of courage and devotion the widest publicity, which is this book, generous France proved once more its unfailing attachment to the colonial empire that it always loved. Our great leader, the Marshal Pétain, this great Frenchman whose past is imbued with glories, warmly appreciated the colonial army in the inscription he made in this book."[13]

Pictures of the Marshal accompanied by a short citation were distributed among Africans. The first, dated October 1941, was handed out to schoolchildren returning from their summer vacation. A quotation from Boisson was inscribed below: "He is the father and he is the leader. Upon him all our hopes and all our certitudes rest." Later that year a twenty-two-page brochure entitled *Images du Maréchal et de ses collaborateurs* was printed and distributed among Africans.[14]

The Vichy administration often used printed material as counterpropaganda against the British and the Gaullists. In refuting hostile propaganda it opted for the use of ostensibly authentic African voices. An illustrative example is a pamphlet supposedly written by a Muslim of Tukolor origin who was born in French Guinea but grew up in the British colony of Sierra Leone. He recounts his pilgrimage to Mecca, describing the Islamic cities he saw along the way. This account, which the Vichy authorities believed would attract Muslim readers, includes testimony against the British in favor of the Vichy administration. The pilgrim concludes his account by saying that he long wished to return to FWA but the British would not permit him to do so. He somehow managed to cross the border, however, and tells of his "happy ending" in these words: "Entering the French territory I saw that there was no suffering in the French colonies, as the British claimed. I saw that the Germans did not rule the French colonies, as the British wanted us to believe. After being able to appreciate exactly the fate of the natives of Sierra Leone, I chose the Marshal who, whatever the British may say, protects and guards our colonies for France."[15]

Vichy invested massive resources and effort in printed propaganda, insisting on its worth despite the high costs and technical problems.[16] Educated Africans were also targeted through lectures. The documents consulted do not convey how exactly Africans were enticed to these apparently tedious lectures, which lasted two to three hours, but they do report huge attendance.[17] The lectures concerned National Revolution issues or the importance of the empire to France. The speakers were usually members of the colonial administration and occasionally important Vichy figures who had come from France for this purpose, such as Minister of Propaganda Phillip Henriot, who gave several lectures in the main cities of FWA in April 1942. At one lecture, in Saint Louis, Henriot clarified the main principles of Vichy policy and tried to allay his audience's fears concerning Franco-German relations. He criticized Africans who fled France's "patronage" for the neighboring British colonies, pointing to Britain's betrayal of and hostility toward France. In concluding he highlighted the debt France owed its empire, especially FWA, which had remained loyal to France in its difficult hours.[18]

A more "popular" means of propaganda was radio broadcasts. Radio reached all kinds of audiences, including the illiterate and those in remote areas; indeed, it had been widely used as a major instrument of information and propaganda since the 1930s.[19] The use De Gaulle made of BBC Radio encouraged the Vichy authorities in FWA to broadcast their own propaganda to Africans. Radio, however, had one major disadvantage: the high price of radio sets severely limited the medium's potential audience. A survey conducted in the Gold Coast in June 1943 showed that out of a population of more than 3.5 million, only 650 owned a radio.[20] Presumably, the situation in FWA was similar. The solution in both places was to use mobile radio transmitters located in populated centers throughout the colonies.[21] In fact even the infirm could not avoid listening to Pétain's messages: "Hospital Radio" broadcast federal radio programs.[22]

In addition to Radio Dakar, three other stations operated in federation capitals: Radio Niamey in Niger, Radio Cotonou in Dahomey, and Radio Abidjan in Côte d'Ivoire. Propaganda was spread through the news and other programs, such as *Chroniques de la vie français*, which discussed the political, social, and economic policy of the Vichy government in France, or through programs designed for youth.[23] Some of these, too, were aimed at the African educated elite.

An intriguing element of the attempts of the Vichy administration to use Radio Dakar as a means of propaganda was its attitude toward a series of programs aired every week between October 1940 and October 1941 by Théodore Monod, a botanist and oceanographer who served as the director of the French Institute of Black Africa (Institut français d'Afrique noire) in Dakar. Monod's broadcasts were supposed to address ecological issues such as the flora and fauna of Africa, but through these issues Monod also condemned Nazi ideology and racist theories in general. He turned his weekly program into a "corner of liberty" in which he diffused his antiracist, pacifist, and ecological convictions. Finally the colonial administration in Dakar lost its patience. On 11 October 1941 the director of information services in FWA sent a letter to Monod saying that his messages might annoy the people of the armistice commissions in North Africa, who listened regularly to his program. The letter also suggested that Monod's arguments might be used by the British and the Gaullists. Monod's reply was swift and deeply ironic. He wrote that he saw a fatal conflict between the new orthodoxy and free thought. He expressed his "pity" toward the people of the armistice commissions, who might suddenly discover that they were worshiping idle gods, but added that he doubted whether their conscience would really be disturbed by this revelation. With regard to the suggestion that the British and Gaullists might make use of his arguments, he asked the director if he really believed that scientists in free countries needed Radio Dakar for rejecting racist myths. Following this correspondence the administration did not allow Monod's program to continue.[24]

However effective radio was in attracting Africans, moving images on the silver screen were even more potent. Vichy, like other regimes, found the cinema extremely useful for getting its message across. During World War II the Allies, as well as Nazi Germany, used films for propaganda.[25] What made the cinema so effective was its universality. Both silent films and talkies held a visual appeal that acted on the audience's emotions rather than its intellect. There was also the added attraction for audiences of cinema being a technical novelty and much easier to understand than the written word. For the disseminators of propaganda its advantages included the ability to screen the same film in different places and send copies of films to even the most distant locales.[26]

The Vichy colonial regime used two types of films: outright propaganda movies and newsreels. These were screened either before or after a feature film. A report analyzing the first type stated that, in view of their enormous success, they should be distributed to governors more frequently.[27] In February 1941 the regime began to screen the successful documentary series *La France en marche* in FWA. The introductory episode, *Dakar*, circulated continuously in FWA for a full year, playing at 209 cinema halls.[28]

Feature films accompanied by newsreels were somewhat more problematic for the colonial regime. First, the authorities had to ensure that the newsreels would indeed be projected. Second, they were concerned about the messages the films themselves might convey to the African viewers. The solution was to dispatch to the cinemas a policeman whose duty was to report any failure to screen the newsreels and assess the audience's reactions. The policemen sent weekly reports to the head of their regions. As a consequence of one such report the owner of the Rex cinema in Saint Louis, Madame Philipp, received a pile of angry letters from the local commissar of police between April and June 1942, accusing her of not upholding regulations and of damaging the cause of the National Revolution, as she had failed to screen the newsreels regularly.[29] Another report for the week of 27 July–2 August 1942 suggested sending an Italian film for reinspection by the censorship committee, as scenes depicting attacking rebels had elicited loud applause from the audience. The policeman who watched this film wrote that it was not compatible with the "new spirit."[30]

Censorship was a vital tool in ensuring that films—indeed, any media— would not contradict the messages authorities were trying to convey. In the colonies, in February–March 1942 alone, forty-five films were either banned or limited to viewers over the age of eighteen. In most cases these restrictions were binding only in the colonies. The scenes that were expunged would have, allegedly, encouraged African or other "native" aggressions toward Europeans or aroused feelings of contempt toward Frenchmen or other white people.[31] Films that presented the Germans as victorious and the French as vanquished or weak were also banned. Censorship was enforced with equal verve on Nazi propaganda films, such as *Jude Süss*, which was totally banned in FWA.[32] Presumably, in this case the French were concerned that Africans were incapable of distinguishing among "different categories" of Whites and might thus see no difference between the principal character in *Jude Süss*, a "despised" Jew, and any white man—or Frenchman.[33] Another justification for deleting scenes or banning a film was "concern" with impinging on the morality of African viewers. Scenes of Tarzan and Jane bathing together, for example, were cut from *Tarzan Escapes*.[34]

The fact that certain films were allowed in France but banned or censored in FWA points again to the regime's paternalistic attitude. This is well reflected in an article written in Vichy-period France by G. de Raulin: "In France," he wrote, "tolerance toward cinema is great, but in the colonies we should be aware of the potential damage to French prestige of films that make us laugh."[35]

Other visual means of propaganda used in the colonies included official ceremonies. Although far less amusing than the cinema, these had their own special appeal. In Vichy France tremendous importance was attached to the staging of official ceremonies marking holidays and memorial days. On Joan of Arc Day (10–11 May), for example, the Vichy regime used

FIGURE 2. Cub Scouts parade on Joan of Arc Day in Dakar, 11 May 1941.
Photo by Lapi/Roger-Viollet.

the revered French martyr as the model of the new order's virtues.[36] Joan was seen as prerevolutionary, young, physically and morally healthy, and eager to sacrifice—even her life—for France.[37] Her veneration was to represent the wish for conciliation among all Frenchmen. As of 1941 this became the official "national day" under Vichy and was celebrated annually with great pomp in both occupied and nonoccupied France.[38]

The Vichy regime made sure that this holiday and others, such as Labor Day, were commemorated throughout the empire. On 13 May 1941 Boisson dispatched a report to France describing the Joan of Arc Day celebrations in FWA. He noted the massive participation of both Europeans and Africans. Black and white schoolchildren marched in parades, and wreaths were laid next to statues of the heroine. Radio Dakar dedicated three hours of broadcasts to the figure of Joan. Other cables to Vichy that week described Labor Day celebrations. Official demonstrations, sports meetings, and other events were organized in all of the colonies, with the participation of legionnaires, farmers' unions, artisans, schoolchildren, youth groups, African chiefs, and notables. In the days leading up to and following the event the social policy of France in the empire was discussed in newspapers, the cinema, and schools and on the radio. Other holidays associated with the empire included the Imperial Fortnight, Imperial

Week, and Memorial Day, recalling those who fell in the Gaullist-British attack on Dakar.[39]

A September 1941 report on Imperial Week (15–21 July) in Dahomey summarizes events there. Discussion groups and lectures focused on issues such as French history in relation to the colonies; France's civilizing mission; its medical, social, and economic accomplishments in the colonies; the geography of France and its empire; hygiene; agriculture in France and the empire and the return to the soil; and morality—the family and the village, the fatherland France, and patriotism. Sports events, folklore performances, songs, and tam-tam drumming were also featured. The report mentions the special success of the song "Papa Pétain," written by an African schoolteacher, whose lyrics highlight the figure of Pétain as a loving father of his African children:

> Maréchal Pétain, nous écoliers de Dahomey
> Nous te saluons—nous te saluons encore
> Aujourd'hui. . . .
> Afin d'achever l'oeuvre commencé
> Sauver la France entière
> Nous autres, travaillerons avec ardeur et confiance
> Et tu sera fier de nous
> Notre Maréchal Pétain, notre Papa.[40]

We also learn from the report that the topics discussed publicly during the holiday reflected the main ideas of the National Revolution—work, family, the fatherland, and the return to the soil—and emphasized the bond between France and its empire and the achievements of French colonialism.

Official ceremonies were also an integral part of the education system. The Vichy government ordered that, beginning on 10 March 1941, a daily ceremony would be conducted in every school of the colony. During this ritual the French flag would be raised to the sounds of choral music. In informing his regional administrators of this the governor of Dahomey stated: "This symbolic action, so beautiful in its simplicity, should add to the certainty of our little Dahomeyans that, in spite of the difficult times, France is still great and full of life and has more than ever the right to be treated with respect, love and gratitude by its adopted children."[41]

Interestingly, while the Vichy administration developed and intensified the use of official colonial ceremonies, its members did not attend Muslim celebrations, as had been the custom in previous years, since 1936.[42] No official explanation for this change in practice could be found. It could have stemmed from unwillingness to continue a custom initiated by the Popular Front's administration. It does not, however, necessarily reflect a negative attitude on the part of the Vichy regime toward Islam. While the Vichy colonial administration acted to keep "dangerous" Islamic elements at bay, it also made gestures toward this religion, such as donations to Muslim orders and the authorization of pilgrimages to Mecca during wartime. [43]

Official ceremonies were of course conducted in FWA before Vichy. However, the republican tradition prevented the French from imbuing these events with the monarchic splendor that prevailed in British colonial ceremonies in Africa and in those of imperial Germany prior to the loss of its colonies in World War I. [44] The establishment of an authoritarian and paternalistic regime in France offered the French an opportunity to endow their ceremonies with just such flamboyance. Pétain gave the French colonial regime the figurehead of a paternalistic leader; it could present him as a father figure for the Africans, something that did not exist under the Third Republic. Indeed, it is hard to imagine a refrain like "Papa Pétain" written in honor of any republican prime minister. Under the Vichy regime Africans could direct their "respect, love, and gratitude" toward a real person, not only toward the abstract and distant concept of the "fatherland."

The Vichy colonial regime, then, invested efforts in spreading the values of the National Revolution among its African "children." Propaganda was one of the means used. Its effect on Africans, especially from the Western-educated elite, will be examined in part III, where Vichy relations with various African sectors will be discussed. I now turn, however, to probe another means of spreading desired values—the education system.

The National Revolution in the Colonial Education System

The line between propaganda and education is sometimes unclear even in democracies, not to mention in a regime like that of Vichy, which was not only authoritarian but also had to defend itself constantly from accusations of collaboration. If we add in the colonial context, the difference between education and propaganda becomes rather minimal.

In the early twentieth century, when the French colonial regime decided to establish an education system in FWA that would expose African children to French education, it confronted a major dilemma. [45] On the one hand the ultimate justification for French colonial rule was the "civilizing mission," and spreading civilization necessitated education. On the other hand education was dangerous for colonial stability: it brought with it new ideas that could be turned against France. It also had the potential of alienating schoolchildren from their society. In spite of the rhetoric of assimilation, most educators did not really believe that Africans could become French even after receiving a "proper" education. Even those who did believe this was possible in the long run, for at least some Africans, did not see this as a specifically desirable goal. In any case, most African children were perceived as possessing an extremely limited intellect. George Hardy, the general inspector of education in FWA, appointed in 1914, wrote in his 1917 book, *Une conquête morale*, that any curriculum demanding abstract knowledge would be too complicated for Africans, resulting in a waste of time and possibly even stirring up problems. [46] The basic racist assumption common at the time, influenced mainly by the writings of Gustave Le Bon, was that the intellect of the African child was not as developed as that of the French child, and therefore the African did not have the same capacity to learn as the average pupil in France. [47]

Gail Kelly, who examined school texts designed for African children in FWA in the interwar era, claims that the colonial educational system created African elites who were separated from their own societies, as well as from the French. While those who graduated from this system did not usually wish to go back to their former lives, they could not expect to belong to the French society in the colonies either and had to forgo any aspirations they might have had to develop brilliant careers. The best they could expect was to live among other Africans in better conditions. This educational system made African pupils feel ashamed of their cultures and even of their physical appearance but at the same time discouraged them from attempting to be something they were not—French. [48]

The dilemma the colonial education policy confronted was this: when the African child received a French education, he might develop undesired pretensions and start viewing his retarded environment with contempt. The challenge facing the colonial educational system was, thus, how to give the African child a basic education that would allow him to improve his environment while accepting it and not wishing to leave it. How could the aims of the civilizing mission be realized, by forming a small elite of African auxiliaries, and at the same time ensure that most African children continued to live as before, while taking advantage of the most basic tools French civilization offered them? Hardy claimed that the answer lay in what he referred to as moral education (*education morale*). In *Nos grands problèmes coloniaux* he wrote: "In the colonies, more than anywhere else, teaching must be preoccupied with education for values rather than instruction, as the family's milieu is incapable of backing the school on that point." [49]

The first part of this idea sounds as if it were taken out of the educational reforms the Vichy regime presented in France. In many ways Vichy educational reform—known as the "General Education" reform—was based on principles similar to those that guided the colonial education system in FWA under the Third Republic, in spite of the huge differences in Vichy perceptions of African and French children. But in order to examine the implementation and significance of Vichy educational policy in FWA, it is vital first to discuss briefly the essence of the General Education reform in France.

The Vichy regime saw the French youth that the Republic had not yet had a chance to "spoil" as the essential force for the mission of rehabilitating France. It perceived the republican education system as blameworthy, to a large extent, for France's defeat. The German victory, it was claimed, stemmed at least partly from the better quality of the Prussian teacher; under the influence of secular French teachers the French public school had adopted a pseudo-intellectual culture that undermined the pupils' morals and patriotism. [50]

Indeed, as early as 15 August 1940 the Vichy minister of education declared that of all the regime's tasks the most important was educational reform. The ideal person the National Revolution wished to create was one deprived of his or her natural individualism, someone who knew how to appreciate the beauty of collective effort and integrate harmoniously into his or her social environment and nation. To achieve this ideal the school had to educate and not only instruct. Instruction—meaning what went on in the schools of the Third Republic—was perceived as encouraging two traits the Vichy regime saw as negative: a sense of criticism and independent thinking. Both encouraged undesired individualism, while education aimed to arrest desires and encourage obeisance. [51]

The General Education reforms were meant to repair the damage caused by republican education. Behind the reforms stood the wish to retain within the schools an important place for activities that would complement the theoretical disciplines, such as sports, hygiene, manual crafts, choir singing, excursions, and camping. The belief here was that in order to have a healthy mind and spirit, the child must also have a healthy body. [52]

It is important to note that in spite of Vichy "accusations," the idea that education was also meant to transmit values was not born under Vichy. The republican educational system did not make such a separation between education and instruction; it simply transmitted to the younger generation of French people a different set of values. The General Education reforms were thus intended to replace these republican values with Vichy ones. A good example of how this was done can be found in the changes the Vichy regime tried to introduce to the teaching of history, where it worked to transfer the emphasis from the French Revolution to pre-Revolution eras. The Vichy regime believed that stressing the Revolution divided the French people and even made pupils anti-French.[53]

Although the General Education reforms were conceived to educate French children in France, they were also implemented in the colonies. There colonial educators received them with great enthusiasm. In spite of the different conditions and populations, these reforms were deemed most suitable to the colonial environment, much more appropriate than the republican vision of education.

The focus in the implementation of the educational reforms in FWA was on extending the weekly hours dedicated to manual crafts and sports and introducing the figure of Pétain, as well as other popular Vichy heroes and heroines (such as Joan of Arc), to the colonial curriculum. In fact, as we shall see, changes to educational perceptions in FWA were hardly as dramatic as in France. The reforms in France, however, made it easier to support the already existing colonial educational ideas.

A good example of the welcome metropolitan educational reforms received can be found in a 1941 report by a Mr. Barbieri, the principal of the *école normale* for rural education of Sevare, in French Sudan. He praised the new reforms and said that in African schools, too, the curricula were often too comprehensive and encyclopedic. Simple curricula such as those the Marshal encouraged, without a theoretical character that distracted students from their real goal, were also desperately needed in Africa. However, the principal emphasized, the problems of education in Africa were very different from those in France because colonial education was aimed at children coming from a backward environment in which the intellect was still "sleepy" (*en someil*).[54]

The General Education reforms encouraged the colonial aspiration to "promote the African pupil in the framework of his environment." The colonial administration was aware of the inherent contradiction in this aspiration; advancing within a framework is in fact a kind of cul-de-sac. It was not the potential of each child that dictated the limits of advancement but rather the colonial administration itself. The administration feared that when African children were exposed to French education they would sense the huge gap between the school and the "backwardness" of their own environment and thus begin to feel contempt toward their milieu and even toward their parents. Their main goal would then be to leave this environment. Such a goal was deeply undesirable in the eyes of the colonial regime, which did not wish to create a class of educated and frustrated Africans whose desires were frustrated by the regime itself. During the Vichy period the fear of such frustration increased in light of the sensitive situation and the British-Gaullist propaganda that was targeting exactly this fertile soil.[55]

Mr. Barbieri, inspired by the idea that education in France must stay connected to the environment of the pupils (without of course considering this environment to be backward, as was the case in Africa), suggested minimizing the gap between African schools' curricula and the pupils' environment. He proposed two examples, pertaining to the teaching of French and history. French, he maintained, must turn into a familiar and simple means of expression and not into obscure and pretentious jargon. To achieve this the pupils must be asked to write about what was closest to their hearts—their land, their village, or their parents— and required to listen to stories, legends, and proverbs in their own homes and then translate them into simple French. They must be asked to write freely about subjects that interested them, such as everyday stories and scenes from the village and the fields. With regard to history the principal maintained that only local history should be taught. He stressed that the facts regarding the colony and France's activities in it could not be taught only through books. The pupils must be encouraged to study by themselves the history of their region by questioning the people around them. In this way they would know how their family lived in the past and would learn to respect France more.

The aim of the headmaster's suggestions was to confine African children to their milieu and steer them clear of any menacing ambitions. The basic assumption here was that the only way African children could be happy was to stay in their environment. This happiness would indeed be modest, as the principal put it, but such modest happiness was the most African children could aspire to. They had to be taught to criticize their way of life, but in a gentle way that would not destroy it but only improve it slightly. Although he presented them as stemming from Vichy reforms, these ideas of keeping children close to their surroundings and teaching them appreciation existed in the colonial sphere well before Vichy. Still, these notions were similar, at least in some aspects, to ideas promoted in France at the time. The Vichy regime, for example, reproached republican education for trying to efface the differences among various regions of

France and thus distancing the French child from his or her local traditions. However, it must be emphasized that there was a huge difference between Vichy educational reforms in France and the ideas promoted by this colonial headmaster. The environment of the French child was not seen as backward but as unique, with its own cultural variants, whereas the African child was perceived as belonging to an underdeveloped society that he or she must gradually improve. Objections to the excessive use of books in both France and Africa were also based on different motives. In the French case such book-based education was seen as encouraging independent thinking, as being harmful to the system's ability to mold the French child according to the values of the National Revolution. In the African case there was another reason for avoiding the use of books: the assumption that African children lacked the intellectual capacity for this means of instruction.

Yet in spite of these differences the Vichy reforms in France were a great relief for the colonial administration in FWA. It was much easier to promote an educational policy that avoided intensive teaching of facts, that maintained pupils' relation to their local environments and encouraged physical activities, such as agriculture, manual crafts, and sports, when this was, more or less, the basis of the educational system in the fatherland. The Vichy inspiration to discourage critical spirit and independent thinking among pupils had existed in FWA ever since the establishment of its educational system. Individualism was never desirable in the colonial system. Its rejection in France simply legitimized a preexisting view regarding the required goals of the French civilizing mission among the schoolchildren of FWA.

It is not surprising, then, that the colonial regime in FWA undertook the full implementation of the General Education reforms. The regime's seriousness in this area is well reflected in an October 1941 seminar on the reforms that was conducted in Dakar for European and African teachers from various colonies in the federation. The seminar ran for two weeks and included lectures and demonstrations on General Education activities and visits to schools.[56]

The reforms not only endorsed existing colonial notions but also gave them a serious boost. During the Vichy period efforts were made to improve physical conditions in the federation's schools in order to enable sports activities. After visiting the city's schools in September 1942, a representative of the governor of Dakar recommended that a swimming pool be built at Faidherbe High School and proposed extending the sports area of the Van-Vollenhoven School by destroying the adjacent cinema and a few "natives' huts." He stressed that this could achieve two goals: a range of sports activities would be possible on the school grounds, and the cinema, an immoral nuisance, would be removed from the eyes of the pupils.[57]

Although General Education subjects were included in the federation curricula long before Vichy, the new reforms added substantial emphasis to these subjects in FWA. While the education decree of 1924 established that one weekly hour apiece would be dedicated to "morals" and to sports, a new 1942 decree set aside for each of these subjects seven and a half weekly hours for boys and six for girls.[58] The encouragement of sports activities in colonial schools was also related to Boisson's wish to return to the évolués a sense of physical work.[59] However, according to the testimony of an African who was a schoolboy during these years, sports sessions became unbearable under Vichy. The pupils had to run great distances uphill, and they all resented this demanding physical activity.[60]

The contents taught under the subject heading "morals" were also totally "Pétainized." The new programs for the écoles premiers supérieurs established that this subject would include values that the National Revolution promoted, foremost the trinity "Work, Family, Fatherland." Lessons addressed the main duties of the child to himself, to those closest to him, and to God (without specifying religion), as well as the qualities required of the pupil in school life: respect, obedience, work, courage, honesty, and loyalty. Teaching material emphasized the family as the basic unit of society and the promoter of all values, encouraged respect toward it, and stressed the pupils' duties to it. Lessons also included lectures on the role of the (colonial) state, duties toward the state, and loyalty to it and to its leaders.[61]

Another existing trend that was reinforced in the Vichy period was the emphasis on basic education that allowed only a few pupils to continue their studies beyond this level. The 1942 decree stated that the village school must not be perceived as a first stage of education, leading to more advanced learning. It clarified the regime's intention: after four years of primary school, children would return to their families. Some children might be allowed to continue their studies, but this was not to be encouraged as it would result in dangerous alienation of children from their natural environment.[62] This reinforcement of the tendency to prevent African children from pursuing their studies beyond primary school was referred to in a report regarding education in the federation from 1944, after the Vichy period in FWA had ended. The report stated that one could not avoid being amazed by the small number of Africans in the EPS, which limited considerably the ability to select from among them a genuinely worthy elite.[63]

As noted, the principles at the basis of the Vichy General Education reforms were not a novelty in FWA. In fact they resembled those already found in the colonial education system in the federation. Nevertheless, the reform in the French educational system boosted these ideas there. Vichy allowed the colonial regime to repair everything that was still perceived as inadequate in the local education system. Most of the budget was directed to programs in the areas of General Education, such as sports and crafts, while higher levels of education were totally neglected. The gap between the declared goals of education in France and those in FWA became narrower. The values of the National Revolution had already been present in the colonial schools, then, but under the new regime they received a clearer and more organized framework. There is no doubt that colonial educational administrators found it much easier to explain to African schoolchildren the trinity "Work, Family, Fatherland" than its precursor, "Liberty, Equality, Fraternity," which totally contradicted the colonial reality in which they lived.

Social Organizations as a Means to Spread the National Revolution in FWA

The Vichy regime in France used social organizations to interact with the French public. The organization that was chosen to carry the flag of the National Revolution was the Légion français des combattants, which was established on 29 August 1940.[64] The legion was in fact supposed to act as a liaison between the regime and the French people. Pétain rejected the usual tool used for this purpose in fascist regimes, the political party, because he feared losing control to people who favored such a party, such as Pierre Laval and Marçel Déat. Communication between Pétain and the French population was, thus, created through the veterans' organizations of World War I and those who took part in the 1939–40 battles. Pétain officially presided over the legion, which became the only veterans' organization once all others had been abolished. The legion was supposed to supplant the old political parties and prevent their reestablishment.[65] In fact it was the legion that incarnated the Pétainist version of the National Revolution. It was the only mass organization that existed under Vichy, and its militants were the most convinced supporters of the Marshal's ideology.[66] Support for the legion was enthusiastic, as the numbers prove: by February 1941 it included 668,801 members in the free zone.[67] The legion put itself in the service of the Marshal and his

FIGURE 3. Legion Day celebrations in Dakar, n.d. Photo by Roger-Viollet.

National Revolution. One of its local presidents defined it as "a national elite, gathered around the warriors, at the command of the Marshal, to take upon itself and to lead the National Revolution until that revolution was realized."[68]

The legion's activity was not limited to metropolitan France but extended to the colonies as well. Its FWA branch, which had operated unofficially from the end of 1940, was officially inaugurated on 13 February 1941 as the French Legion of Combatants of Black Africa (Légion française des combattants de l'Afrique noire). The legion's establishment was marked the following June in the stadium of Dakar's Van Vollenhoven High School with the participation of two thousand black and white legionnaires.[69]

Boisson presided over the group, which was run by a committee of ten people, nine Europeans and one African. The legion had eight branches in the federation: in Dakar, in Saint Louis (responsible for Senegal and Mauritania), and in each of the other colonial capitals. Conditions of entry were identical to those in France: Jews and Freemasons were rejected, and every new member had to carry a warrior card from 1870, World War I, or the battles of 1940; declare alliance to France and the principles of the National Revolution; and accept the disciplinary rules of the organization.[70] Membership in the legion was hardly voluntary.

Boisson clarified to his subordinates that those who would not join its ranks would be considered hostile to the National Revolution.[71]

The aims of the African legion were to enhance support of Pétain's political philosophy and direct public opinion in FWA against the British and "enemies from within," that is, Jews, Freemasons, Gaullists, and Communists. Its intensive activity included organizing ceremonies, holding lotteries to collect funds for prisoners of war, and distributing propaganda material. The legion also pushed the personality cult of the Marshal.[72]

The law that established the legion in France did not take into account its possible activities in the colonies. This is quite clear from the formulation of its aims. The minister of the colonies was not at all pleased with this oversight. In September 1940 he complained to the organization's secretariat, saying that it appeared that the legion had been established only for the benefit of metropolitan France and that the colonies were to be excluded. He maintained that it would be regrettable if France created among its colonial population the feeling that, after being called to take part in two wars, they were alienated from an organization of this type. The minister remarked that the only person who would gain from such a policy would be De Gaulle.[73]

Following these complaints additional goals were formulated to allow and justify activities in FWA. These included mutual aid among all veterans and assurance of the cooperation of veterans in the subdivisions, circles, and colonies that composed FWA. The section of the law addressing the general organization of the legion referred to its adjustment to the territorial structure of FWA. It was decided that each colony would have its own legion branch whose president would work out of the governor's office. The number of members in each branch was limited to one hundred Europeans and two hundred Africans, with a minimum of thirty Europeans and sixty Africans. A branch that did not have this required minimum had to be merged with the one geographically closest to it.[74]

The legion served as an important tool for the colonial regime in FWA, spreading Pétainist propaganda in the colonies through assemblies, lectures, and conversations in which Africans took part. The colonial regime called this "propaganda from mouth to ear." The approach was perceived as effective, since it bypassed the obstacle of illiteracy and allowed access to a relatively wide audience.[75] The legion also organized charity events and social aid and provided moral and material assistance to African soldiers and prisoners of war who returned home.[76] In August 1942 the legion included 12,892 members, of whom 4,836 were Africans.[77]

Two other organizations served as instruments of Vichy ideology in

FWA. The first, the Groupement de Pétain, was not established by Boisson but served his purposes well. This group was responsible for spreading propaganda in the colonies and kept Boisson informed about the attitude of various segments of the population and their political tendencies. [78] The second was an extension of the Service d'ordre légionnaire (SOL), established in FWA in early 1942. The aim of the SOL, founded in France the previous October, was to assemble the legion's elite. [79] It continued to support Pétain's regime after the Allied landing in North Africa in November 1942 and declared its willingness to fight with anyone who would set foot in FWA. The SOL was even more extreme in its demands that Vichy laws be implemented than the legion. It made accusations against administrators and created an atmosphere that worried Boisson. Its activity in FWA aroused such resistance among some legion members that it resulted in their resignation. [80]

In addition to such controlled activity, more spontaneous organizations of French Pétain supporters surfaced shortly after the establishment of the Vichy regime in FWA. While these organizations were indeed based on the initiatives of French inhabitants of the federation, the colonial regime closely supervised them and used them for its own ends. Moreover, whenever the colonial regime decided that a certain organization was not fulfilling its role, it was abolished. [81]

In fact the legion was the only organization whose necessity and loyalty were undoubted. Other groups' activities, whether metropolitan or local, required authorization. The colonial regime hesitated about whether to approve social organizations because it feared that these might eventually, in spite of their initial declarations, act against its interests. In fact one of the Vichy administration's first moves in FWA was to dismantle all social bodies and trade unions. During 1941 most requests to form new organizations were denied. The colonial administration claimed that these organizations had a political character and might act against the aims of the National Revolution. During that year only two organizations were approved in Côte d'Ivoire. One was an agricultural syndicate and the other the tennis club of Abidjan. [82] The new regime also acted harshly against what it referred to as "secret societies." On 13 August 1940 the Vichy regime in France outlawed all organizations whose members were asked to conceal the nature of their activities from the government. This law also applied in the colonies. [83]

Even metropolitan organizations that endorsed the ideology of the National Revolution did not easily win approval from the colonial administration. Boisson refused, for example, to authorize the foundation of a branch of the metropolitan movement Progrès social français in FWA.[84] In a circular to the governors of the colonies he explained that he preferred to deny a political organization authorization, even when it had the "right" political tendencies and was permitted in France, because any political activity might impair the unity of the empire.[85]

The Scouts movement (Éclaireurs français), which was extremely active and important in France under Vichy, encountered difficulties when it tried to avoid the requirement that it receive authorization in each and every colony. On 15 March 1941 a regional commissar of this youth movement applied to the Directorate of Political and Administrative Affairs, asking that Scout activity throughout the federation be authorized, thereby avoiding the need to depend on the colonies' governors. Two days later Boisson denied this request, claiming that for security reasons each colonial governor had to authorize the Scout branches in his colony.[86] It is probable that in this case the request was denied not because of fear of subversive activity, but in an attempt to guard the autonomy of the governors with regard to the *métropole*.

Boisson's inclination not to authorize metropolitan organizations had two main motivations. One was concern about the proliferation of organizations in the federation whose activities might create divisions or reactions that were not always easy to predict. The other was fear of losing control over the colonies. Boisson was worried that groups related to metropolitan movements would not feel any obligation to report to him or to his governors.[87]

If it was difficult for a metropolitan organization to receive authorization to act in FWA, for local African organizations it was almost impossible. We can see how complicated the process of investigation and examination was for such requests through the example of one group that chose a name that would reflect its loyalty: Boisson's Youth Society (Société jeunesse Boisson). In September 1941 the vice president of this organization, a teacher in the French-Arab school in Dakar, wrote to Boisson and asked him to authorize both the organization and its name. He explained that the group's aim was to bring together all the young Africans who supported Boisson and Pétain. Boisson ordered an investigation to be conducted. The subsequent report stated that the writer of the letter, Abdoulaye N'Diaye, born in 1921 in the region of Sine-Saloum in Senegal, arrived in Dakar in 1935 to study. He worked as an educator in the French-Arab school from December 1940 to August 1941 but resigned because the salary was not adequate; he then applied for a post in the public service. The organization, according to the report, was designed to bring together young African men and women. Its leaders were not yet known, but it was decided that a membership fee of ten francs a month should be charged. The report concluded that N'Diaye's name did not appear in the archives of the security services and that he enjoyed a good reputation. Nevertheless, it stated, this was one of the native societies whose activities included mainly tam-tam drumming and dances, and it was only a matter of time before its members wasted all their funds on "nonsense." The request to establish the organization was finally denied in spite of the conclusion that N'Diaye posed no danger to the colony's security.[88]

The Vichy colonial administration wished to ensure that all African organizations would be subject to it. Therefore it was highly suspicious of bodies established through African initiative, even if they had operated before the war. The Great Chain (La grand chaine) was one such organization that the Vichy regime persecuted and finally dissolved. It was established in 1938 by Scouts who were graduates of the William Ponty School. Its objectives were to maintain contacts among Scout graduates and to spread the movement's ideas. Although the Vichy colonial regime also aspired to spread the values encouraged by the Scouts, this organization was soon denounced by the police services of Boisson as a "dangerous association with a nationalistic character," suspected of being associated with the Islamist Hamalliyya movement.[89] These accusations led to its dissolution. The administration was worried by the adaptation of "Scoutism" to African realities through the use of totems as symbols of different internal groups and by the organization's efficient communications network all over FWA through letters, circulars, and periodic bulletins.[90] Some African organizations, however, did receive authorization, such as the Foyer France-Sénégal, whose president thanked Jules Brevié, the minister of the colonies, in a letter dated July 1942, for the Marshal's confidence in his organization.[91]

International groups, too, found it difficult to act in FWA. The Vichy administration hesitated, for example, about whether to authorize the activity of the Rotary Club in FWA. Boisson consulted the minister of the colonies on the matter in 1941. He reported that the club had renewed its activity in Dakar after a few months' break following the war. Boisson wrote that the aim of the organization was to spread France's good name throughout the world, especially in the United States, and to develop among its members abroad an awareness of French Africa. He added that the subjects of the organization's propaganda were acceptable but asked the minister's opinion before he authorized the club. The minister's reply was that, in the current circumstances, it was not advisable to authorize organizations with international ties. However, the minister did not object to a reorganization of the French sections of the club, on condition that they detach themselves from all foreign influence.[92]

Youth movements received special attention in the Vichy period in FWA. Such organizations were meant to round out the colonial education system by reaching African children in their free time. Apart from the metropolitan youth movements that acted in FWA, such as the Scouts and the Catholic youth movement, Association catholique de la jeunesse française, the administration established a colonial youth movement called the Empire's Guards (Gardes d'émpire). This movement targeted African children aged ten to thirteen and aspired, unsuccessfully, to attract African children who did not belong to the modern urban elite.[93] The wish to organize African youth stemmed from a desire to use them to spread the ideology of the National Revolution among their older relatives. It also reflected a desire to control the activities of young Africans, especially educated ones, who might be exposed to Gaullist propaganda and, due to their youthful energy, encouraged to act in a way that might unsettle the colonial regime. These movements, however, did not succeed in reaching the rural areas of FWA. Saliou Samba Malaado Kandji, who lived during the war in a small village in Senegal, did not recall any youth movements acting around his village. He said they existed only in the cities. Other activities for youth that were planned according to the metropolitan model, such as the "maisons de jeunesse," were also absent.[94] Even in the cities the Scouts did not hold much appeal; many young Africans had had enough of the difficult physical activities demanded of them during school hours and did not even consider joining the movement in their leisure time.[95]

The issue of the establishment of social organizations in FWA demonstrates the problems that were created by the desire to implement the National Revolution there. Even organizations that were free of all suspicion of being anti-Vichy were not welcomed on African soil. There were two reasons for Vichy reluctance: Boisson feared the stirring of political agitation among Africans in such organizations, and he was concerned that they would declare allegiance to their French headquarters rather than to him. Boisson's harsh experiences as a soldier in World War I and his consequent abhorrence of Germany, reflected in his resolution to reject all of its demands regarding its lost colonies, suggest that he also may have had personal reasons for prohibiting the activity of Nazi sympathizers in his colonies. Although he believed that the National Revolution as a whole was suitable for Africa, he probably felt that at least some expressions of the National Revolution should not be exposed to colonial subjects.

The special significance the empire had for the defeated *métropole* was expressed both in the Vichy regime's discourse in France and in its perception of the empire as an integral part of the fatherland. This view entailed the extension of the new regime's ideology to France's colonies. The same tools that were used at home to spread the values of the National Revolution were also used in FWA, and in some ways this propagation was even easier in the colonies than in the *métropole*. Unlike in France, where the new regime had to explain why the abrogation of democratic parliamentary rule was essential to rehabilitate the nation, in the colonies there was no democratic culture to efface. In fact the new values of the French state did not in any way contradict the colonial reality. The changes the Vichy regime brought with it were much less dramatic and radical in the colonial environment than in the *métropole*. On the other hand, in spite of the compatibility of National Revolution ideology with colonial rule, its importation to the colonies met with some difficulties. Neither part of the term *National Revolution* suggested ideas that colonial rulers wanted to encourage. In addition, some colonial administrators were concerned about demeaning the Third Republic before the "natives." They believed that criticism of the republican regime must remain among the French, as criticism of any French regime might be harmful in the colonial context.

Another important aspect of the new regime in France, aside from the political and social ones, was the economy. The war and the consequent defeat and occupation brought with them economic hardships that had to be confronted. As we saw earlier, the Vichy regime perceived the empire as an economic lifesaver. The next chapter examines how this was addressed through Vichy economic visions in FWA.

5.

"Thinking Big"

Vichy Economic Visions in FWA

As in other areas, the Vichy regime aspired to introduce a new order to the French economy. However, it faced difficulties when trying to implement far-reaching reforms because of the circumstances of the war and the diversity of economic views and ideas among the regime's politicians. The dominant motive of Vichy economic policy was economic survival. The regime wished to make optimal use of the existing manpower, goods, and factories and at the same time curtail German attempts to control French industry. A secondary motive was to introduce structural changes by establishing *comités d'organisation* that were to replace trade unions and employers' associations. In addition the Vichy regime created a special body for economic planning, the Délégation générale à l'equipement national, which was assigned to draft a ten-year economic plan that included the French colonies.[1]

The difficult economic situation in France caused by the war and occupation led the regime to look for remedies in the empire. One aspect of Vichy imperial propaganda emphasized the great economic potential that lay in the colonies and presented the empire as the feeder of France. The French colonies constituted a vital source of the raw materials and food products that France so urgently needed. The Vichy regime believed that this potential had not previously been realized and that by using metropolitan funds and expertise it would be possible to build up Africa's ability to produce.[2] This, however, did not prove so simple. The British blockade prevented the transfer of products from the African colonies and created severe shortages in FWA itself. So while the Vichy regime in France was considering how to better exploit Africa's economic sources, the colonial administration in FWA was concerned with tackling the economic crisis in the colonies to prevent severe food shortages that might lead to political turmoil.

The Economic Situation in FWA under Vichy

When asked about the Vichy period or World War II in general, all of the Africans interviewed for this study recalled the grave economic difficulties of the period: food shortages, rationing, and the shortage of fuel and other basic products. One informant, who lived in rural Senegal at the time, even used the word *hunger*. Others, who then lived in Dakar, did not refer to hunger but stressed that the food sold to Africans was mostly impossible to digest. Boubacar Ly remembered his excitement at eating white bread for the first time three years after the war ended.[3] Another informant stated that Africans could eat only rice.[4] Someone else spoke of dire shortages in basic imported products, such as wheat and textiles.[5] The textile shortage was so grave that, according to another informant, people would sneak out to cemeteries at night to steal burial shrouds from newly interred corpses in order to make clothes.[6]

Adding to the strain caused by the war, nature was not especially considerate during this period. Vast areas of rural Senegal, for example, suffered a disastrous drought in 1941, a locust scourge in 1943, and poor harvests until 1944. The only "consolation" was that the endemicity of plagues was relatively low during these years, as rats did not have much to survive on.[7] These difficult conditions made the Vichy colonial administration realize that before contemplating any economic reforms or projects, it had to deal with the situation at hand to avoid further deterioration and protests from the African population.

The maritime blockade the British imposed on FWA in 1940–42 entailed a large degree of autarchy in the federation and decreased trade.[8] In his economic report for 1940 Governor Hubert Deschamps noted that after the signing of the armistice there was a sharp decline in trade. In 1939 export to France totaled 178,352 tons; in 1940 it declined to 110,316 tons. Imports declined even more drastically: to 59,108 tons, compared to 122,752 the previous year. The immediate solution to the deficiency in vital products, such as fuel, was rationing, but this, according to Deschamps, would only extend a limited supply. It would not solve the problem of the transfer of merchandise that was stockpiled in stations far from railways and ports. This situation, Deschamps cautioned, would have severe implications for the colony's economy: lacking any significant industry of its own, it was totally dependent on imports.[9] A later financial report from Senegal also pointed to the severe economic difficulties in the colonies after the armistice. The major problem was, on the one hand, the supply of food and clothing to the inhabitants of the colonies and, on the other hand, the supply of groundnuts to France.[10]

These two reports expose the problematic situation in which the colonial administration found itself due to the lack of local industry. Although the scarcity of products like fuel was extremely challenging, the lack of food products was no less alarming. The colonial administration feared that food shortages might cause the African population, already aware of the crisis within the colonial power, to react with violence, leading to instability. To prevent food shortages the colonial administration had to persuade Africans to keep their excess crops rather than selling them. A chamber of commerce report from February 1941, for example, exposes the fear that from May to September there would be food shortages, as Africans who wished to get rid of their debts would sell their excess crops. The decline in imports of rice from Indochina would make a sufficient supply impossible. Governor-General Pierre Boisson and the governor of Senegal were asked in the February report to take steps to save excess crops, for example, by assisting Africans in repaying their loans, and at the same time to make every effort to import certain products, especially rice. Another concern raised in this report was the uncontrolled sale of livestock in the colonies without seeing to the animals' reproduction first. This oversight, according to the report, might liquidate this agricultural sector altogether as the number of livestock had already dwindled in the colonies due to foot-and-mouth disease. The shortage of meat in France further exacerbated this problem.[11]

The colonial administration also tried to prevent food shortages by encouraging African farmers to continue to cultivate their old crops while also attempting new ones, such as rice.[12] The administration used the influence of marabouts for this purpose. In May 1941, for example, the governor of Senegal reported to Boisson about a meeting he had held with the marabout Babacar Sy and his younger brother Mansur Sy. The governor asked the two brothers to grant their disciples means and land so that they could grow crops and thus help solve the problems with the food supply. Babacar Sy, in return, reported to the governor that every day after prayer he recommended to his followers that they invest their efforts in agriculture. He asked them to plant millet, yams, and other crops and demanded that they start cultivating rice, which they had not done before. Along with this economic propaganda the marabouts disseminated political propaganda as well. He and his colleagues, Babacar Sy said, continued to explain to the population that France was not defeated but was like a man who had been hit on the head and was getting up and recovering, because as long as Frenchmen like Pétain and Boisson existed, France would continue to live.[13]

The most popular step taken to prolong food supplies, however, was also the most common recourse of governments, particularly in wartime: rationing. Rations were imposed as early as June 1940, immediately after the armistice was signed, but in 1941 they were extended in FWA to include more products (bread, wine, sugar, soap, rice, corn, millet, milk in boxes, textile, imported oil, butter, and quinine).[14]

Food rationing and shortages are among the period hardships most vividly remembered by Africans in the interviews I conducted. The scarcity of palatable food, especially in the cities, and the long lines before empty stores, together with the harsh discrimination that accompanied food rationing, were subjects raised in all of the interviews. While white people received five kilograms of sugar and ten kilograms of bread a month, Africans were allocated only three hundred grams of sugar and two kilograms of bread. Butter and milk were reserved for Whites only. Complaints about discrimination can also be found in a letter, intercepted by the Vichy colonial postal control, from a student at the technical school in Bamako (French Sudan) who criticized the school and its attitude toward African students. He wrote to a friend that Africans were going barefoot and suffering from malnutrition. On the morning of Labor Day, he said, they did not get any food because "here it is clear; Blacks do not have a right to bread anymore. We are very miserable, but we suffer in silence and no one complains."[15] A.D.M. also recalled the separate lines for Blacks and Whites in the grocery stores. He remarked that even *originaires* had to stand in line with the rest of the Africans.[16]

These clear memories of economic difficulties and discrimination demonstrate that at least this colonial fear of the effect food shortages would have on Africans was justified. The fear of violent reaction, however, was much more unfounded. Africans managed to cope with the economic difficulties using mostly nonviolent methods. One popular strategy to attain food and other items that were missing in Vichy-ruled FWA was smuggling.

In 1942 Boisson's secretary-general reported to the governor of Senegal on a smugglers' network operating on the Senegal-Gambia border. The smugglers sold agricultural products in Gambia in return for textiles. French customs agents claimed that this trade was regulated by the British administration and that a barter rate had been set so that a given quantity of textiles was equated to a certain portion of groundnuts, millet, and other products. The agents also reported that even Africans who lived far from the border were involved in the smuggling.[17]

The British did indeed encourage smuggling from FWA. One of their motives was that they considered it an efficient way to destabilize the Vichy colonial regime by devaluating the French franc. Another benefit was the connection they succeeded in establishing between this economically motivated activity and espionage. The British in neighboring colonies appreciated the potential of Africans smuggling goods into British territory as suppliers of information or spreaders of propaganda in their own colonies. They therefore allowed smugglers from Vichy territories easy access across borders and, in turn, often used them as secret agents.

Most Africans who played a part in these networks lived close to the borders and had commercial connections in the British colonies. During the Vichy period at least seventy-five Africans were convicted of espionage.[18] The connection the British had created between smuggling and espionage is key to explaining the motivation for African participation in resistance networks. There is no doubt that being part of such a network made illicit trade with the British colonies much easier. Financial benefit was gained, then, through the payment Africans received for the transfer of information or propaganda, as well as through the smuggling itself. This is not to say, of course, that political motivation was totally absent. The fact that one out of every two Africans who belonged to resistance networks was a French citizen attests to the will of these Africans to act against a colonial regime that denied them their former privileges and was deeply and manifestly anti-assimilationist.[19] It is also possible that some of these Africans were motivated by their love for the defeated republican France.

The British in the Gold Coast saw smuggling itself, even without the addition of espionage, as a form of "economic and financial subversion" that would distort the balance between supply and demand in the Vichy colonies and thus further damage the Vichy economy. Thus they not only allowed smugglers to act but even sent "traveling agents," including women, into Vichy territory to spread the news that merchandise could be sold in frontier villages at advantageous prices and that a good market existed for livestock, gold, silver, diamonds, and a wide range of other products. Sellers of such goods were to be paid at least one-third more than prevailing frontier prices.[20]

Another means Africans resorted to when faced with food shortages was black-market trading. In May 1942 an African member of the *conseil colonial* in Kaolack (Senegal) was accused of selling sugar without asking the buyer to present the necessary authorization and of raising prices illegally. He was sentenced to three months imprisonment and fined twenty-four thousand francs. The governor of Senegal expressed his wish that the official be fired as well. He stated that not doing so would have severe repercussions for the local population, who would see a man who had committed fraud continue to serve in a political post.[21]

Only one major instance of a violent reaction to colonial steps to prevent food shortages can be found: the "rice revolt" in Casamance, in the south of Senegal. The Floups of Casamance revolted when faced with the military demand that they hand over seven years' worth of rice reserves, and when the army tried to take these reserves by force, the Floups threw poison arrows at them and then tried to cross the border into Portuguese Guinea.[22]

The shortages caused by the war and the British blockade emphasized the need to reconsider the colonial economic future of FWA. The Vichy regime conceived (optimistically, in retrospect) a ten-year economic program for the African colonies that took into consideration the difficulties discussed above. Since the Vichy regime in France, and more so in FWA, did not last that long, most of these economic ideas and projects remained unimplemented. Nevertheless, exploring them will increase our understanding of the way the regime perceived some of the main issues in the colonial economy: the need for and scope of industrialization, the development of grand-scale projects, forced labor, and European agricultural settlement.

Vichy and Industrialization

One of the factors that slowed down economic development in France's African possessions before World War II was reluctance to industrialize Africa.[23] The notion of developing industries in the colonies was discussed in France in the 1930s, especially during the rule of the Popular Front. Louis Mérat, the director of economic affairs in the Ministry of the Colonies, believed that industrialization of the colonies would solve the problems raised by the economic crisis. He wanted the colonial economic policy of the Popular Front to give precedence to the needs of the colonial population.[24] Nevertheless, the promoters of colonial industrialization faced fierce resistance from the weak sectors of French industry. For textile producers, for example, industrial development in the colonies was simply out of the question. They maintained that this would damage the textile industry in France and create unemployment at a time of economic stress. No less important were political objections to the industrialization of the colonies. The fear of the emergence of an organized working class that might threaten French sovereignty in Africa made colonial administrators reluctant to encourage industrialization. In March 1938 Minister of the Colonies Marius Moutet expressed his fierce objection to industrialization. He maintained that an artificial industrialization would be dangerous, as it would raise the level of unemployment in France. He also expressed his fear that the emergence of an exploited and discontented proletariat might endanger French sovereignty.[25]

Indeed, until World War II, industrial activity in the colonies was limited to those practices supporting the import-export trade, such as ship-repair workshops, refrigeration facilities, and electrical generators. Entrepreneurs who were interested in developing light industries were usually denied credit. Some food factories that made soft drinks and cookies—for local consumption—were built in Senegal in the 1920s, as were a few groundnut-oil refineries, also mainly for local use.[26] The producers' lobby in France, however, later curbed the development of the groundnut-oil industry by demanding that the government raise the taxes on imported oil to an impossible level. This happened only a short while after Senegal began producing small amounts of oil for export to France.[27] Until World War II state support of the industrial sector in the colonies (excluding the French colonies of North Africa) was merely 0.9 per cent of the overall budget for the colonies. Even during the rule of the Popular Front no substantial industrialization plan was offered. Moutet was convinced that the future of the Africans lay in the rural areas.[28]

The debacle of 1940 left France in such a severe economic slump that the Vichy regime was motivated to develop an economic plan. The colonies played an important role in this plan. The Vichy minister of the colonies, now Admiral Réné Charles Platon, presented the ten-year plan in December 1941. He declared that the disaster that had befallen France in June 1940 would not put an end to France's economic projects and that Pétain's regime was determined to continue the colonizing mission. Industrialization of the colonies occupied an important place in this plan. Platon believed that the colonies should be industrialized and that there was no reason that this should weaken French industries. The arrival of technology in the colonies, he claimed, was inevitable, and the war proved that it would be wise for the nation to decentralize vital industries. Vichy economic planners saw other advantages in colonial industrialization as well: the development it would entail would increase the purchase power of the colonial subjects and solve the problems of economies that were based on only one agricultural product.[29]

In the text of the ten-year plan the minister explained that its foremost purpose was to develop exports by improving agriculture, as well as roads and means of transportation, thus facilitating the transfer of export products to the coast. The second stated purpose was encouraging at least some form of industry in the colonies. He regarded industrialization as one of the ways to ensure the social, political, and economic development of each colony. Another aspect of this development was investment in health, hygiene, education, and urbanization. The development of basic industries—for construction materials, substitute fuels, electrical energy, and so on—was meant to ensure a minimal vital autonomy that would enable economic survival in all conditions, according to Platon. In fact the ten-year plan went beyond the stage of basic development. It suggested extending local industries even further, so that raw materials would receive primary treatment locally until they reached the level of partly finished products, even wholly finished in some industries. Platon, however, was cautious about such "revolutionary" change and said that the industrialization he suggested was natural and would only slightly affect metropolitan industries.[30] The plan envisaged a sum of eighty-four billion francs as an investment in the colonies. Out of this total 18.1 percent was to be invested in the industrial sector. Although this might not sound so impressive in view of the regime's stated ambitions, it was nevertheless the first time that a French government invested in financing the colonial industrial sector.[31]

These ambitious plans to industrialize the colonies were not seriously implemented due to the short life span of the regime and the colonial administrators' fear of introducing such major changes in the colonial economy. This reluctance to industrialize FWA is reflected in a book Boisson published in 1942, entitled *Contribution à l'oeuvre africaine*. Africa was rural, he wrote, and to maintain its political stability it should remain rural. He emphasized that it would be a serious mistake to make Africa proletarian and industrial, as the emerging proletarian class that would be the result of such a policy would jeopardize the stability of the colonial regime. This political motive for limiting the development of local industries in the colonies was accompanied by an economic one: Africa possessed, Boisson wrote, immense and concealed resources and raw materials that were vital to Europe, but these were not being exploited due to a shortage of manpower. It would therefore be completely unreasonable to divert some of the limited existing manpower, which could help find these resources, to local industrial production that would compete with metropolitan industry. Boisson concluded that it should first be determined which industries to develop and that local industrialization should then be limited to these fields.[32]

A slightly different approach was expressed in a metropolitan newspaper, *La vie industrielle*. A May 1941 article from this journal, published on the occasion of "France Overseas Week," attacked pre–World War II colonial industrialization policy for being inconsistent and for allowing duplications in certain industries and shortages in others. The writer emphasized that for some of the colonies these shortages could be lethal. Black Africa was mentioned as an example. In the colonies no development of substitute fuels was encouraged, the writer explained, and as a result the British maritime blockade suffocated their economies. He concluded that industrialization of the colonies was necessary and should be coordinated with metropolitan industries. He was also in favor of individual industrialization enterprises but stressed that these should be closely supervised.[33]

It is important to remember that the promotion of agriculture, rhetorically at least, flourished in France under Vichy as well. In fact the regime attributed to agriculture a significance that went beyond economic considerations. Agricultural work represented a desirable and healthy way of life. Vichy ideology emphasized the "return to the soil" and demonstrated hostility toward the city and urbanization, which were seen as the source of at least some of France's ailments. Pétain believed that only the encouragement of agriculture would deliver France from its economic difficulties. "The soil does not lie" (la terre ne ment pas), he declared, calling upon the French to return to tilling the land. The regime's propaganda accorded the farmer a place of honor and the image of the warrior worker, one that equated the farmer with none other than Pétain himself.[34] Nevertheless, the regime did encourage industrialization in the *métropole* in spite of its propaganda.

Vichy ideology, then, reinforced the dislike of urbanization and industrialization that already existed in the colonial context. Vichy colonial policy regarding industrialization in FWA was ambivalent despite the obvious need for local industries. While some steps were indeed taken in the direction of industrialization, these were limited to the region of Dakar, the capital of the federation, and to several industries that were especially needed during the war years. However, the grave difficulties that emerged during the Vichy period due to the lack of local industries did give rise to a certain extent of industrialization in the colonies, although this was done reluctantly. On 30 March 1941 the Vichy government published a decree that created a committee to coordinate colonial industrial production

Table 1. Wood coal industry in Senegal, 1937–1941

Year	Production in tons	Value in FF
1937	27,889	138,831
1938	33,371	168,795
1939	28,723	227,954
1940	50,156	291,104
1941	168,762	1,138,134

Source: AN, 2G41/22 (200mi/1829), Rapport sur la situation économique du Sénégal, 1941

with metropolitan industries. This body, the Coordination Committee of Imperial Textile Industries (Comité de coordination des industries textiles de l'empire), clearly focused on the textile industry. Its main duties were to examine all proposals to establish new textile industries in the framework of "a rational plan of industrialization in the colonies" and to find the means to reduce the problems that would arise from the competition between colonial and metropolitan industries in the same markets.[35] In other words, the committee was meant to ensure that the emergence of new industries in the colonies would not pose any substantial threat to parallel metropolitan industries. It also had the authority to determine who would be entitled to set up textile plants in the colonies.

The textile industry was only one of several sectors the Vichy regime encouraged in FWA. In fact top priority was given to substitute-fuels industries because of the severe fuel shortage that practically halted trade in the colonies. The major substitute fuels were manufactured from wood coal, refined groundnut oil, and groundnut shells.[36] Senegal's annual economic report for 1941 pointed to the rapid development of the local wood-coal industry. This industry received a boost especially in the region of Casamance, where massive forests enabled extensive production. Table 1 demonstrates the acceleration of the wood-coal industry in 1941.[37]

The substitute-fuels industry was also encouraged in Côte d'Ivoire; already in 1940 the creation of two new groundnut-oil refineries was planned.[38] It was also suggested that additional palm trees be planted to extend the already existing palm-oil industry into Côte d'Ivoire and Dahomey.[39]

Additional industries that the colonial administration tried to develop were small factories for cigarettes, soap, cookies, conserves, and sweets. In June 1940 the Bata shoe company asked for permission to establish a branch in Dakar. Its request was approved, and the company invested half a million francs in the creation of a subcompany, African Bata Company

Ltd. In a letter to the minister of the colonies dated March 1941 Boisson reported that the company produced 250 pairs of shoes a week and employed four Europeans and sixty Africans. He noted that as soon as additional machines arrived in Dakar, the European and African staffs would be increased.[40]

Local industries in FWA did receive, then, a certain push during the Vichy period, in spite of the regime's basic reluctance to industrialize Africa. This push was not ideological. The circumstances of the war, especially the British blockade that almost brought trade in FWA to a standstill, left the regime no choice but to invest at least some efforts in industrialization. The Vichy regime invested in research on various production techniques that could be implemented in the colonies, such as production of alcohol from the fruits of the baobab tree; established professional committees to address the issue of industrialization; and tended to authorize requests to set up new industries in FWA.[41] Its investment in the industrialization of FWA comprised 9.4 percent of overall investment in the federation.[42] While this figure does not seem too impressive, it is still considerably higher than France's investment in the industrialization of its colonies prior to World War II.

Vichy and Grand-Scale Projects: The Trans-Saharan Railway and the Office du Niger

Trains have fired the human imagination ever since they existed. Even today when there are other, faster means of travel, the train has a special appeal. In Victorian England the train was a symbol of progress and modernization, an incredible product of the industrial revolution.[43] All over Europe train stations became, with their magnificent architecture, the new "cathedrals" of the age of technology.

In the colonial sphere the train was even more symbolic. It was a means of conquest, a way in which the supremacy of the colonial powers over the conquered territories and their peoples was clearly manifested. The railroad was the means to spread commerce, technology, and European values. It enabled colonizers to reach formerly inaccessible places.

Of all the railroad projects the French colonizers contemplated in Africa, the Trans-Saharan railway was the most presumptuous. Here the "iron snake" was not only conquering an African territory by crossing it; it was also conquering the Sahara Desert. This vast desert, described as separating the land of the Whites from the land of the Blacks, had a special place in the imagination of the French people. Their view of the Sahara is well expressed in Antoine de Saint-Exupéry's classic *The*

Little Prince (*Le Petit Prince*), written in 1943. Saint-Exupéry describes this desert as a huge territory vacant of any life forms: "The first night, then, I went to sleep on the sand, a thousand miles from any human habitation. I was more isolated than a shipwrecked sailor on a raft in the middle of the ocean." [44] In the Vichy period the Trans-Saharan railway demonstrated that the motives for such grand-scale projects often went beyond the domain of economy.

The idea of constructing a railroad across the Sahara first appeared in 1876, three years after the explorer Paul Soleillet and the engineer Adolphe Duponchel took part in an expedition to the Tuat oasis. Duponchel publicized the idea of a railroad linking Algeria to the Niger and attributed to it quasi-magical powers. Such a railroad, he claimed, would create "a vast colonial empire . . . a French India rivaling its British counterpart in wealth and prosperity." [45]

The idea appealed to the then–minister of public works, Charles de Freycinet, who endorsed it for several reasons. He explained in a report he sent to the president, Jules Grévy, that the project would put France at the head of the movement to conquer Africa. He added that the project was certainly feasible, the proof being the railroad from New York to San Francisco, built not long before by the Americans. A year later the Tuaregs (a nomad people living in the region) massacred the members of an expedition that left Algeria in the direction of Lake Chad. It was then decided to delay the project until the territory had been fully secured in French hands. The idea resurfaced about ten years later, and the project proposals became even more elaborate and fanciful. However, they all encountered the same obstacle—overly high costs of construction and the knowledge that the Trans-Saharan railway would never cover its own expenses. [46]

On 21 February 1928 the French government appointed by law a research committee to examine the technical feasibility of the project. [47] The committee reached the conclusion that the project was indeed possible. It presented five motives:

1. The Trans-Saharan would spread the French spirit around the entire African continent.
2. It would give France military security by allowing the transportation of a large number of soldiers.
3. It would ensure a political, economic, intellectual, and moral liaison with France.
4. It would favor the *mise en valeur* of the African territories and the supply of primary materials for French industries.

5. It would allow, by the creation of new prosperity, improvements to the hygiene and productive power of the black race.[48]

The order in which these motives were presented demonstrates that the railway's main importance was cultural and political; its economic significance was ranked fourth. The advantages the railway was supposed to bring to the Africans were ranked last.

Due to financial problems, however, the Third Republic governments never executed this project. On 22 March 1941 the Vichy government published a decree ordering the immediate commencement of work. For Vichy this was an incredible opportunity to show the French people the great difference between a regime that talked and a regime that acted and to demonstrate the greatness of France despite its defeat.

The government authorized the company Mediterrané-Niger to execute the project.[49] A further decree, dated 19 May 1941, allocated FWA a loan in the range of 1.69–3.12 billion francs for this purpose.[50] A review of the Vichy press from the time shows clearly that for the regime the Trans-Saharan railway was much more than just an economic project. Some articles discussed economic issues in the wake of the profits the railroad might bring, the costs of its construction, the lack of fuel and water along its tracks, and so on, but these aspects were certainly not the focus of the debate. The Trans-Saharan railway was also a tool of propaganda, used to emphasize the greatness of the Vichy regime.

Jean Marguet, a reporter for the Cri du people, published in March 1941 the proposed route of the railway. He invited his readers to lean over the map of Africa with him and chart the course of the future Trans-Saharan: "From Oujda—the northern terminus of the line will later reach the coast at Nemours and Oran—we reach Colomb-Béchar and Kenadsa. Then Benni Abbès—where the great soul of Father Foucault lies—Ardar, Reggan, Bidon V, Tessalit, before arriving at the bend of the Niger in In-Tassit. From there one branch will go toward Timboctu and Segou to join the already constructed Senegal line and the other eastward to Gao and Niamey." Marguet expected the line to be completed by 1945 and even humorously advised his readers to start thinking about booking seats for the inaugural journey from Oran to Timbuktu.[51]

In a report referencing the decision to finally begin working on the railway, the situation before Vichy was depicted in these words: "From 1859 till 1941, only discussions, only commissions, only studies, only wishes! And only wasted time!" The reporter quoted the Vichy minister of communications, who said that if the railway had been constructed in 1936, as planned, the French would have been laughing today at the English blockade. [52] But the project was not realized, the reporter continued, because the Third Republic was too weak to perform such a courageous task. "For more than eighty years," another journalist wrote, "the Trans-Saharan was one of those miraculous projects like that of the tunnel under La manche. There were some discussions around it, but then other issues such as electoral struggles drew attention away from the project. Then a new leader arrived—one who was not concerned with electoral struggles—a leader who did not talk but acted. The strong will of Marshal Pétain turned the illusion into reality." [53] For still another reporter the Trans-Saharan was the ultimate proof that indeed something had changed for the better in France. [54]

Some of the articles published in the Vichy press in France about the Trans-Saharan project compared it to the Suez and Panama Canals. The only difference was that France was "at home" in the region of the Sahara and did not need to cooperate with international companies, which was, of course, considered a huge advantage. Descriptions of the project and its actors were imbued with virtues from Vichy ideology. Its director-general, for example, represented a replica of the ideal "new Frenchman": "Young, sporty, the face tanned by the Saharan sun, this was the appearance of Mr. Chadenson, the director general of the 'Mediterrané-Niger,' who came yesterday to tell us about the magnificent act of faith accomplished between the burning dunes of the desert by those who would not despair of the grandeur of their country." [55]

Other participants in the project were depicted as young and brave Frenchmen willing to defy all the dangers involvement in this "adventure" posed, such as hunger, thirst, sandstorms, and epidemics. The text also emphasized the fact that the motives of these brave young Frenchmen were not financial, as they were being underpaid; rather, they endured all the difficulties because of their sporting spirit. [56] The menacing list of threats was probably partly exaggerated, as it is difficult to imagine that the French government did not provide basic nutrition, for example, for at least its French workers.

The French heroes who were to embark on the great project of constructing a Trans-Saharan railway also had another important role. They were to conquer the symbolic Sahara desert and prove to the French people that their image of it was distorted. The desert, as one reporter claimed, was for most French people a land of fear—a place where dangers, real and magical, lurked everywhere. It was also often seen as the tomb of a marabout, a palm tree, and a camel lost in thousands of dunes. [57]

The Trans-Saharan railway was presented as the tool with which the riches of the empire could save France, but also as the means to enhance France's position within Europe. One of the articles in the Vichy press claimed that it was futile to restart the debate for or against the project. The decision to construct the railway had been made. It might begin to be profitable in the future, but in the meantime the important thing was to use this project as an opportunity to cooperate with other European countries. Africa, it was said, was about to become a suburb of the old continent. The writer encouraged the Vichy government to take this step. He claimed that such a wise diplomatic move would help France financially and have an excellent effect on French, European, and even American public opinion. It would also be a sign to the world that Europe was conscious of its unity and solidarity and was not going to relinquish Africa. Such cooperation on the construction of the railway would later allow cooperation in the exploitation of various railways throughout Africa. Thus France might one day become interested in exploiting the Cape-Cairo railway, just as Italy, Spain, and Germany might like to use the Trans-Saharan line.[58] The Trans-Saharan was thus perceived as a means to ensure that the French empire in Africa had negotiating power after the war. The French would not stand by with bare hands while Germany and its allies divided the loot among themselves; it would have something to offer, as well as an important role in the designing of a new Europe, of which the African continent would become an immediate extension.

Some indication of the impression the Trans-Saharan propaganda made in other parts of the Vichy-ruled French empire can be found in a letter, quoted by Eric Jennings, that was seized by censors in Indochina. It was written by a Vietnamese called Bui Lang Chien, who referred to this project as a symbol of the importance the Vichy regime attributed to FWA: "Some are claiming that Vichy is contemplating . . . abandoning Asia so as to retain Africa. . . . As proof, they point to the [Vichy] decision to [resurrect] plans for the Trans-Saharan railroad, while Indochina is to benefit from no significant grand project, either for the present or the future."[59]

Nevertheless, using the Trans-Saharan as an instrument of propaganda had to be backed up with at least some economic justification. And indeed, the Vichy government also discussed and published the economic motives behind this grand project.[60] On 2 May 1941 the Comité de la France d'outre-mer held a conference dedicated to the Trans-Saharan railway. In its conclusions the committee listed its economic advantages. The train, according to the committee, would allow for the transfer of three hundred thousand tons of merchandise a year and the import of important products from North Africa that were missing in West Africa—for example, wheat that could substitute for millet, which was considered an inferior product. To this one could add products the European population of FWA needed, such as wine, fruit, and vegetables. The committee members noted that apart from these economic advantages the train would also contribute to the advancement of the civilizing mission because it would reduce the distance between FWA and Europe. The existence of a railway, they claimed, would help in civilizing the local population, and the best example of that was the perception that since a railway had been constructed in their colony, "the inhabitants of Senegal had become very civilized."[61] An illustration of the way the French linked the construction of railways in their colonies to the economic and cultural development of Africans can be found in a lecture given in the framework of "France Overseas Week" in 1941. The lecturer compared two train journeys he had made in FWA, one in 1913 and the other just before his lecture. The conditions of the journey had greatly improved, he said. Whereas on the first one the train was crowded and he had to sit on uncomfortable wooden benches, with nothing to drink but warm water, on his recent trip the wagons were comfortable and he was able to eat and drink chilled beverages in the restaurant wagon.[62]

The ostensible economic advantages the construction of the Trans-Saharan railway entailed, however, did not convince everyone. In a critical article published in the metropolitan newspaper *Révolution*, a writer described the enormous technical hurdles that awaited the builders of the railway. The main problem was not, he wrote, the shifting sands, as most of the route was not sandy at all, but two other critical problems. One was the lack of accessible fuel in the Sahara. If the train had to carry its own fuel for three thousand kilometers, it would not be able to carry anything else, and constructing gas stations along its route would be, he stated, superhuman. The second problem was how to cool the engine. The train's engine needed a large quantity of water, and the wells in the Sahara were barely even sufficient for the herds that inhabited the desert.[63]

In view of the voices that doubted the utility of the project, it was necessary to further justify it. Another grand project planned well before Vichy but enthusiastically endorsed by the regime added to the needed economic rationalization. This was the project of the Niger Delta, for which the "Office du Niger" had been established in 1932. In fact this was the only project that survived after the 1923 publication of the Albert Sarraut program for the "mise en valeur" of the colonies. The Niger Delta program had been developed two years earlier, its aim to open the interior of FWA to French trade and produce certain crops in colonies that seemed suitable. This was the first time that the need to invest resources in order to develop production in the colonies was raised. [64] The main aim of the Office du Niger was to cultivate cotton in the region of the Niger Delta so that FWA could become the main cotton supplier of the French textile industry, which received all of its cotton from foreign countries. In 1919–20 a special research expedition was sent to the region. The original plan was to irrigate an area of 75,000 hectares and transfer to the scantly populated region 1.5 million people from the Mossi region, in Upper Volta. In 1924 another expedition decided that rice should also be cultivated in the area to tackle the scarcity of food in Senegal, Upper Volta, and Niger. The Trans-Saharan train was perceived as vital to this goal, as it would be able to transfer the cotton to North Africa and the rice to the populations that needed it in the south. [65]

Emile Bélime, the colonial engineer who envisioned this grand project, planned to develop 1,850,000 hectares. But even after the establishment of the Office du Niger the project had many critics in FWA who believed that it drew resources away from more worthwhile development efforts. The main problem was the sparseness of the population in the region and the difficulty of recruiting the immense manpower needed for the project. In response to this critique Bélime claimed that the advantages of the project would attract farmers back to the region. He did not wait, though, until this happened and instead adopted a policy of *colonisation indigène*. Under this policy entire families were recruited to settle in the Niger Valley, where they had to cultivate the land under the supervision of Office du Niger management. As only few Africans were ready to volunteer for the scheme, until 1946 the vast majority of these farming families were forcibly recruited, and the close supervision over the farmers was not instructive but oppressive. This coercive policy attracted criticism. During the rule of the Popular Front numerous government reports, the press, and some books denounced the forced recruitment and the poor conditions in which the African workers lived. But it was only after World War II that this policy was actually reconsidered.

The same decree that allocated substantial funds to the Trans-Saharan train line also assigned a sum of six hundred million francs to the Office du Niger, designated for the preparation of 200,000 hectares of irrigated soil for the cultivation of cotton and rice in the Niger Delta. This was an area almost three times vaster than that originally planned, a fact that demonstrates the Vichy government's enthusiasm for the project. Under

Vichy, however, conditions at the Office du Niger deteriorated further, as the project expanded and more settlers were recruited.[66]

Vichy policy regarding these two grand-scale projects marked a major change from the Popular Front's reluctant view of such activities. The reason for this shift was not necessarily economic, but rather political. The Vichy regime needed to show that it was different from its predecessor. The Trans-Saharan railway and the Niger Delta project, both of which had been born during the Third Republic, gave it an opportunity to demonstrate the power of a regime that was not preoccupied with electoral struggles. France's dire economic situation and the doubt often expressed about the economic value of these projects did not deter the Vichy planners. For them propaganda was far more important than economic rationale.

The Trans-Saharan railway and the irrigation of the Niger Valley were grandiose projects that depended on the constant use of forced labor. Both, therefore, failed to survive the postwar reforms that prevented the continued use of forced labor. The Office du Niger continued to exist after the war, but the initial grand project of resettling the area with African farmers had to be abandoned when not enough volunteers could be found. The Vichy period was both a climax of such grand imperial schemes and also their swan song.

Vichy and the Question of Forced Labor

The revival of the two grand-scale projects demanded a great deal of manpower, though this was not easily recruited. Consequently another economic issue was brought to the fore: the question of forced labor. Forced labor had existed in FWA since the beginning of the twentieth century. With the formal abolition of slavery in FWA in 1905, the need to create an alternative workforce arose. Although republican France believed in the superiority of free labor, in the colonial sphere forced labor was preferred. The justification given was that Africans were lazy and that forcing them to work was the only way to develop the colony, which would eventually also benefit the Africans.[67]

The term *forced labor* (*travail forcé*) is not to be confused with the term *service de travail obligatiore* (STO), established by the Germans in France in 1942. Forced labor in FWA covered several legal categories: public works, work that substituted for payment of taxes (*prestation*), work that could usually be traded for money, and army recruitment for public works. In certain areas women and children were also recruited for forced labor. The service was for short periods, which enabled the colonial administration to exempt itself from supplying health services, nutrition, accommodation, and transport. Punishments given for refusal to work or unsatisfactory labor were sometimes harsh. Especially difficult was the position of Africans, who were forced to work far away from their homes in climatic conditions to which they were not accustomed and with people whose language they could not speak.[68]

The system of forced labor persisted in FWA until its formal abolition in 1946. Until the end of World War I forced labor was not legal, and the colonial administration was the sole employer. After the war laborers were recruited to work in private enterprises as well as in public works. At this time the colonial administration also added two other forms of forced labor and institutionalized forced labor as a form of punishment. In 1930 an international conference convened in Geneva heavily criticized France and ruled that forced labor was actually a form of slavery. France rejoined that it had saved Africans from their barbarity. The only step it took following the conference was to replace the term *forced labor* with *obligatory labor* (*travail obligatoire*).[69]

The worst system of forced labor was created in the regions where Europeans needed the greatest amount of manpower, especially in the fertile forest areas of Côte d'Ivoire, where European planters had settled. In these regions the population density was low, and planters had to import labor from the more populated regions of northern Côte d'Ivoire, Guinea, and Upper Volta to fell trees and plant cocoa, coffee, and bananas. Toward the end of the 1930s Africans had also begun to develop plantations and to compete for workers with European planters and the colonial administration.[70] When World War II erupted it became more difficult to recruit workers because of immigration to the neighboring British colonies, and competition for plantation laborers thus intensified.[71]

The Vichy colonial administration was deeply concerned about the difficulties in recruiting workers. The attempts to resurrect the Trans-Saharan railway and the Office du Niger projects required a large number of workers. The administration was also under pressure from European planters, who felt especially loyal to the new regime and expected it to satisfy all their economic needs by ensuring that they received enough workers even in wartime. On the other hand recruitment itself created two problems. First, the administration was worried about taking away manpower from the villages and leaving them without enough farmers to produce crops that were in high demand. Second, the administration did not want to create too much resentment by intensifying forced labor, as this resentment could have dangerous results.

Table 2. Needs in wartime

Colony	Number of workers for private projects	Number of workers for public projects	Total number of workers
Senegal	15,000	12,000	27,000
Dakar	5,000	5,000	10,000
Sudan	10,000	20,000	30,000
Guinea	17,000	22,000	39,000
Côte d'Ivoire	75,000	20,000	95,000
Togo	7,000	8,000	15,000
Dahomey	5,500	20,000	25,500
Niger	5,000	20,000	25,000
Total	139,500	127,000	266,500

Source: ANS, 17G/396 (126), July 1942

The regime, then, took some steps to address these two problems. On 10 September 1941 the colonial administration decided to conduct a workers' census in the region of Upper Volta (then a part of Côte d'Ivoire). The aim of this census was not to confirm how many available workers lived in this region but to examine the extent to which it was possible to reduce the number of African farmers in the area by allocating workers to the project of the Office du Niger, without damaging agricultural output.[72] In July 1942 a special Service obligatoire du travail (Obligatory Labor Agency) was established in FWA. A report sent to Boisson regarding this new agency attempted to find a solution to the two main problems related to the recruitment of forced laborers. The report distinguished between the period in which it was written, defined as a time of limited economic activity, and normal times. It presented two tables, one with the required number of workers in each colony for private and public projects in wartime and the other with the same data in normal times.

Several interesting conclusions can be drawn from these two tables. If we assume that the data for normal times were at least partly based on the administration's need for workers before World War II, it seems that the Vichy administration required fewer workers than were necessary before. A closer look suggests that there was a significant difference between the private and the public sectors. Whereas the demand for laborers in the public sector drastically decreased in the Vichy period (to only 56 percent of the number of workers in normal times), the decrease in the required number of workers for the private sector, at least in certain colonies, was not so significant (to 82 percent of the total number of workers required in normal times and 88 percent of this number in Côte d'Ivoire).[73]

Table 3. Needs in normal times (according to the Ten-Year Plan)

Colony	Number of workers for private projects	Number of workers for public projects	Total number of workers
Senegal	20,000	40,000	60,000
Dakar	5,000	5,000*	10,000
Sudan	13,000	30,000	43,000
Guinea	24,000	39,000	63,000
Côte d'Ivoire	85,000	45,000	130,000
Togo	8,000	13,000	21,000
Dahomey	9,500	32,000	41,500
Niger	5,000	20,000*	25,000
Total	169,500	224,000	393,500

*No evaluation (numbers correspond to current needs)

Source: ANS, 17G/396 (126), July 1942

The report also attempted to address the colonial concern with exhausting the agricultural working power of Africans. To do so it collected data about the maximum number of workers who could be taken from each colony without damaging its working power and dangerously depopulating it. The total number of such workers in the federation was estimated at almost two hundred thousand. These were divided among the colonies in the following manner:

Table 4. Maximum number of workers to be recruited from each colony

Senegal	21,100
Sudan	46,400
Guinea	26,200
Côte d'Ivoire	50,000
Dahomey	17,000
Niger	23,000
Total	183,700

Source: ANS, 17G/396 (126), July 1942

The report also suggested reforming the recruitment method so as to reduce the damage to the producing power of African villages and to avoid, as far as possible, resentment from the African population. It recommended prolonging the periods of recruitment, which up until then had extended for a maximum of six months, though they sometimes lasted only one or two months. According to the report, if the colonial administration recruited permanent laborers for longer periods—two years, for example—the need to recruit more laborers would decrease. This would create a situation in which only 1.2 percent of the African population would be far removed from their homes. The report estimated that such a small percentage would be harmless.

The other stated purpose of this new proposal was to reduce the resistance of the African population to forced recruitment. The report explained that the recruitment of laborers had been negatively received until then for several reasons. First, the recruits were always drawn from the same marginalized elements within the African population: poor or unwanted persons and foreigners. Often these people were married and had children. Second, the recruitment was often renewed, to the displeasure of the laborers. The report noted that the workers became undisciplined during their working period and remained so when they returned to their villages, to the point where village heads could not wait to send them out to work again. According to the report, the new recruitment system would prevent these problems, as it would reduce the number of workers needed and allow them to learn their jobs properly. The longer recruitment period would also save money. Moreover, longer service would ensure that the same person would not be recruited again. The new system would not only extend the service but also be enforced on all young, fit, unmarried Africans.

These proposals and the report on which they were based expose the colonial regime's interest in exploiting African labor while avoiding the potential for revolt that recruitment might create. According to these data, in view of the economic slowdown during the Vichy period in FWA, recruitment to private enterprises did not decrease. Especially if we compare the Vichy period to that of the Popular Front, when the use of forced labor was very limited, what was happening in FWA was an expansion of forced labor, especially in the private sector, for the benefit of European settlers in Côte d'Ivoire and Guinea. Over 90 percent of recruits in this period were for private enterprise, slightly under half of them for coffee and cocoa plantations.

It is also probable that the report's proposals regarding the improvement of work conditions for forced laborers were not closely followed. In fact, according to the testimony of Africans who lived in Dakar during the Vichy period, the conditions in which forced laborers were kept bore no resemblance to the idyllic descriptions in the Vichy reports. A.D.M. remembered seeing forced laborers who had been recruited in French Sudan and elsewhere brought to Dakar. They lived not far from the Medina quarter, in a large camp, in deplorable conditions. The structures in which they slept were made of straw, and they were provided with extremely low-quality food, primarily cooked millet with some sort of vegetable to which dried fish and water were added. This food caused some of them grave indigestion problems. Some had to steal food to survive. [74] One informant referred to this forced labor as slavery and emphasized that the Africans were not paid for their work. [75]

Most informants, then, remember forced labor under Vichy as harder and crueler than it had been previously. This was especially true in areas where white settlers used African laborers, as it was in these areas that they were needed the most. The case of private forced labor in Côte d'Ivoire is especially interesting as it bears a relation to postwar political developments in this colony.

European and African Planters and the Use of Forced Labor: The Case of Côte d'Ivoire

The region of West Africa in general and the French territories specifically did not attract European agricultural settlement. West Africa received the unwelcoming name "white man's grave" because of its difficult climatic conditions and its many diseases. Only certain colonies, mainly Côte d'Ivoire and Guinea, attracted some European settlement. When the colonial administration saw the success of the British in the Gold Coast in cultivating coffee and cocoa, it tried persuading Africans to substitute these cash crops for their traditional food crops. [76] When that failed it tried to attract European farmers to the region. After World War I European settlement in Côte d'Ivoire received a strong incentive. The rise in global prices made agricultural plantations in tropical regions most attractive, especially for French people whose aspirations to progress in France were blocked. The settlers usually came from the lower classes, economically and intellectually. At first they established farms only along the coast because they feared the difficult conditions in the hinterlands. Later, when colonial rule was effective in all parts of Côte d'Ivoire, some settlers set up farms in the hinterlands as well. Some of the European farms were so small that one person managed them. Others were huge plantations belonging to companies that sent representatives to supervise them. Before World War II there were two hundred European settlers who owned seventy-five thousand hectares of land, about two-thirds of all cocoa trees, and an even larger share of coffee trees. [77]

The colonial administration saw the European settlers, from the time of their arrival in FWA, as allies. Colonial officials believed that their presence benefited the economic development of the colonies. This approach made them ensure that the Europeans received enough African workers, even at the expense of the number of workers allocated for public projects. Although the idea of forced labor was justified by the claim that workers thus recruited were designated for work that would benefit the colony's development, the administration did not hesitate to enable private European employers to use this method of obtaining manpower for their own benefit. This, too, was justified by the claim that European agricultural settlement benefited the entire colony.

The alliance between the settlers and the colonial regime was only reinforced during the Vichy period. Most settlers were ardent supporters of Pétain and hoped to gain from the establishment of the Vichy regime in FWA. Their hopes for a more authoritarian rule that would guarantee their position vis-à-vis African planters and African workers were more than satisfied.

In his 1942 book, *Destins de l'Afrique*, André Demaison described the crowds of settlers he saw in his vision who would come to Africa to explore new areas of economic competition and form a "white" line between Algeria and Transvaal.[78] A report written in FWA in the same year shared this enthusiasm regarding the benefits of white settlement, although it did relate some of the dangers inherent in the European presence. The disadvantages the report presented included the massive transfer of African manpower from populated areas; the isolation of African workers; their working conditions; and the influence of European culture on them, which might create an unwanted "black proletariat." However, the report maintained, the advantages of European settlement were far more substantial. It could contribute to the colony's economy by increasing production and improving its quality. The presence of one European in one corner of the forest, it went on, gave the African an example of a better way of life and better treatment of his crops that no school could ever provide. The report emphasized this point by using the British case, in which almost every family had a representative in the colonies. This fact underscored the British imperial sense. It concluded by noting that on the day every French family also had a representative in the colonies, the feeling of grandeur of which the Marshal had spoken would be much stronger.[79]

Boisson himself also believed that European settlers in FWA should be assisted. In his book he noted the difficulties Europeans had in recruiting manpower for their plantations and maintained that the only solution was to force Africans to work for them.[80] Nevertheless, he also believed that economic development in Africa could be achieved only if Africans were allowed to remain farmers, and this made him object to the extension of white settlement in FWA. He was critical of European employers who relied on the colonial administration for a steady supply of workers without investing any efforts in attracting these workers, satisfying them, and keeping them. He believed that although workers should be supplied to the existing European settlers, further settlement should not be encouraged and the number of forced laborers should be limited. [81] Nevertheless, Boisson too saw European settlement in FWA as a generally positive phenomenon. The settlers fervently supported the new regime, which granted them substantial advantages, especially the "generous" allocation of African forced laborers.

As noted earlier, the practice of recruiting forced laborers to work on European-owned concessions had long existed in certain parts of West Africa, including Côte d'Ivoire, without any legal foundation. In 1925 it was semilegalized in the first labor code, which aimed to institute a uniform system of individual wage contracts that would be supervised by the administration. The code inspired a regulation of conditions for Africans working on European farms or concessions. While wage contracts were supposed to be voluntary, the code did not deny administrators the right to recruit forced labor in case European entrepreneurs lacked workers. In fact the 1920s saw a rising demand on the part of Europeans in Côte d'Ivoire for African workers due to the new awareness of the economic potential of this colony. It was not easy, though, to find voluntary workers because of the difficult nature of the work and the low salaries that Europeans were prepared to offer. Competition with the wages offered in the neighboring British colony of the Gold Coast also made recruiting voluntary workers difficult. The preferred solution for European employers was not to try to compete on a free-labor-market basis but rather to pressure the colonial administration to recruit forced laborers for their farms and plantations. They insisted that it was the administration's responsibility to reroute the migrant laborer away from British and onto French colonies. They also demanded that the administration make efforts to prevent the desertion of Africans, which, they stated, was a chronic problem that stemmed from their "lazy" nature.

Despite the conflict between the administration's interests in recruiting Africans for public projects and the interests of European private employers, efforts were made to supply Europeans with forced laborers. The colonial belief was that working on European farms would improve the habits of Africans and thus benefit the economic development of the federation as a whole. The new labor code was ambiguous regarding the recruitment of workers when voluntary workers were difficult to find.

It also protected employers from desertion of workers by instituting a system known as the *pécule*, which allowed employers to withhold a portion of the laborer's salary until the work was finished. The *pécule* system also created a fund from which fines could be collected as a form of punishment. The paternalistic justification given for this system was that African workers usually wasted all their wages on nonsense and that this was in fact a way to save their money for them.[82]

When white planters began reaping profits from cocoa and coffee plantations in Côte d'Ivoire, Africans soon realized that they could do the same and, defying the stereotype of the "lazy African," indeed set up their own plantations. White settlers, in addition to their struggles over the allocation of forced laborers and their efforts to keep these workers from running away, now also had to compete with African planters. African cultivation methods were different. Africans usually had smaller parcels of land that were scattered in the forest area. Initially African planters did not need many workers. But gradually, as their plantations developed, they started competing with Europeans over African manpower. Until World War II African planters paid their workers the same low salaries paid by Europeans and had some access to forced laborers. However, the shortage in both imported products and forced laborers caused by the war soon made the colonial administration systematically prefer Europeans, and African planters stopped receiving workers. Moreover, African planters themselves were often recruited to work on European-owned plantations. These Africans' plantations were ruined when they could not find anyone else to look after them. On top of all these other problems the colonial administration created "sanitation" crews during the war that destroyed African plantations, claiming that they were "nests of parasites."[83]

A demonstration of the discrimination practiced against African planters can be found in the solutions the governor of Côte d'Ivoire suggested to the problem of finding forced labor in his colony. In his political report for 1941 he suggested reducing the allocation of forced laborers for African planters. Instead he proposed demanding that these planters recruit workers from among their family members or use volunteers. He did not propose to do the same with relation to European planters.[84] This harsh policy against African planters, which followed the Popular Front's relatively liberal one, made this part of the African elite hostile toward the Vichy regime. African planters who had previously benefited from the forced labor system were not only compelled to abandon their plantations but also found themselves often forced to work on European ones. Their loss of privileges forced them to identify with the African masses.[85]

The discrimination against African planters did not end when the Free French took over FWA in 1943. One of the results of administration policy was the establishment of the Syndicat agricole africain (SAA) in 1944, which was headed by Félix Houphuët-Boigny. This organization initially protected African planters against discrimination in allocation of forced laborers. Houphuët-Boigny soon realized, though, which way the wind was blowing and started to fight against the concept of forced labor per se, until he brought about its abolition in 1946. In the same year the SAA turned into a political party, the Partie démocratique de la Côte d'Ivoire (PDCI).

The period of the Vichy regime in France was too short to allow it to implement long-term economic plans and thus allow us to evaluate its measure of success. In FWA this period was, of course, even shorter. However, the examination of Vichy economic visions in FWA can teach us a great deal about the regime's perceptions on central issues. In general Vichy colonial policy was guided by two elements: the difficult economic situation in both France and the colonies, especially the British maritime blockade, and the ideology of the regime. The Trans-Saharan railway project, which could not have been a profitable enterprise, is an example of the central role the regime's wish to restore French grandeur played in its economic considerations. The issue of industrialization, on the other hand, shows that economic necessities caused by the war and the British blockade could sometimes make the regime act against its ideological beliefs.

The political and economic importance of the empire was reflected in the Vichy regime's attempt to extend its ideology to the colonies. However, as we have seen, this attempt was not always successful. In the three spheres discussed in part II, the political, social, and economic, a large degree of continuity had been preserved. The major change was, in fact, that the new metropolitan ideology was much better suited to the colonial reality. Part III will examine to what extent this new ideology and the attempt to extend it to FWA affected relations between the colonial regime and various sectors of the African population.

PART III

Vichy Encounters with African Society

The Vichy regime invested real efforts in importing the National Revolution to its French colonies in Africa. Through propaganda and education it tried not only to maintain the loyalty of the colonial subjects but also to win their hearts. The ideology of the new regime in France was presented to Africans as one that better suited their needs, aspirations, and traditions than the one that preceded it. Nevertheless, the colonial administration was well aware that the new circumstances threatened the colonial order. It understood that counterpropaganda networks in the neighboring British colonies were also doing their utmost, sometimes successfully, to win the hearts of the Vichy-ruled colonial subjects. This dual concern, of holding on to the loyalty of Africans while preventing them from acting against the colonial order, dictated a policy that cautiously moved between the "carrot" and the "stick."

Part III addresses encounters between the Vichy colonial regime and African society. But first a distinction must be made among the different groups or sectors within this vast and diversified society. Such categorization is never easy. The following chapters, therefore, focus on several groups within African society that may be divided into two sectors. For the sake of convenience these sectors will be termed the "modern" and the "traditional." The "modern" sector includes African groups or communities that were created by the policy of assimilation, while the "traditional" sector contains those groups that the colonial regime saw as related to the African precolonial reality.

I make this distinction in spite of its potentially problematic implications and inaccuracy because this was how the colonial regime perceived African society. The advantage of using such artificial colonial divisions is that it helps us understand the inner logic of colonial policy toward the groups in each sector. The distinction between "modern" or assimilated Africans and "traditional" ones, and the preference for the latter, existed within the French colonial administration in FWA before Vichy. So did the invention of African traditional institutions and concepts. Still, it is interesting to examine the attitude of the Vichy colonial regime to "tradition" and "modernity" in light of the Vichy metropolitan ideology. The adoration for the peasant as presenting the antidote to urban decadence, rooted in the traditional social hierarchy, existed long before Vichy and flourished between the wars. Just before World War II Drieu la Rochelle wrote against the too urbanized Third Republic: "La France du camping vaincra la France de l'apéro et des congrès."[1] The Vichy regime adopted this reverence toward the French farmer. It suited the regime's ideology of promoting the values of "the good old France," as well as the dire economic circumstances that necessitated the encouragement of the agricultural sector.[2]

The Vichy regime in France expressed deep nostalgia for the values of the past. It called upon the French to practice old customs and study local languages; it tried to resuscitate French folklore by reviving abandoned ceremonies and encouraging popular art. The regime declared that by doing so it hoped to rehabilitate the "real France," whose inhabitants were attached to its soil and in which no uprooted foreigners lived.[3] This is not to say that the Vichy regime was conservative and backward looking. Alongside this rehabilitation of the values of the past it also considered modernity a vital element.[4] As described in chapter 5, however, the encouragement of modernity in agriculture and industry in the colonial sphere was marginal in spite of the economic difficulties. The next two chapters examine the extent of colonial continuity in Vichy relations with "modern" and "traditional" elements in African society.

In the modern sector, that of the "products" of assimilation, I include the African elite of the *originaires* and the *évolués* and Africans who had converted to Christianity. These groups sometimes overlapped. In the "traditional" sector I include African chiefs, both precolonial kings and leaders and appointed colonial chiefs, and Muslims, especially the leaders of the Sufi orders. A third group included in this category is soldiers, or as they were called, *tirailleurs sénégalais* (although they were recruited all over FWA). This is the most difficult group to characterize: clearly a product of colonialism and in some ways "modernized" by their experiences in Europe, most soldiers were Muslim and lived in rural areas and therefore were perceived by the colonial regime as belonging to the "traditional" sector of society. By using this categorization I hope to cover most elements within African society. Unfortunately an examination of the entire society is not possible, especially not in a colonial context. The story of some groups within this vast society—such as women, for example—remains untold due to the lack of sources.

Vichy encounters with the various sectors of African society are examined from both directions. While part II discusses primarily the colonial perspective, here I also look at the various African responses to the new colonial regime. Such responses are examined for each of the abovementioned groups after Vichy policy toward them has been probed; chapter 8 then summarizes the discussion while focusing on the measure of continuity and change in colonial relations under Vichy rule. It also presents some examples of subtle responses to Vichy policies that cannot be attributed to the specific sectors outlined here.

Any discussion of the Vichy regime and responses to it could easily fall prey to the temptation to employ such notions as "resistance" and "collaboration." The debate around these notions has been at the core of Vichy historiography ever since the end of World War II. The Gaullist myth that emerged after liberation about the fierce resistance of the French to the occupation pushed historians of the Vichy period to concentrate on the issue of resistance. This emphasis characterized research during the twenty years that followed. With the publication of Robert Paxton's *Vichy France: Old Guard and New Order* in 1972, and its translation into French a year later, the resistance myth was broken and replaced by its opposite—the notion that the "true France" was that of Vichy; that members of the resistance made up a tiny minority; and that most of the French, notwithstanding their view of the Germans, were "functional collaborators."[5]

Paxton's book played a key role in the transformation of the model of understanding the Vichy regime. The picture of Vichy France that emerged from this book was described as one painted in "dirty grays" rather than the black and white of previous efforts. Ever since its publication historians who study this period in French history have added more colors to the picture. They have advanced a more nuanced view of the almost endless fragmentation of French public opinion under Vichy.[6] Toward the end of the 1970s the focus of research moved from the nature of the regime to the people who lived under it. In the decade that followed historians began to study the departmental level and discovered an almost universal hostility toward the Germans and a rather rapid disenchantment with the Vichy regime. These studies challenged the oversimplistic categorization of public opinion and claimed that the dichotomy between "collaboration" and "resistance" was too crude to accommodate the diversity of responses to the regime.[7]

During the 1990s new tendencies toward the study of resistance emerged. More emphasis was put on the experience of nondominant groups, such as women and immigrants. An attempt was made to study resistance within its social context, that is, to study the social history of resistance.[8] According to H. R. Kedward, the narrow definition of resistance as being a quality only of those men and women who belonged to a movement or an organized network ignores attitudes and actions that clearly signify a spirit of resistance. Although he does not deny that resistance in Vichy France was a minority phenomenon, he indicates that newly discovered documentation shows a range of rural support networks operating in the period, voluntarily providing, for example, food, clothing, lodging, and transport; concealing parachuted weapons and ammunition; and refusing to divulge information during Gestapo investigations.[9] Such subtle forms of resistance also existed in FWA, as we shall see later.

Another new tendency is to examine the relations between the Vichy regime and the resistance movement. Recent studies have proved that not all of the resistance organizations in France necessarily challenged Pétain's authority or alienated themselves from the regime's policy and institutions. Few of the resisters condemned in one breath both the Nazis and Vichy. Some were definitely anti-Nazi or anti-German but generally held a positive view of Pétain.[10] The view of the Vichy regime, then, is much more ambivalent now than in the past. According to Pierre Laborie, the simplistic alternatives of Pétainism versus Gaullism, and collaboration versus resistance, can only provide highly reductionist images of the experiences of people under Vichy. It is known, for example, that most French people grieved the defeat but supported the signing of the armistice and that they could be hostile toward the occupier without joining the resistance. In an interview with L'express in October 1997 Simone Weil expressed the complexity of the Vichy period when she said that some of the French behaved well, some badly, and most behaved well and badly at the same time.[11]

The dichotomy between "collaboration" and "resistance" is even more problematic in the colonial context, because responses to Vichy colonial rule were not necessarily different from responses to colonial rule in general. Recent colonial historiography rejects such notions and contends that responses to colonial rule should be viewed mostly as forms of accommodation.[12] The establishment of the Vichy regime in FWA was not such an acute transformation for Africans, who had not exactly lived under democratic rule before. Therefore, African responses to Vichy policy should be examined as responses to any other colonial regime would be, without the connotations usually evoked when we hear the words *resistance* and *collaboration* in the context of World War II.

6.

Vichy and the "Products" of Assimilation

Citizens, Western-Educated Africans, and African Christians

When in the 1880s the French government began to officially endorse colonization and view it as an important political goal of France, it had to decide upon a theory with which to rule its colonies. Until the last years of the nineteenth century the leading theory was that of assimilation. Its principle was that the colonies should be considered as provinces overseas, extensions of the fatherland, and therefore should have similar institutions to those of the *métropole*. French people who immigrated to the colonies were to retain all their rights as citizens, including the right to vote for the National Assembly. This theory was implemented with regard to foreign settlers of European descent and in some cases applied to original inhabitants of the colonies, aspiring to turn them into Frenchmen; the four communes in Senegal are examples of this impulse.[1]

The theory of assimilation was in opposition to the colonial ideology upheld by the British, who perceived their colonies as foreign lands and anticipated, though only in an unforeseen future, their separation from Britain. The French approach intended to prevent the possibility of self-rule by considering the colonies as an indivisible part of France.[2] The French civilizing mission played a crucial role in this theory. Local cultures were looked upon with contempt or were even completely ignored. The idea of the civilizing mission, which had existed in different forms since the sixteenth century, suggested that the power France possessed to conquer and rule "inferior" peoples should be used to advance these peoples until they attained the intellectual and cultural level of the French people.

And yet there was no general agreement among the colonizers regarding the interpretation of the civilizing mission. Some politicians accepted only the material definition of civilization. They claimed that France should give the peoples of the empire civilization only in the modern meaning of the word. That is, the French should teach them how to work so that they could spend money, buy goods and services, and exchange products. But they should not transmit to them moral values that would not bring them or France any benefit.[3]

Even during the years in which assimilation was the official theory of the government of France, its supporters were skeptical of the possibility of fully implementing it. As the nineteenth century drew to an end, the criticism of assimilation became harsher. This stemmed from the fact that the colonies France added to its possessions during this period did not attract European settlement, and it was therefore difficult to implement the theory there. Those who rejected assimilation found support for their views in the new social sciences, especially psychology and sociology, which warned against the dangers of interfering with the laws of social evolution.[4]

The retreat from the policy of assimilation was in direct proportion to the growing French admiration of foreign colonial methods.[5] The French were impressed by the Dutch method, which enabled a small number of Europeans to rule efficiently over their immense empire in Indonesia. They related the Dutch success to their development of a colonial policy based on the conservation of native institutions. British colonial theories were now also viewed with admiration. The French especially appreciated the British distance from their colonial subjects.[6]

In the early twentieth century several new programs that were supposed to replace the theory of assimilation emerged. They were all essentially similar and were assembled under the term *association*. The theory of association was never defined, but there was wide agreement regarding the general ideas it was supposed to embody. Its merit lay in its simplicity, flexibility, and practicability. Contrary to the rigidity and universality of the doctrine of assimilation, the policy of association emphasized the need for variety in colonial practices. One of its basic principles was the idea that the decisive factors in any colonial policy had to be the geographic and ethnic characteristics and specific conditions of social evolution in a given region under foreign rule.

The changes in French colonial policy in the interwar era reflected transformation in metropolitan France, as well as the needs of the colonial state. The challenges of the revolts that erupted during World War I, and the demands of the *évolués* for equality with French citizens, clarified to the colonial administrations that it was a mistake to ignore precolonial

institutions and strip the chiefs of their authority. The policy of association was accompanied by the appearance of new themes in the ideology of
the civilizing mission. These themes remained within a republican framework, but their emphasis was totally different. The colonial administration no longer claimed that it had an obligation to release Africans from
their "feudal chains" by systematically divesting traditional elites of their
power. It now claimed that African society would advance better if chiefs
were to remain in their positions while the French consulted with them
and guided them regularly. Thanks to this guidance chiefs would be able
to both civilize the African rural masses and represent them. Through the
concept of "association" the colonial administration in FWA adopted a
much more positive approach to the political and social organization of
West Africa than ever before. This new policy stemmed from the need to
control the *évolués* and reestablish discipline among colonial subjects in
general. It was also influenced by the atmosphere that reigned in France
after World War I, marked by a wish to reconstruct the "old order" and
a growing respect for all types of hierarchy—social, sexual, and racial.

Association, though, was not a new idea. It was, rather, a variation
on the notion of the "noble savage" that had already been applied in
parts of the French empire well before World War I. This policy was
based upon common interests—a fraternity without equality. The colonial
theoretician Jules Harmand believed that *association* was a synonym of
cooperation, a policy that committed the conqueror to developing the
conquered region but also made it responsible for the physical and mental
welfare of the colonial subjects. It was a sort of a contract between two
societies, but with no equality between them. Although some of the basic
elements of association, such as the tendency to respect local political
institutions and the reluctance to accord French citizenship to too many
colonial subjects, existed in FWA before World War I, the policy did entail
a significant change. A certain obligation to the idea of the universal
man, equal everywhere in his potential and deserving emancipation, had
disappeared.

And yet the new policy did not contradict the idea of the civilizing
mission but only modified it. According to these ideas the conquest of
a colony still demanded a moral obligation to improve the material and
cultural status of the "native," but this was to be done without changing
the way of life of colonial subjects and without attempting to turn them
into Frenchmen.[7] It is important to bear in mind, though, that association
was not an unrepublican concept, and its advocates did not necessarily
hold more racist views than those who tried to promote assimilation. In

fact, until the Vichy period, association and assimilation could indeed coexist.[8]

The new policy did not manage, however, to solve the problems that the policy of assimilation had created. The elite of the *évolués* continued to demand further rights, and the chiefs' authority was not enforced. On the contrary, the younger generation began to challenge the chiefs' leadership. The colonial administration refused to recognize this failure. Admitting that the chiefs could not serve as intermediaries between the administration and the African population would have obligated the French to replace them. But they did not want to do that because European substitutes would have been too expensive, and the only other possible local rulers— the African Western-educated elite—might have demanded more political participation than that demanded by the chiefs. Toward the end of the 1920s there was a proposition to create a sort of *elite d'indigènes*—a new legal category between subjects and citizens whose members would not be citizens but would be allowed to vote in local elections and be exempted from the *indigénat*. This idea never materialized, though, because of the objection of Governor-General Jules Cadre (1923–30). He claimed that the creation of such a class would disrupt his work and be accepted in the more politically advanced regions as a refusal to accord citizenship, thus perhaps bringing about turmoil.

Association was, then, an attempt to deal with the growing power and demands of a Western-educated elite. Nevertheless, throughout the interwar era the theory of assimilation continued to exist in FWA, especially in Senegal, where most of the Africans holding French citizenship resided. Although this right to citizenship was often contested, the new policy of association never abolished it. In the federation of FWA Senegal was the oldest colony. Its four coastal cities, known as the four communes— Dakar, Saint Louis, Gorée, and Rufisque—were an "experimental laboratory" for the theory of assimilation. In these cities a privileged African elite had emerged that profited from the implementation of this theory during the whole history of the colony, even when the competing doctrine of association held the upper hand.[9]

The first political institutions to emerge in the four communes, beginning in the middle of the eighteenth century, were municipal. A century later, in 1848, the inhabitants of the four communes were granted for the first time the right to elect a representative to the National Assembly in Paris. In 1879 the General Council (*conseil général*) was established, its members elected through direct and universal suffrage of the communes' inhabitants. The General Council had real powers and even approved a part of the colonial budget. It was politically active and animated. Real debates were held that did not hesitate to question colonial policy. Partly due to this activism the colonial authorities re-formed the council in 1920 and changed its name to the Colonial Council (*conseil colonial*). The number of members was enlarged to forty, but only twenty were elected; the rest were appointed from among the chiefs who were loyal to the colonial administration.

In the early twentieth century a new generation of colonial administrators, who did not adhere to the theory of assimilation, began to contest the political rights of Africans. A real attack on their civic and political rights evolved in this period. In 1907 suffrage was limited to the *originaires*, meaning Africans who had been born in the four communes.[10] Two years later the *originaires*' rights were limited to the territory of the four communes; as soon as they traveled outside of these borders, their rights were automatically revoked.

This limitation provoked the *originaires* to wage a battle for recognition of their French citizenship. They succeeded only when the first African, after a long line of *métis*, was elected as the deputy of Senegal. This was Blaise Diagne, who in 1915 and 1916 managed to pass two laws that accorded the *originaires* and their descendants full French citizenship. They now had duties such as military service but also fundamental judicial and political rights. They could publish newspapers and establish political parties, which made political life in the four communes much livelier than before. What French objectors to assimilation had the most difficulties with was in the judicial domain: the Muslim *originaires* were subject to Islamic law in private affairs such as marriages and inheritances.[11]

On the eve of World War II there were more than twenty thousand Africans who were eligible to vote. The modern African elite, however, was larger, as it included Africans who were not *originaires* and therefore were not entitled to French citizenship. This elite was formed through its members' education and way of life, as a result of which they received from the colonial authorities some recognition, but no specific privileges. The colonial administration called these Africans *évolués*. This designation stemmed from the discourse of assimilation, which suggested a salutary "evolution" toward a sociocultural European model.

From the beginning of the French presence in Senegal a part of the African population found itself closely associated with the Whites and their lifestyle. More or less voluntarily they adopted certain economic and cultural standards from the civilization that the colonizers imported. This minority faction became the core of a new colonial elite attached to the colonizer. In the twentieth century this elite was defined in cultural terms and not in judicial ones. The *évolués* were the new educated elite of the colonial system.[12] While most Africans holding French citizenship were Senegalese, *évolués* also lived in other parts of FWA. Dahomey, for example, had a relatively large proportion of western-educated Africans because missionary education had continued in this colony even after the separation of Church and State in France in 1905.[13]

The French colonial regime was ambivalent toward this new elite from the outset. This attitude reflected in a way the general French ambivalence toward the idea of assimilation. The regime needed this elite desperately in order to rule effectively. Most members of the elite served as civil servants, which solved the problem of finding enough local French personnel to fill the colonial posts. Also, the salaries of African civil servants were significantly lower than those of French civil servants, saving the colonizers large amounts from their coffers. On the other hand the colonial regime was worried by the creation of "detribalized" African elites who would eventually feel frustrated by their inability to advance beyond a certain point. The administration's concern was that this frustration and the feeling of not belonging anywhere—neither to the traditional milieu nor to the colonizer's society—would make these Africans direct their anger toward the colonial regime, resulting in its destabilization. This concern actually reflected the disbelief of most French colonials in the possibility of assimilating Africans into French civilization.

Vichy and the Doctrine of Assimilation

While republican rhetoric corresponded to the doctrine of assimilation, at least in theory, Vichy ideology completely contradicted it. Its leaders objected to the ostensible republican attempt to abolish differences in the world and join all nations under French civilization.[14]

In a lecture entitled "La politique coloniale positive," which is cited in a book about the French empire from 1941, the colonial expert René Maunier described the mistakes he believed had been made in the French colonies prior to the Vichy period. The biggest was the idea that the colonies were a tabula rasa and that there was only one truth suitable for controlling all countries and all climates. This idea, he held, resulted in the total destruction of local cultures and customs, which administrators treated as if they were contagious diseases. Maunier explained that as the empire was not homogenous and contained diversified populations with different levels of civilization, the colonial policy must also be diversified and adjusted to the reality on the ground. He also rejected importing

French institutions per se to the colonies, claiming that such copycat replication turned these institutions into caricatures.[15]

Maunier called upon the Vichy colonial administration not to implement the same policy for the very civilized, the civilized, the less civilized, the little civilized, and those who were mistakenly—according to him—called uncivilized. He stressed that there should be a clear distinction between those who accepted France and those who rejected it. The greatest attention should be given to the évolués, for whom it was necessary to create, even at that late stage, a special status.[16]

In another of his articles Maunier explained what he meant by a "special status" and why its accordance was already impossible in certain cases. For him it was a substitute for the undesired option of granting French citizenship to colonial subjects. He explained that he was against giving French citizenship to the Muslims of Algeria without them first renouncing their personal status, meaning their right to be subjected to Islamic law in matrimonial affairs. These Muslims, he clarified, could even be polygamists, could hold amusing and irritating beliefs such as the notion of the "sleeping child," and still take refuge in their French citizenship when they so desired.[17] It was absurd, he said, that French citizens were subject to two legal systems while Algerian Jews who had lost their French citizenship continued to be subject to French law. Citizenship, he wrote, should be accorded only to those who really wanted it and then only on the condition that they realized that being French meant adopting French customs and the French lifestyle and observing French law. Maunier then searched for a solution that would enable granting a special status to the colonial subjects who became closer to France, without making them full-fledged citizens. He suggested creating a "citizenship of the empire" that was in fact a second-rate citizenship.[18]

Maunier did not clarify, though, the meaning of such citizenship. Probably it was different from citizenship in the French union, given to colonial subjects in 1946, as he does not suggest establishing political institutions in the colonies to which Africans could be elected. He noted that he had suggested in the past declaring that the "natives" were French and their nationality was French but that, apart from exceptional cases, they would not be granted French citizenship. He cited as an example the Portuguese, Belgians, and Italians, who accorded to a certain number of their colonial subjects the special status of "half citizen," or as he imaginatively termed it, mitoyen. This status was given to colonial subjects who fulfilled certain conditions. For the Italians in Libya, for example, a mitoyen had to be non-Jewish, over eighteen, serve Italy in such a way as joining its army and even being wounded or decorated, be literate in Italian, spend at least two years in the public service, and so on.

Maunier lamented the fact that in the French empire the fulfillment of these conditions enabled colonial subjects to become full-fledged citizens, while in Libya the Italians only allowed certain rights, such as protection of property and the right to organize, but not the right to elect and be elected or to have command over Italians. The status of semicitizenship allowed the "good" colonial subjects to be compensated, but with an "encouragement price" (*un accessit*), not the "big prize" (*le prix*), which did not compel the subject to forgo his personal status. Maunier questioned whether it might still be wise to do the same at least in some parts of the French empire. He believed that regrettably this was no longer possible, as it would be turning the wheel back.[19]

As we have seen, this special legal category of African *évolués* who were not French citizens but enjoyed some privileges had already been suggested in the late 1920s but was rejected by the governor-general. Maunier, however, did not wish just to add this category between African citizens and the masses of colonial subjects. In fact he wanted it to replace the legal category of citizenship for Africans.

The idea that French citizenship should not be given to those who did not belong to the French nation by blood and race was wholly accepted by the colonial theoreticians of Vichy. While Maunier only alluded to this idea by suggesting a "half citizenship" for non-French people, Jean Paillard, a former *Action Française* journalist and the head of Pétain's Bureau des corporations, recommended that "the title of French citizen can belong only to a son of a Frenchman, carrier of the blood representative of the genius of his race." Paillard found the idea of giving "natives" the right to vote appalling and dangerous, as it would eventually lead to the domination of the colonized over the colonizer.[20]

Maunier and Paillard, two of the most influential colonial theorists under Vichy, totally rejected, then, the doctrine of assimilation, and their view widely represented that of the regime in general. However, the Vichy colonial authorities in FWA still had to address the consequences of the limited implementation of this doctrine under the Third Republic.

Vichy Policy toward *Originaires* and *Évolués*

Adopting the idea of citizenship as based on blood ties and race meant that the Vichy colonial regime necessarily rejected the idea of according French citizenship to Africans. Still, the authorities knew as well as Maunier did that they could not turn the wheel back, though this did not prevent them from attempting to snag it. There was no technical problem with revoking the citizenship of all Africans who possessed it. Such a measure had been taken against the Jews of Algeria, who were granted French citizenship in 1871 by the Cremieux Decree. [21] However, the colonial administration did not wish to take such a radical measure against a population that belonged to the colonial elite and thus presented a potential threat to colonial order. The administration did, nonetheless, undermine their privileged status through official and discriminatory measures. In fact Africans holding French citizenship were no longer allowed to exercise any of their political rights, such as the right to organize or publish a newspaper. [22] The Vichy administration often expressed its opposition to French citizenship for Africans and its reluctance to authorize their naturalization. The already small number of Africans who were naturalized just prior to the Vichy period (thirty-eight in 1939 and thirty-two in 1940) declined even further under Vichy. In 1942 only five naturalizations were authorized, and these were primarily motivated by propaganda. One example was Seidou Tall, a *médecin indigène* who was wounded in the British-Gaullist attack on Dakar and who was also a relative of the influential Tijani grand marabout Seidou Nourou Tall. [23]

Vichy notions of a return to the soil and the regime's general dislike of intellectuals reinforced the previous negative colonial attitude toward educated Africans. However, the administration knew it had to be very careful when dealing with them; members of the modern African elite had to be relatively content and yet kept under tight control. This attitude manifested itself in several ways. Some of these have already been discussed, such as the special propaganda designated for the educated African elite and the encouragement of young Africans to join youth organizations whose activities were planned and controlled by the regime.

Another means of keeping this elite content without losing control over it was via the press, which has already been discussed as a propaganda tool in FWA. The supplement of *Paris-Dakar*, *Dakar-jeunes*, added in 1942, targeted particularly the elite *évolués*.

The colonial administration occasionally used the journal to allow educated Africans to express themselves at a time when other channels of expression were blocked. One such attempt was made in 1942 when the colonial authorities encouraged a literary discussion in the pages of this newspaper focusing on whether or not educated young Africans should aspire to assimilation into French culture. This debate is especially interesting, as some of the contributors became local political leaders after the war. [24]

The debate, which one of the participants defined as concerning "any educated African," was launched with an article by Outhmane Socé Diop entitled "L'évolution culturelle de l'AOF" (The Cultural Evolution of FWA).[25] The article presented two basic views. In the first, supported by the writer, the assimilation of Africans into French culture was seen as both inevitable and desirable. Adherents of the second view Diop presented, such as, at the time, Léopold Sédar Senghor, were against assimilation. Proponents of this second view claimed that the attempt of black people in Africa to adapt to a civilization that was not created by them and for them would be a mistake. Diop saw all civilizations as results of *métissages*, a view that Senghor himself came to accept after the war. Africans, Diop maintained, could not escape this determinism.[26]

The response to Diop's challenge was enthusiastic, and many young Western-educated Africans began to submit their own views on the desirable future relation of African cultures with France. Joseph Baye, for example, proposed a solution that was, as he himself acknowledged, as complex as the problem itself. He opposed assimilation but believed that it was possible to reach a harmony between the two views that Diop had presented. On the one hand, he said, *métissage*, if meant to be permanent, was a renouncement of the African personality; on the other a pure black culture at this stage of history was impossible. Therefore, *métissage* was inevitable, but it should be seen not as an end but as a means to reach a culture that was essentially black.[27]

Mamadou Dia believed that the black mind had no problem with assimilating to Western culture, as this was a universal culture, beyond races and borders.[28] But he asked whether it would not be better if, instead of going to study at the Sorbonne, Africans tried to understand who they were and explore their own still-unknown historical heritage. No doubt, he explained, an educated black man would know how to appreciate the beauty of classical music, but this could not compare to the enormous inner excitement that the sounds of African musical instruments he had known from birth would evoke in him.[29] Emile Zinsou, who became Dahomey's president after independence, also claimed that absolute assimilation was impossible because some elements objected to it, for instance, Islam, with its Semitic origins. He also emphasized that the question of whether Africans should assimilate to French culture was not only cultural but also political.[30]

This point became clear to the colonial administration when, after several months of publishing articles on this subject in *Dakar-jeunes*, it decided to suspend the debate, as it feared it might become too heated and have dangerous political repercussions. This decision came about after an article by Charles Béart, principal of the William Ponty School, regarding the supposed inability of educated Africans to write French literature, caused deep resentment and protest among African readers. In his article Béart explained to the young educated Africans that there was no point in their investing effort in writing French literature, as even if they mastered the French language they would not understand its mechanisms. He added that he, for example, was not in the least amused by British humor, but he still understood its mechanisms. According to him young Africans should concentrate on the important mission of reconstructing African stories, myths, and legends. At the same time he warned them against developing naive pride and reminded them that while their oral literature might be rich and varied it was not equal in value to any European written literature. [31] The strong reaction to Béart's article troubled the administration to the point that it called for a special intelligence report to probe the subject. [32] It demonstrated how the policy of allowing educated Africans to express themselves could easily spin out of control.

Vichy policy toward the African educated elite was as ambivalent as that of the previous colonial regime. However, it put greater emphasis on this elite. If before Vichy the colonial regime was worried about the creation of a "detribalized" elite that would become frustrated and thus act against the colonial regime, in the Vichy period, when the Anglo-Gaullists directed their propaganda at this group, these fears were exacerbated. This led to unprecedented attention being given to educated Africans. The Vichy regime, then, rejected educated Africans on the one hand while embracing them on the other. This attitude was met with similarly ambivalent responses from the elite. But before we turn to discuss these responses, let us look at another African group that drew the attention of the Vichy administration and that had been created by an additional aspect of assimilation—converts to Christianity.

Vichy and African Christians

Africans who converted to Christianity were usually (though not always) considered to belong to the "modern" African elite. Most of these Africans were mission educated and had a European way of life. But unlike non-Christian members of the elite they were part of wider networks of either Protestant or Catholic missions, whose members sometimes felt they had to protect them from the secular colonial regime whose interests often contradicted their own. Most of the Christians among the Africans were Catholic simply because the Catholic mission was more active in the French territories than its Protestant counterpart. [33] Nevertheless, there were also many African Protestants. In 1941 there were around one hundred thousand African Catholics and sixty thousand Protestants in Côte d'Ivoire, the colony with the highest percentage of Christians in FWA. [34] In spite of representing only a small fragment of the total population of the federation, African Christians posed two problems for the colonial administration during the Vichy period. The first pertained to the Protestant missions, and the second concerned Vichy relations with the Vatican.

The status of the French Protestant church, headed by Pastor Marc Boegner, was unclear in the immediate aftermath of the debacle, when the regime's policy was still unknown. Some Protestants were worried that the National Revolution might show hostility toward them. They feared that they might be next in line after the Jews and the Freemasons. [35] The reason for this trepidation was that Protestants had been a minority that had been persecuted in France in the past (on the eve of the war there were six hundred thousand Protestants in France). [36] But although the French nationalistic press often mentioned the Protestants in the same breath as the Jews and other "anti-French" elements, the fears of persecution appeared to be baseless. [37]

This does not mean that relations between the Vichy colonial administration and the Protestant missions in FWA were in any way relaxed. On the contrary, these missions were viewed with suspicion due to their close ties with Anglican missions in the neighboring British colonies. In a letter dated 30 June 1941 Minister of the Colonies Réné Charles Platon reminded Pastor Boegner of the conditions under which the Protestant missions were allowed to act in the French empire. Platon clarified that he was prepared to ensure freedom of action to the missions on the condition that their activities would always be limited to the religious domain and that they would remain loyal to France. He added that evidence showed that this was not always the situation. Many mission stations, he wrote, were situated near British colonies, from which they received financial support and even operational directives. Such instructions were sometimes politically motivated and opposed to the line of the Vichy government. Platon made it clear that he would not tolerate such phenomena. He cited as an example a case in which the Protestant missions in Lomé, the capital of Togo, received ostensibly religious booklets, in fact Anglo-Gaullist propaganda tracts, and informed Boegner that he had ordered colonial administrators to closely supervise missions that had contacts with the British. [38] The case Platon cited occurred in 1941, when a bulletin entitled *Pour la liberté* (For Liberty), sent by air from London to the missionary station in Lomé, was intercepted by the postal control in the city.[39] Another incident in which Protestant priests were suspected of cooperation with the British took place in July 1942, when two African priests from a Protestant missionary station in Guinea were arrested for espionage.[40]

Unlike the Protestants, who were concerned to some extent by the National Revolution, the Catholic Church saw its three pillars—Work, Family, and the Fatherland—as its own values. The Catholic Church emerged strengthened from the defeat of June 1940. The Marshal had promised order, hierarchy, discipline, and respect for religious and traditional values. The defeat was perceived as a moral one, which stemmed from the decayed values of the Third Republic and its rejection of religion. The enthusiasm of the Catholic Church for Pétain and his regime was not a result of any material benefit but of the change of atmosphere that Vichy inspired. It was certainly Christian symbolism that Pétain relied upon when he spoke of the suffering and sacrifice that the French people would have to endure to bring salvation.[41]

The Vichy regime also aspired to improve relations with the Vatican, which had been rather strained since the separation of Church and State in France in the early twentieth century. To do so the government tightened its diplomatic relations with the Vatican; abolished laws that prohibited some forms of religious activity; and promoted cooperation among the State, the French Church, and the Vatican.[42]

This wish to retain good relations with the Vatican may explain the seriousness with which the Vichy government handled a request the Vatican forwarded through its ambassador in France that the legal status of Catholic communities within France's overseas territories be regulated. The request was transmitted to Governor-General Pierre Boisson, who conducted a comprehensive examination of the subject and consulted all of his governors. He sent them a summary of a circular that Governor-General Jules Brevié (Vichy's third minister of the colonies) had formulated on that issue in 1935, representing the colonial stand regarding the status of African Christians, then expressed his own view on the subject and asked for their opinions.

The prevalent view found in the 1935 circular included several points. First, appreciation was expressed for missionary activity; it was stated that conversion to Christianity contributed to the moral development of the "natives." African Christians were to be accorded full freedom of faith. However, it was emphasized, it was vital to ensure that African

Christians would not form a separate social group on the margins of African society. To prevent family disputes the administration would verify that no African minor would be baptized without the consent of the head of the family. The main problem that was raised, though not solved, was the same question that bothered the Vatican, namely, what the legal status of the African Christian should be. While converts could not be judged by the customary legal system, as they rejected the principles upon which it was based, if they were not citizens they could not be judged by the European legal system either.

With this circular Boisson noted that the letter that the Vatican ambassador had delivered to the Vichy government raised a political question to which France could not remain indifferent. He presented a view that had been raised before the war—that African Christians should be judged in matrimonial affairs according to Christian laws. Boisson was reluctant to accept this view and asserted that it should not be forgotten that the indigenous customs in the federation were alienated from the Western habits with which the Catholic Church was imbued. The solution, according to him, was to try to compromise between the laws of the Church and local customs to create a law that would harmonize the spiritual and social rules of the Catholic religion with the exigencies of the local African environment.[43]

In the course of the following months seven governors sent Boisson their opinions on the question of African Christians' legal status. Hubert Deschamps, the governor of Côte d'Ivoire, the colony in which this issue was the most relevant, noted that most of the African Christians in his colony remained tied to their local customs and that their new religion had not abruptly changed their social organization. Although he admitted that on some points Christianity contradicted local customs, especially in matters of marriage and divorce, he objected to the formation of a special legal status for Christians. He claimed that such a step would only result in a rapid disintegration of African society that would be against the missionaries' interests. Instead he suggested implementing a few rules that would help solve the problem, such as following the custom of the individual person in question, in divorce cases that of the wife. He also proposed adding to the African judges in the native courts two Catholic and two Protestant representatives.[44] This was the general tone of the answers of all the governors: none was in favor of creating a special legal status for African Christians, and all pointed to the harm that such status might cause to the stability of African society.[45]

While conversion to Christianity seemed to the colonial regime, even during the anticlerical Third Republic, a step toward civilization, it clearly created problems within African society. Just like citizens and the *évolués*, African Christians were colonial subjects who crossed the boundaries between the colonized and the colonizer, and such subjects were the most difficult to handle. The French were not prepared to accord these new Christians French citizenship or grant them other privileges, even at the price of rebuke from the Vatican. The Vichy administration was even firmer in its anti-assimilationist stand, but the new atmosphere in the *métropole* regarding Christianity made it at least reexamine the problem. The few changes the governors proposed were mostly cosmetic, but the attention given to African Christians—a minority in FWA—at a time when other more pressing problems bothered the administration reflected the Vichy regime's desire to keep the Catholic Church content.

The Modern African Elite's Perceptions of the Vichy Regime

In order to understand the ways in which the African Western-educated elite perceived the Vichy regime and its policies, it is vital to highlight the close ties of most members of this elite to republican France. Most of the Africans I interviewed, who were part of an entire generation of educated Africans on the verge of adulthood when World War II broke out, recalled the moment they heard about France's defeat and said they were devastated by the news. Bara Diouf, who was eleven when the war began, had wanted to join the French Army. He cried on the day of the armistice, believing he had lost something good. He described the feeling he and his friends felt toward France as a "sentiment très élévé, très beau, très noble," which was based on a myth of an admired republican France.[46] A.D.M. described a similar sense of loss; he and his friends felt that the defeat of France was their own.[47] According to Peggy Sabatier, this reaction was typical of members of the modern African elite. In her study of this elite, stretching from 1903 to 1950, she concludes that most of them felt French or had feelings of deep affection and admiration toward the colonial power. As proof she provides several testimonies of informants who said they shed tears when they heard France had been defeated.[48]

The ambivalent treatment the Vichy administration offered to African elites, created by the implementation of assimilation, is reflected in the ways these Africans perceived the new regime. While at least part of this elite felt deep frustration at their loss of privileges and their new experiences of discrimination, which became a part of their everyday life, the members of the modern African elite were also flattered by the immense attention that the Vichy regime accorded to them and were attracted to the ideas of the National Revolution.

According to the testimony of Africans who belonged to the Western-educated elite and lived under Vichy, Vichy colonial propaganda generated a large degree of responsiveness. All informants questioned about their responses to Vichy propaganda admitted that they had been attracted by Pétain's messages. Most started spontaneously singing the hymn "Marechal, nous voilà," remembering the lyrics even sixty years on. One of them even recited the first five sentences of one of Pétain's speeches he had had to memorize in school.[49] Bara Diouf described this propaganda as brainwashing. Schoolchildren were encouraged to join the Scouts and collect money for France. At the time he was so impressed by this that when he found a coin in the street one day, he did not hesitate for a moment before giving it to the school principal as a donation for the Marshal. Two days later a circular was distributed in all classes praising Diouf for his good deed, and his name was posted on the distinction board. Diouf also recalled that they were told in school that the Third Republic had been wicked and that Pétain had signed the armistice to save France. He said that this sounded logical to him then. Only after the war did he realize that he had been misled. A.D.M. explained that Pétain was perceived as the hero of Verdun. No one spoke about the Germans because the colonial authorities knew that Africans saw the Germans as enemies.[50]

Similar evidence of the enthusiastic responses of young Africans to Vichy propaganda can be found in memoirs written by Africans after the Vichy period. The vivid and detailed descriptions of songs, statues of Pétain, and ceremonies found in these books illustrate the deep impression this propaganda made on young Africans at the time. Abdourahmane Konaté, then a pupil, and Léopold Kaziende, a teacher, both recount that the Pétain cult was extremely powerful in the schools. Statues of the Marshal stood proudly on the school grounds, the French flag was hoisted every morning, and the children often sang the hymn "Maréchal, nous voila."[51] Kaziende, who was about thirty when he was posted to a regional school in Niger, admits that he truly believed the Marshal would save France and that he had total confidence in him.[52] This obviously sincere testimony demonstrates the potential influence of Vichy propaganda not only on youngsters but also on their teachers.

Further evidence of the effect of Vichy propaganda on young Africans is given in the Lucien Lemoine biography of the Franco-Senegalese artist Douta Seck. Lemoine notes how Seck, while studying at the William Ponty School, revealed his artistic talent in a portrait of the Marshal. This painting so strikingly resembled Pétain that the headmaster sent it to the French leader. The young artist received a personal letter from Pétain in response. The author goes on to explain to his readers that there was no reason to censure Douta for being a Pétainist: "Who could think of reproaching him for it? At the moment things were happening everyone was Pétainist, all those who did not know [what was going on], those who were in Verdun, or whose fathers were, and those who still believed in the 'camouflaged resistance' of the Marshal."[53]

The enthusiastic response of educated Africans to the colonial idea of launching a cultural debate in *Dakar-jeunes* may also point to a certain support for the regime. After all, a relatively safe way to express discontent would simply have been to ignore this literary discussion. Similar enthusiasm can be gleaned from a report written by Mamadou Dia, a teacher who took part in a seminar organized by the Vichy authorities on the General Education reforms. Dia, who became the first prime minister of Senegal after independence, described the seminar in which he participated in highly complimentary terms.[54]

Such reactions could be interpreted as stemming from obligation rather than enthusiasm. In the case of Dia, he had to write a positive report if he wished to keep his post as a teacher in a school for soldiers' sons in Saint Louis. In the case of the literary debate, it is possible that educated Africans who wanted to express themselves chose to participate because all other means of expression were blocked to them. Nevertheless, it seems that members of this elite showed some interest in the messages of the new regime and tried to discuss their cultural dilemmas in this new light. As the discussion in part II shows, the Vichy propaganda designed for this elite did not fall on deaf ears. At least some aspects of it seemed convincing to its African audience.

However, enthusiasm for the new regime and its ideology was also accompanied by feelings of frustration, resentment, and even anger, stemming from the combination of economic hardships produced by the war and the policy of discrimination, which members of the African educated elite, including the *originaires*, were feeling for the first time. Complaints about discriminatory measures appeared in letters written by educated Africans in the Vichy period. These letters were intercepted by a special postal-control service that was established in the colonies as well as in metropolitan France, with the aim of following dangerous shifts in public opinion. The *service du contrôle technique* had, in fact, been established in France before Vichy, on 12 December 1939. Its role was to appoint "postal control commissions in time of war" (*commissions de contrôle postal en temps de guerre)*. The activity of these commissions went into high gear, though, only in the fall of 1940. Postal control took place only in the unoccupied zone. Every week 320,000 to 370,000 letters were read. The postal-control service chose letters randomly or explicitly (in the latter case, when the writers of the letters were suspected of hostility toward the regime), steamed them open, and copied parts or even the whole text. Later the letters were sent on to their original destinations.[55] The process of postal control in the colonies was similar. The *service du contrôle technique* there transmitted to the governor-general a monthly general report about the letters that had been read. Usually the contents of the seized letters were described in a few words. Only when a letter was considered important was it copied. Most of the intercepted letters dealt with personal matters and did not discuss the political situation. Censure reports from 1941 state that *évolués* complained about the rise in rent, which had doubled during 1941, and expressed their distress at having lost all rights to receive bread.[56]

The policy of segregation did not always stem from food shortages. The Vichy authorities also encouraged it in cases that had no relevance to the economic situation. Such was the case of a certain beach in Dakar. The authorities posted a sign stating "plage des blancs" at the entrance to this beach. This sign later symbolized for some informants the rabid racism of the Vichy colonial regime.[57] After the war the name of the beach was changed to Plage de la plante, but according to Boubacar Ly, a philosophy professor at the Cheick Anta Diop University of Dakar, his generation still refers to this beach as Plage des blancs.[58] A.D.M., who was born before Ly, clearly remembered, however, that this beach had been reserved exclusively for Whites before the Vichy period as well.[59] If that is true, then the real change was posting the official sign, which left no room for doubt and put the educated Africans and even those holding French citizenship in the same category as all colonial subjects.

Segregation was not an unknown phenomenon in FWA before Vichy. In an article that compares British segregationist policy in Freetown to that of the French in Conakry, Odile Goerg states: "Fundamentally influenced by the assimilation theory . . . French colonizers could not use an overtly segregationist discourse to impose changes in colonial cities. Therefore, they adopted a more subtle policy, legally based not on race, but on living standards and cultural characteristics."[60]

The Vichy colonial administration did not see itself as in any way obligated to the discourse of republican assimilation. It therefore had no problem implementing a policy of segregation based on race rather than on other more blurred categorizations.

These examples demonstrate that the real change experienced by the African educated elite in the Vichy period was an outbreak of a previously latent racism. After all, as we have already seen, no real change of personnel occurred in FWA. The same is also true for the education system—a central space for younger educated Africans. According to the testimonies of some who studied in the colonial schools during the Vichy period, schoolteachers and headmasters were not replaced, and some began to openly express racist opinions that they had previously concealed. A.D.M., for example, recalled one teacher who compared his African students to animals and made fun of black people who supposedly wore a tie on their naked bodies. The same teacher reversed his attitude completely after the Vichy period was over. Diouf recalled similar experiences regarding the manifested racism of teachers, although, being younger than A.D.M., he could not say whether this marked a change compared to the previous regime. He also recalled an especially humiliating incident that happened out of school. He had gone to visit his sick aunt in Dakar's hospital, and when he came out of the hospital he crossed the path of a white couple to whom he did not pay much attention. Unfortunately for him, they were the governor of Senegal and his wife. The governor's wife ran after him, grabbed his hat, and threw it on the ground, while screaming at him, "You must salute when you see the governor!" When I asked him if he thought that racism like this was new in FWA, he answered that racism had existed before but that this was a new kind—a dogmatic and Hitlerian racism. The French, he said, were not dogmatic racists before Vichy, but they began to believe the doctrine of the superior race during that era.[61]

Vichy's new type of racism was not of course felt only in the cities by Western-educated Africans. The atmosphere that allowed colonial officials to express their latent racist attitudes flourished also in the rural parts of FWA. Saliou Samba Malaado Kandji tells the story of the head of Tivaoune subdivision, a man called Cau, who was, according to Kandji, known to be a racist before Vichy but was encouraged to express his racism more openly by the defeat of republican France. After the establishment of the Vichy regime he declared to the elders of the village, "Your France is dead! Be warned, your France does not exist anymore!" Ironically, it was the regime he so admired that dismissed him. His uncontrollable behavior evoked many complaints against him, and the Vichy colonial authorities were worried that he might cause a popular insurrection in his circle.[62]

In spite of these evident feelings of frustration, and harsh criticism toward the Vichy regime and its policies, attitudes were not translated into real action. Most Western-educated Africans, including politicians whose status remained void of any meaning, either supported the new regime or tried to ignore its harsh consequences. Some évolués joined Anglo-Gaullist espionage networks, but the risks this kind of activity involved deterred most of them from doing so. The absence of action against the Vichy regime is easy to understand and does not imply real support of the regime.

Perhaps the best example of this blend of latent criticism and ostensible support can be found in the figure of Galandou Diouf, who was elected as Senegal's representative to the National Assembly in 1934. Six years earlier Diouf had formed an opposition party to the party of Blaise Diagne. When the latter died in 1934, Diouf succeeded him in the National Assembly. Although he did not work closely with French people, as had Diagne, who was a customs inspector, and in spite of having mobilized many anti-French forces to win the election, Diouf presented in Paris the perfect image of an assimilated African in a three-piece suit. He took with him only the youngest and most chic of his four wives to help him "conquer" Paris. When World War II broke out, he declared that he could reinforce the French Army with four hundred thousand African soldiers.[63]

Diouf's pro-French stance was reflected in the following declaration he published in April 1940 in France-Soir: "France is our mother. . . . All its benefits the black people cannot forget, and this is why, by the hundred thousands and soon by the millions, our tirailleurs sénégalais will join their youth and their force with yours, farmers, workers, bourgeois of France . . . A white race? A black race? Maybe, but also men, united Frenchmen by the defense of the same ideal and a beloved fatherland that spread its protective genius under all the skies of this vast universe."[64]

On the day after the Anglo-Gaullist attack on Dakar Diouf wrote a personal letter to Pétain in which he expressed his fright at the "appalling" assault and his wish to express the loyalty and commitment of the Senegalese population to France.[65] Nine months later Diouf sent another formal letter, this time to the minister of the colonies, Platon. Opening with "Mon cher Amiral," he then quoted a proverb in Wolof (the lingua franca of Senegal): "Those who wait for the rain to fall before they buy an umbrella risk getting themselves wet." Diouf hoped by this quote to explain why it had been vital for him to return to FWA. Diouf presented himself in the letter and in a telephone conversation that preceded it as the perfect intermediary between the regime and the African population. He wrote that, with the help of some people who knew FWA well and enjoyed the appreciation and trust of its inhabitants, he could transmit to his black brothers advice that would light the road ahead. He emphasized that his authority among the Africans did not stem from his position as a member of parliament; rather, it was a traditional authority related to the important place his family held in the history of Senegal.[66]

These two formal letters might present an image of an African politician who, despite being denied his privileges, accepted the new regime and even wished to embrace it. But personal letter that Diouf wrote to his son in 1941, intercepted by the postal-control service, presents an entirely different picture and probably reveals Diouf's true feelings toward the Vichy regime and its ideology. The following excerpt illustrates the degree of Diouf's discontent with the "new" France:

> With regard to the assimilation of the clerks of the superior cadre—it is an iniquity—the valiant Mandel was going to level all this because he recognized only merits. Unfortunately, the defeat occurred. The sooner I confront the Admiral with this question the better . . . because this is a disgrace. This is a battle to fight, as there are only Negrophobes in the colonies. To work and die for France, the Negroes are considered good Frenchmen and good brothers. But when it comes to granting them some of the advantages enjoyed by some of their white brothers, we are good-for-nothing dirty Negroes. For now, there are the ordeals of the moment. I am certain that everywhere we, the Negroes, will be the last ones to rally around the tricolor flag. When I hear French people here say: Let us throw all the colonies to the Germans so that they leave us in peace, let us jettison them—and to think that without the empire where would they be today? This is the mentality of some of these people. So how are we to obtain assimilation with such characters? Fortunately, alongside such bastards there are good Frenchmen who think otherwise. . . . In any case, we are ready to perish with the tricolor flag as we are French, it is not the color of the skin which determines who is a good Frenchman.[67]

Several interesting points emerge from this excerpt. It is clear that Diouf was imbued with deep emotion toward France as a country. His criticism is directed against certain Frenchmen whom he refers to as "bad," but not against France or the French nation as a whole. He even claims his loyalty to be stronger than that of most white Frenchmen. Although the word "Vichy" does not appear in the letter, the praise given to a republican

and Jewish minister of the colonies, George Mandel, regarding the issue
of assimilation suggests that Diouf believed that the Vichy administration
opposed assimilation. In the last paragraph he describes to his son the
situation in France: "Here in France there is nothing to bite. We would
have better died than let this country deteriorate to such an extent. This
is the moment to send all the shirkers and cowards to suffer the disgrace
of hunger. *But the pigs now find the climate good*" (emphasis added).[68]

Here the criticism is even sharper. Diouf clearly says that the armistice
was a mistake. He criticizes those Frenchmen who, unlike their black
"brothers," were too cowardly to stand up to the Germans and even
wishes them the disgrace of hunger. The last sentence is especially interesting: "But the pigs now find the climate good." We can assume that
the pigs are those "bad Frenchmen" mentioned earlier. They have always
been around, but the fall of the Republic and the new regime provided the
right environment for them, and they began to feel they could act upon
their wishes.

The example of Diouf, who can undoubtedly be shown as a representative of the African elite, sheds light on the disappointment and disillusion-
ment of this elite with French colonialism. While the doctrine of assimilation did not always prevail before Vichy, and while even Africans who
held French citizenship had to reassert their rights once in a while, under
Vichy assimilation was blatantly rejected for the first time. According to
G. Welsley Johnson, Diouf, who died in 1941 and did not see the return
of the Republic, was convinced on his deathbed that the French had lied
to him and that the principles of 1789 were only for metropolitan French
and had never been meant for black people.[69]

Vichy's total negation of the theory of assimilation dictated to a large
extent the regime's attitude to those who were perceived as the "products"
of this theory. The idea that assimilation was dangerous, as it created a
group of Africans who were detached from their "natural" milieu, had
existed well before this era. However, the accentuated and visible racism
of this regime, which refused to accept foreigners as French by either
blood or race, as well as the delicate circumstances of the war, made
the Vichy colonial authorities deeply concerned about this elite. After
all, educated Africans had the tools necessary to understand France's
real situation and follow the events of the war. They were also those
most exposed to British-Gaullist propaganda because of their ability to
read. The potential danger related to them made the Vichy colonial policy
toward them ambivalent. On the one hand their privileges disappeared,
and they often encountered racism and contempt. On the other they

received a great deal of attention from the authorities and were influenced by its inclusive propaganda.

The manifested racism of the Vichy colonial regime and its harshness—previously unfamiliar to most educated Africans—made them recognize the inherent racism that exists in any colonial rule. These young Africans who grew up during the war believed, like their parents, that the "fatherland's" defeat was their own. But unlike their parents their encounter with the colonial establishment, mainly through their teachers, occurred at a time when the concept of assimilation, though never fully endorsed before, was totally nonexistent in the colonial discourse. The economic hardships of war accentuated colonial racism. For these Africans the masks of French republican colonialism had all fallen away, and colonialism was exposed for what it truly was. The Vichy period changed for them in large part the rosy view they had held with regard to the period that preceded it. Vichy's manifested racism highlighted the fact that racism was, in fact, an inherent part of the system, and that system had to be at least reformed, if not completely overthrown.

The effects of Vichy policy toward this elite and the way its members perceived the regime will be discussed later in relation to the impact of the Vichy period on postwar political developments in FWA. Let us turn now to the no less complex relations between the Vichy colonial regime and the more "traditional" elements of African society.

7.

The Vichy Regime and the "Traditional" Elements of African Society

Chiefs, Soldiers, and Muslims

There is no other African institution so closely related to the concept of "tradition" in the French colonial discourse than that of the African chief. From the outset of the colonial takeover of West Africa the administration vacillated on the question of the chiefs—that is, whether to leave the traditional chiefs in power and govern the population through them or to appoint new chiefs who would ensure the continuity of African tradition but also be under tighter, more efficient control. Ultimately the French preferred to appoint chiefs loyal to them who underwent administrative training. These chiefs were integrated into the lower levels of the colonial administrative hierarchy.[1]

In the 1930s, however, the French also began to fear that the chiefs would lose touch with their subjects. As a result of the practice of educating Africans, a new elite was emerging that tended to be less subservient to the colonial regime and whose members were eager to replace the chiefs as the leaders of the African population. The new policy sought to entrench the chiefs more firmly in local society by strengthening their traditional legitimacy.[2] As we have seen, the policy of association aimed to restore the chiefs' power and encouraged colonial administrators to treat this elite with respect so as to use the chiefs as intermediaries between the government and the rural African masses.

During the Vichy period the colonial aim of strengthening the chiefs' authority became even more crucial. The new and dangerous circumstances allowed African chiefs greater room to maneuver, and the colonial administration was deeply aware of this. The pressure the Vichy administration was under made it endeavor to maintain both the chiefs' status and the respect of the population toward them. Colonial dependence upon the chiefs grew even stronger under Vichy, when it became much easier to move to British colonies. The chiefs, for their part, were encouraged by Vichy propaganda on the issue of tradition, particularly the importance of maintaining traditions in Africa. The new regime emphasized an already existing colonial preference for "traditional" elites over "assimilated" Africans. It seems that the new circumstances, in addition to the new rhetoric, encouraged chiefs to apply for new nominations and/or improved salaries.[3] While most were content with aiming for minor goals, some of the more influential rulers took the opportunity to fulfill greater political ambitions. The following two cases each demonstrate a chief's ability to manipulate the new situation to his own advantage.

Playing between the Two Frances: The Kings of the Mossi and the King of the Abron

Manipulation of the new circumstances was especially easy in areas that were adjacent to British colonies, where the Free French forces were active. Even before Vichy areas that were close to British borders were sometimes problematic for the French due to Africans' attempts to cross over to escape forced labor, a practice that was abolished in the British West African colonies in 1927. Such immigrants were not welcomed by the British, as they too did not want open borders between their colonies and those of the French. In the Vichy period, however, the rules of the game changed. Such immigration now took on a different meaning: even when the motives of Africans who wished to cross the border remained the same as before, the very act became political and even ideological. For the British and Gaullists this provided a way to undermine Vichy authority and stability in West Africa, and they used the phenomenon as an effective propaganda tool. As for the Africans, they were happy about the relative ease with which they could now cross into British colonies and evade both the hardships of forced labor and the severe economic conditions in their own areas.

The cases of three superior chiefs, two successive Mossi kings and the king of the Abron, all of whom lived near the border with the Gold Coast, demonstrate the newfound ability of African rulers to maneuver between the "two Frances" and to use this situation to advance their own political agendas. These cases are also interesting because they demonstrate two different directions in which such tactics could lead. In the first case the two Mossi kings remained, at least formally, loyal to Vichy, while in the second case the Abron king "defected" to the Free French camp, leaving the governor of Côte d'Ivoire in an extremely embarrassing position.

In precolonial times the political system of the Mossis included a loose association of relatively autonomous kingdoms, each pyramidal in structure with a *naba* (chief) at its head. These kingdoms were situated in the area that is today northern Burkina Faso (Upper Volta in the colonial period). The Mossi of Ouagadougou, the strongest of the kingdoms, considered their ruler, the Moro Naba, superior to all Mossi kings. He had the status of a sacred king. Following the French conquest of his kingdom in 1896 he sought help from the British in the neighboring Gold Coast and even signed a treaty of friendship with them. When the British accepted French sovereignty over Mossi territory, the Moro Naba chose exile in the Gold Coast. His younger brother, however, soon submitted to French rule.[4]

Although the French intended to introduce direct rule in the Mossi region, they soon discovered that this was going to prove difficult. They encountered resistance from village chiefs who refused to cooperate. To convince the Moro Naba to cooperate they retreated somewhat from their stated policy of direct rule and gave the Mossi ruler limited authority, allowing him, for example, to collect taxes. In 1905, after the death of his father, sixteen-year-old Moro Naba Kom was chosen as the new Mossi leader; he would still be in his post at the beginning of the Vichy period. The French saw in him an exemplary auxiliary. During World War I he helped the colonial administration recruit thousands of Mossi soldiers. Later he was very helpful in recruiting workers for colonial projects, such as the construction of railways. The French decision in 1932 to break up the colony of Upper Volta and divide its circles among its neighboring colonies made Moro Naba Kom very bitter. He felt that he was losing control over his kingdom and resented the fact that people in Côte d'Ivoire were controlling his kingdom's capital, Ouagadougou, as well as the Mossi laborers. In the years before World War II he acted to change this decision.[5]

On 13 May 1941 the governor of Côte d'Ivoire asked Boisson to satisfy the Mossi king's request that he be allowed to appoint the head official of financial services as a canton chief. The supreme administrator of Upper Côte d'Ivoire, to whom the request had been submitted, emphasized to the governor of Côte d'Ivoire that the local practice regarding the appointment of chiefs should be honored and reminded him that when the land of the Mossi was conquered the French had promised to uphold their customs so long as they did not infringe on the public order or violate the principles of French civilization. Thus, he claimed, "one should satisfy the request of the Moro Naba, who demonstrates every day his loyalty and devotion to France."[6] The regime also responded positively to an additional request of the Moro Naba concerning the son of one of the heads of the provinces in his kingdom, the Balum Naba, who was studying at Faidherbe High School in Saint Louis. The son had not received a scholarship for the 1940–41 academic year because his grades had not been high enough. The Moro Naba wrote to Boisson requesting the scholarship, noting the loyalty and good services of the student's father, as well as the fact that the father's difficult financial situation did not enable him to finance his son's studies. The governor of Côte d'Ivoire recommended to Boisson that he fulfill the request because of the loyalty that the father and the Moro Naba had always shown.[7]

British and Gaullist intelligence reports about this ruler and his disdain for the Vichy regime, however, give a different picture regarding his ostensible loyalty. According to one such report from April 1941 Moro Naba Kom told his council that he was displeased with things as they were and that he would welcome British intervention. The report went on to state that all indications pointed to the "growing unrest of this numerous and warlike tribe." Just over a month later another report indicated that forced labor was one of the principal grievances in the Mossi region. The Moro Naba was said to be in trouble with the authorities on account of his openly expressed contempt for the Vichy regime. By June it was reported that the unrest among the Mossi was giving way to a state of fear caused by administrative threats against anyone working in conflict with the Vichy regime. Another report stated that during a meeting between the Moro Naba and the governor of Côte d'Ivoire, Hubert Deschamps, the Moro Naba had asked the governor whether his colony was French or German. Based on these reports the Free French made efforts to persuade Kom to support De Gaulle. The Moro Naba agreed to send a messenger to a British district officer in the Gold Coast. After this meeting the district officer expressed the opinion that "if we were to go into their country the Mossi would be one hundred percent with us."

But the Moro Naba had other plans. His primary political goal was still to see Upper Volta restored as a separate colony. He died before he could achieve this. His death was announced on Vichy Radio on 14 March 1942. There were rumors, perhaps spread by the Free French, that he had committed suicide because he did not wish to continue living under Vichy tyranny. Another rumor said that the Catholic Church, profiting from the Vichy regime's support, tried to force the Moro Naba to divorce all but one of his wives, and he preferred death.[8] The Vichy administration insisted, however, that he died of natural causes. The new Moro Naba,

Saga II, pledged full allegiance to the Vichy regime and showed respect to the Church. Nevertheless, he continued to pursue the goal of a separate Upper Volta and, like his predecessor, kept his options open.[9]

Saga II did not wait long after the end of Vichy rule in FWA to express his enthusiastic support for De Gaulle. Only two days after the departure of Boisson he wrote a long letter to G. F. Blan, the head of the military mission of the Free French in British West Africa, in which he assured Blan that he had always believed that France's capitulation was a mistake and that the "real France" would eventually regain power. He wrote that he was very happy to hear that De Gaulle was now in control in Algiers and that Boisson had been dismissed. He went on to ask Blan for some advice. He told him that he and the other superior chiefs of FWA had been invited to Dakar to meet the new governor-general to discuss the reconstitution of a governmental council. How should he conduct himself? he asked. He then wrote that he would be grateful if Blan would answer him promptly so that he could collect useful information before his departure for Dakar. He concluded the letter by expressing his and his people's loyalty to France.[10] The Moro Naba's wish to express his loyalty to De Gaulle as quickly as possible and his claim that he had been a Gaullist from the outset are not surprising. What is interesting is the fact that he chose to write this letter not to the new governor-general but to the head of the Free French mission in the Gold Coast. Furthermore, he asked Blan, whom he probably knew, for advice on how to approach the new governor-general.

Blan forwarded the letter to Governor-General Pierre Cournarie, who answered the Moro Naba about a month later. He assured the Mossi ruler that he knew his attitude was loyal and that he had never really accepted the capitulation to Germany and told him that the bonds of friendly trust between the French administrators and the Moro Naba were still as strong as before. However, it is obvious from the two last paragraphs of the letter that Cournarie was not at all pleased with the fact that the Moro Naba had sent his letter to the Free French mission in the Gold Coast. He therefore diplomatically explained that the military mission in Accra had terminated its role and that the Moro Naba should in the future receive instructions only from the governor-general and the colonial authorities in Côte d'Ivoire, which were the only recognized command.[11] What the governor-general was actually saying was that from then on there would no longer be two Frances, but one, and that the days when the Mossi king could maneuver between two authorities were over. Behind the sweet words expressing gratitude for the king's ostensible loyalty to the Free

French were hidden a warning and a declaration that a sole colonizer was again in command.

It seems that both Kom and Saga II attempted to play a double game. They "flirted" with the British and Gaullists and were even ready to send messengers to meet their representatives, and occasionally they criticized the Vichy regime in front of their subjects. However, they decided eventually not to gamble on the British and Gaullists and not to make the irreversible move of aligning with them. They both believed that they could better secure their political interests by staying loyal to the Vichy authorities. From Cournarie's letter to Saga it is clear that the Free French accepted this kind of conduct, understood its motives, and were more than willing to forgive and forget. This is also true for the Vichy attitude to both Moro Nabas: the administration was probably aware of their relations with the British and Gaullists but was prepared to turn a blind eye so long as the kings did nothing drastic and remained officially loyal to Vichy.

The better-known case of the Abron king demonstrates the other alternative that superior chiefs had—"defection" to the other camp. The Abron king was one of the few traditional rulers who were allowed to continue to rule after the French conquest. The colonial administration referred to him as a superior chief, and he ruled over the canton chiefs. While most of his powers had been taken away from him, he was still allowed to collect customary tributes from his subjects and had been appointed according to the customs of the Abron people, as these were perceived by the French. Kwadwo Agyeman, the king who moved to the British-Gaullist side, had ruled over the Abron kingdom since 1922. When World War II broke out, he declared his allegiance to the French and even sent three of his sons to fight so as to set an example for his subjects. Following France's defeat the king expressed his loyalty to the Vichy authorities.[12] But on 17 January 1942 the Abron ruler crossed the border to the Gold Coast with his son, three canton chiefs, and up to four thousand of his subjects. British administration officers received the king, and he and his son spoke on Radio Accra, declaring their intention to pursue the fight against the Germans. They stated that Marshal Pétain and the governor of Côte d'Ivoire were no more than liars working in the service of the Germans.

In spite of these dramatic announcements the real motives behind this "defection" were different. The background of the king's decision to move to the Gold Coast was the tense relationship he and his son (apparently the real initiator of this move) had with the colonial administration regarding two matters: the king's wish to preserve certain precolonial customs and his desire to change others. In the first case the king had held the right to impose fines, called "gifts," on his subjects. The commandant of the Bondoukou circle, M. Robert, did not approve of this practice and ordered that the so-called gifts be returned.[13] The Abron king was angry about this attempt to undermine his authority. His anger only increased when Robert, who also served as the president of the Circle Court, supported divorce each time a woman came to complain about her husband.[14] In addition the king's son was troubled about the question of his inheritance. According to the customs of the Abron inheritance was matrilineal (the eldest son of the eldest sister of the king inherited the throne), but it also rotated between two dynasties, the Zanzan and the Yakassé. The king's son, who was apparently a highly ambitious person, could not therefore assume the throne in any way, except by acting against custom. He hoped that through good relations with the colonial administration he would succeed in convincing them to ignore Abron tradition and appoint him as the new king when his father died. On 6 November 1941, only two months before the crossing, the king's son asked the governor of Côte d'Ivoire to make him responsible for the equipment of the colony in the hope that such an appointment would be a step toward his later enthronement. Deschamps refused, as he was worried that such an appointment would upset the other dynasty. This refusal probably convinced the king's son that the French would not allow him to ever become king.[15]

In normal circumstances the king's son would have probably renounced his ambition to succeed his father. But the Vichy period offered new possibilities. The willingness of the British and Gaullists on the other side of the border to receive with open arms any African ruler who was ready to publicly denounce the Vichy regime offered him a path to the fulfillment of his political ambitions.

The political decisions the Mossi and Abron rulers made had nothing to do with notions of resistance or collaboration in the metropolitan meaning. These rulers had their own political agenda and the skills to take advantage of the new situation, which offered unprecedented possibilities. In some way the circumstances under Vichy resembled those of the era of colonization, when the West African territory was not yet divided among the colonial powers and African leaders could still maneuver between Britain and France and exploit these two powers' rivalry. After several decades in which the modus vivendi between the two countries prevented such maneuvers, the Vichy period again offered a chance for African chiefs

to achieve their political goals. The attempt to present the Moro Nabas'
ties with the British and Gaullists and the Abron king's "defection" to
the Gaullist camp as acts of ideological resistance is meaningless. So is
the presentation of both Moro Nabas' decisions to stay loyal to Vichy
as collaboration. The dissimilarity between these African rulers' actions
and the acts of resistance or collaboration in France during World War
II also becomes clear when we examine the postwar implications of these
two opposite modes of conduct. Both the Moro Nabas and the Abron
king's son achieved their political goals even though they chose different
methods of action. The colony of Upper Volta was again separated from
Côte d'Ivoire in 1946, and when the king of the Abron died in 1953,
his son was named his successor. The eventual success of both political
choices demonstrates that the Vichy period did indeed offer African chiefs
wide room to maneuver. Moreover, the heavy dependence of the colonial
administration, both Vichy and Free French, on the local rulers created a
situation in which these chiefs could not go wrong. Whatever they opted
for, loyalty to Vichy or "defection" to the Gaullists, they eventually won.
    African chiefs provided for the Vichy colonial administration a double
challenge. The regime tried to limit the chiefs' ability to take advantage
of the new situation, but the chiefs were a vital link between the colonial
regime and the African rural population, and therefore it was vital that
their authority be maintained. The governor of Guinea, for example,
offered in 1941 a practical way to enforce the chiefs' authority. His idea
was to install in front of the chiefs' houses official signs with the tricolor
painted on them. He believed that such a step would be efficient in light
of the "sensitivity of the natives to such external symbols." To reassure
the administration he also suggested that the expenses incurred by this
exercise be extracted from the chiefs.[16] At the same time the Vichy colonial regime reacted harshly against chiefs who did not fulfill their duties
properly or were suspected of disloyalty. A canton chief from Kolda circle
in Guinea, for instance, was imprisoned for three years for distributing
Gaullist tracts, while the chief of Oussouye province in Senegal was dismissed for displaying apathy toward the mobilization efforts that were
made in his province in December 1941.[17]
    In fact it is possible to ascertain that it was mainly the war and the
new circumstances it created that influenced Vichy colonial policy toward
African chiefs. The new metropolitan ideology had little to do with the
colonial view of these so-called traditional rulers, which basically remained the same. The Vichy colonial regime's main concern was one
that had also existed under the Third Republic—namely, the process

that started before the war of a decrease in the chiefs' authority and an increase in that of the modern African elite. The chiefs' loss of respect and, consequently, of control was manifested in the rising number of reports of clashes between them and discharged soldiers. It is to this group, especially menacing to the colonial regime, that we now turn.

Vichy and African Colonial Soldiers

The French Army included seven African divisions among the eighty French divisions that defended France's borders in 1939. In 1940 Africans constituted 9 percent of the French Army, compared to only 3 percent during World War I. From the outbreak of the war in September 1939 up to the fall of France in 1940 about one hundred thousand soldiers from FWA were recruited into the French Army. Seventy-five percent of them served in Europe. At the time of the signing of the armistice agreement with Germany, as many as twenty-eight thousand Africans were declared to be missing. Of these almost sixteen thousand had fallen into German captivity. There are no exact figures for the number of fatalities among these soldiers, but Myron Echenberg estimates that about seventeen thousand may have died.[18] (The overall number of soldiers in the French Army who died in the battles of May–June 1940 was approximately one hundred thousand.)[19]

Echenberg focuses mainly on the history of African soldiers on European battlefields and in German prison camps. Here I will consider how the colonial regime in FWA treated these soldiers during their service and particularly after their discharge and return to their villages. I will also discuss how these soldiers viewed the colonial regime after the difficult experiences they had undergone in the attempt to defend France and after they had seen this colonial power, which ruled over almost all aspects of their lives, succumb to another European power.

In examining the colonial regime's treatment of African soldiers, it is necessary to distinguish among three groups: soldiers who were discharged after the defeat, those who fell into German captivity, and those who continued to serve in the army during the Vichy period as part of the defense forces that the armistice agreement allowed the Vichy regime to maintain in FWA (for defending the region in case of attacks by the British and the Gaullists).[20] In regard to the first group—the discharged soldiers—the colonial regime's main concern was that they return to their everyday lives and be reintegrated into their places of residence as rapidly as possible. The colonial administration was aware of the destructive potential of a mass discharge of soldiers who had been witness to France's humiliating defeat, and they sought to keep this group from becoming excessively embittered.[21]

In 1940 about thirty-five thousand soldiers were sent back to FWA via North Africa and arrived in Dakar. An additional twenty-seven thousand awaited their transfer in North Africa. In 1941 the British began to create obstacles to the transfer of the African soldiers because they regarded FWA as enemy territory. Even when they managed to return to the federation, the facilities in Dakar were not adequate for such a large number of soldiers. Grave problems of discipline arose in the transition camps in Africa. The soldiers, who did not understand why they were being delayed, became angry and lost all respect for defeated France; their officers were often replaced, and they waited for discharge payments that usually did not arrive. This situation brought the soldiers to the verge of mutiny. Even after the transportation problems were solved, new hurdles sprang up. Many soldiers lacked identification documents, and the authorities had no means of verifying what their home village was or whether they belonged to the standing army or the reserves. However, the graver problem was the paying of discharge grants. Most of the soldiers insisted that they had been promised they would receive these grants upon arriving in Dakar. They demanded money, not promises. French officers assured them that their grants would be awaiting them when they arrived at their circles, but there they were promised that they would receive the money in their villages. When these commitments were not fulfilled, the soldiers became violent.[22]

In November 1940, in the Kindia district of Guinea, a revolt broke out among 450 *tirailleurs* who were in the process of being discharged. The governor of Guinea reported that the situation remained extremely grave for two hours. The *tirailleurs* were dispersed after they beat many French officers and lightly wounded four of them. A rather large group, armed with rifles, cried out for murderous retribution; threw stones at houses; barged into administration offices, where they assaulted the circle commandant; and subsequently attacked a group of Europeans who escaped to the railway station. After three hours a European team armed with automatic weapons succeeded in overcoming the rebellious soldiers. Three hundred of them were arrested immediately, and thirty-five additional arrests were made the next day. They received sentences ranging from five to twenty years in prison. The governor stated that while the immediate motive for the violent outburst was indeed the delay in the discharge grants, the real reason was the communist propaganda that had been disseminated among the soldiers by the British and the Gaullists, who called on the soldiers to rebel and defect.[23]

Despite the conclusion that the delay in the discharge grants was just the spark that ignited the revolt and not its real cause, the administration acknowledged that this delay was a problem. In January 1941 the governor of Senegal wrote to one of his circle commandants that in light of the grave incident in Guinea special care must be taken to pay the discharge grants. He said it had been decided that the issue would be left in the hands of the circle commandants so as to prevent any unnecessary waste of time. He requested that the circle commandants report to him on the number of discharged soldiers and how many of them had received discharge grants.[24]

Even after the first stage of the soldiers' discharge had ended, the colonial regime was concerned about reintegrating them into daily life, which it saw as necessary for preventing unrest. The first cautious step the French took was to discharge the soldiers to their villages gradually.[25] The second was to see that the soldiers who had returned home were immediately employed. In February 1941 the governor-general turned again to the village governors and demanded that they heed the directive of 21 April 1939, which promised reemployment for discharged soldiers. According to this directive a soldier's previous employer had to rehire him unless he could demonstrate that this was not possible. The directive stated that contracts that had been signed with substitutes for the mobilized soldiers would become invalid upon the discharged soldiers' return. Boisson instructed the governors to intervene in cases where the discharged soldiers' rights were being compromised. About five months later a discharged soldier complained that his job at the Central Natives' Hospital in Dakar had not been restored to him after he had faithfully served France, whereas the person who had taken his place had evaded his military obligations.[26]

The colonial administration ran programs that enabled the employment of discharged soldiers, thus preventing them from creating problems. In January 1942 the governor-general raised the idea of resettling *tirailleurs* who had returned to FWA in territories of the Office du Niger. He said discharged soldiers who had received training and had a connection with French civilization were suitable for such work, and it would enable the utilization of land in the Niger Delta that had become fertile. Boisson suggested disseminating information on the matter among pre-discharge soldiers while they were sailing back to Africa and were worried about the conditions of their return. It was decided that the soldiers would be able to come to the Office du Niger within three to six months from the day of their return to their place of residence and would be employed for a trial period of six months that could be extended. The plan was

to establish villages in the area according to ethnicity and to open a
special instruction center for those with ranks, so that they would become
work administrators or could be sent to look for additional volunteers.[27]
Another plan aimed at creating employment was the professional retraining of three military services—the quartermaster, health, and artillery
services—into civilian bodies; this retraining would also enable the continued employment of soldiers after their discharge.[28] On 5 January 1942
a law was passed that gave priority to employing discharged soldiers in
the tax administration and village police forces. These soldiers would,
however, have to meet certain conditions: they could be no more than
thirty-five years old and must hold a school diploma (brevet élémentaire)
of at least the junior high school (école primaire supérieur) level. On 25
September a job application from a certain discharged prisoner of war
was rejected because he did not meet these two conditions.[29]

In an article on African soldiers from British and French colonies Rita
Headrick asserts that France succeeded in creating a wide group of supporters from among the soldiers of World War II.[30] However, while the
war was still going on, the soldiers were perceived as a menace, especially in the period immediately following their discharge. Even after the
soldiers had been discharged and returned to their villages, the colonial
administration could not relax its control. Most of the disruptive incidents
in which discharged soldiers were involved had to do with refusing to pay
taxes to African chiefs; soldiers behaved aggressively toward chiefs and
made anti-French statements.

It appears that France's defeat, which they had witnessed, led the discharged soldiers to scorn the authority of the colonial administration
and its African representatives. In March 1941, for example, a former
tirailleur was put on trial, charged with attempting to attack the chief
of his canton. The attack was prompted by the chief's demand that the
man pay taxes, including for his two wives and his children. The man
claimed that because he had recently been discharged he did not owe any
taxes. The chief then ordered him to first pay the taxes and then lodge
his complaint with the circle commandant, requesting that his money be
returned to him. The soldier refused and subsequently tried to attack the
chief with a knife but was stopped by one of those present at the scene.
The judge sentenced him to a year in prison and declared that even if he
was indeed exempt from taxes, the exemption did not extend to his second
wife. In a different locale a village chief's son, who was a discharged
soldier, was put on trial. The son and his father, also a former soldier,
had refused to participate in the rubber harvest. Beyond his refusal to toil

physically, in an assembly convened by the chief of the canton he claimed that he had seen and heard everything in France and knew that French authority no longer existed. He added that the decrees of the canton chief were meaningless because they were not in line with those of the new authority that was going to replace the French one.[31] In another report on the same case the governor of Côte d'Ivoire quoted the same former soldier as saying: "The French should not count on me for anything. They took me to fight in a land that is not mine, and the English are the ones who returned me to my land and my family. If the English were to ask me to work for them, I would."

The same report describes some additional cases in which former soldiers refused to obey the orders of African representatives of the administration and even behaved violently toward them. One of the circle commandants in Côte d'Ivoire wrote that this was a widespread phenomenon among soldiers who had returned from the European battlefields.[32] Some of the returning soldiers told war stories in which they described the heroism of the black and British soldiers and the cowardice of French officers who fled the battle while abandoning the Africans, who then fell prisoner to the Germans.[33] An annual political report for 1940 by the governor of Côte d'Ivoire refers to events like those described above as "small and annoying incidents" and emphasizes that there were no organized movements among discharged soldiers.[34] As he and the other administrators saw it, the main obstacle standing in the way of dealing with these "annoying" incidents was the decree of 19 April 1939, stating that former *tirailleurs* were to be tried by European courts.[35] In almost all the reports on incidents involving discharged soldiers the complaining administrator asked that this law be annulled so that the soldiers could be punished severely. One of the Côte d'Ivoire circle commandants explained his demand that the decree be canceled with the fact that in most cases a "native court" could give an "appropriate" punishment of fifteen to thirty days in jail for transgressions of this kind.[36] Indeed, an injunction canceling the discharged soldiers' right to be tried in European courts was published on 5 February 1942.[37]

Unlike the discharged soldiers African prisoners of war who had been in German prison camps did not constitute an immediate threat to the colonial regime. Nevertheless, the regime regarded them warily because of the potential threat posed by their future release. As noted, during the battles of May–June 1940, some sixteen thousand African soldiers had been taken prisoner by the Germans. Most were sent to prison camps in Germany and about a year later were transferred to labor camps in the occupied zone of France.[38] While still in Germany African POWs suffered from Nazi brutality. There is also some limited evidence regarding medical experiments performed on African prisoners. The transfer of most soldiers to camps in France probably saved them from further cruelty, though the Germans continued to attempt spreading propaganda among them. According to Martin Thomas they concentrated their efforts mainly on North African prisoners.

In December 1940 the occupation administration established a Maghreb propaganda bureau. Emphasis was put on the ostensible respect that Germans held for Islam, while France and Britain were presented as enemies of this religion. Some of the most enthusiastic collaborators were transferred to a camp near Berlin and were said to be very well treated.[39] The Vichy authorities were most concerned by the information the administrative police forces gathered on this propaganda and by the transfer of colonial prisoners to a camp near Berlin. According to these reports the Germans allowed the inmates of this camp to wander in the capital, let them sit in the cafés and restaurants, and even "gave them women." About a hundred Senegalese from one of the prison camps watched a German propaganda film and were later taken on a tour of "the great Germany." In addition it was reported that the Germans were using defamatory verbal propaganda and blaming France for all the prisoners' hardships. According to the report of the police services this propaganda was received positively by the Algerians and some of the educated Moroccans. The colonial prisoners who declared that they supported Hitler's regime were not sent to France but instead were kept by the Germans for "future use."

The report emphasized the need to fight this propaganda. It proposed classifying the prisoners who had escaped and, in the future, those who were freed. Those who said they had suffered under the Germans should be sent back immediately to their villages. The prisoners who had been treated well would be kept in France to undergo a counterpropaganda process.[40] In a letter that Boisson sent to the minister of the colonies on this issue he suggested that the best way to neutralize the German propaganda was to struggle against it while the soldiers exposed to it were still in France—that is, before they returned to their homes in Africa.

In this letter he also mentioned an African named Alioune Mamadou Kane, who impersonated a prince and was sent by the German occupation authorities to make the rounds of the prison camps where Africans were being held.[41] News about this "prince" surfaced in September 1940, when the postal-control committee for FWA opened a letter he had sent to a relative in Senegal. He wrote that in June he had been appointed by the French Supreme Command to carry out missions among Senegalese soldiers in France. Now, he said, after being discharged, he was working to improve the fate of the African prisoners, in whom no one was taking an interest. Later in the letter he wrote that the Germans had taken over his apartment in Paris beside Monceau Park, as well as his Buick automobile. On the basis of this and other letters that he sent the security services investigated the matter and discovered that he was a Senegalese adventurer who had changed his name to Alfonse William Kane and was of questionable morals, making a living through machinations. This person, the security services reported, had appointed himself a religious leader of the Senegalese soldiers and was pretending he had been appointed by the French. The suspicions of the security services intensified when they discovered a letter to the former mayor of Dakar in which he wrote that he had transferred to the prisoners of war a sum of 892,000 francs, since it was known that he lacked all means of subsistence. He had, furthermore, been authorized by the Germans to enter the prison camps and hence was suspected of disseminating German propaganda among the prisoners. The Vichy press in France used the affair of Kane's exposure to vilify the former minister of the colonies, George Mandel, who had appointed him the "leader of the black soldiers." A March 1941 article in *Paris-Soir* described how Mandel, who had already renounced his ambition to be popular in France and was seeking, rather, to become "father of the empire," had appointed Kane a leader. The newspaper gave the article the derisive headline, "Mandel turns a con man into Great Marabout!"[42]

There is no doubt that the Vichy regime's main concern in this context was centered on metropolitan POWs. Colonial prisoners were mostly neglected. They suffered from food shortages and cold, and diseases were rampant among them. The Vichy regime and of course the colonial administration in FWA were also aware of the destabilizing consequences the grievances of released colonial POWs might have on order.[43] In January 1941 a report was published in Vichy on the issue of the POWs. The writer attacked both the military authorities in France and the governor-general of FWA for ignoring the African prisoners. He wrote that the social solidarity services were rebuffing them so as to curry favor with their German "friends." Indeed, he claimed, it was thanks to the assistance of a few humane Germans that some of them had been able to flee the prison camps, only to be subjected to disgraceful treatment by their own military authorities when they sought refuge in Perpignan (which was in the area of Vichy control). The writer added that it was most surprising that none of FWA's officials—not the governor-general nor the administrators, nor the plantation owners, nor the European and local merchants—had made any generous gesture toward the black POWs. By contrast he noted, for example, that the governor-general and settlers in Algeria, even though the latter were "known as egoists from the social standpoint," had initiated the dispatch of twenty thousand packages of dates to Algerian POWs. The writer called upon the minister of the colonies to demand that Boisson make a similar gesture. He explained that the African prisoners must be shown that the state was thinking about them and that their victimization was not in vain. He also proposed that the minister of the colonies and the minister of defense, in coordination with the German authorities, expedite the release of those colonial prisoners who were being held in such conditions but because of illiteracy were unaware of their rights.[44] He concluded by noting that it was important that the painful impression of abandonment not prevail among black prisoners of war, because this was not in the national interest or wise from a political standpoint.[45]

Perhaps as a result of this report the general government strove to aid the prisoners whom it had a possibility of liberating. On 19 January 1941, for example, Lieutenant Mamadou Kane (probably not a relation of the abovementioned Kane), who had fallen into German captivity, submitted a request that he be released because he was the father of five. The Directorate of Political and Administrative Affairs reacted by asking Boisson that he ensure that documents be sent to the prisoner proving that he was indeed a father of five, so that he could present them to the German authorities.[46]

On the other hand great importance was assigned to caring for the families of the prisoners, who sometimes were left without their main breadwinner for long periods. These families received rations that were funded by the state budget rather than local budgets.[47] Rations were also given to needy families of soldiers who had not been taken prisoner and were continuing their military service. The governor of Côte d'Ivoire demanded of his circle commandants that they not be niggardly with these rations but also that they ensure that only truly needy families received them, such as elderly people whose sons were in the army and who could not support themselves. In one letter to the commandants he included a table showing the number of requests for rations from each circle; according to these data 7,142 requests were made in all of Côte d'Ivoire from the outbreak of the war until 31 December 1940.[48]

There were two kinds of rations for the families of prisoners: a daily ration that was meant to meet the needs of the entire family and a special ration for wives of prisoners, known as "separation compensation" (*compensation de séparation*). Receiving the separation ration did not preclude receiving a regular ration, and in fact the Ministry of the Colonies saw to it that soldiers' wives also received the daily ration because the separation ration was smaller, and in most cases the husband could not send his pay because he was in captivity. Writing to Boisson the minister of the colonies noted that in some locations the women received only separation rations and demanded that the situation be rectified to ensure that they were not deprived.[49] The separation ration also caused some confusion in the administration in cases where the POW had more than one wife. The Ministry of the Colonies ruled that the ration would be given only to legitimate wives. However, officials of the general government emphasized to the head of the military cabinet that this terminology was inaccurate and injurious to the wives who were defined as illegitimate by the administration. According to African custom any woman who had married her husband according to the law was his legal wife even if she was not his first wife. It was, however, stipulated that even if the additional wives were not illegal, only the first wife was entitled to this ration.[50]

Compared to the prisoners, who constituted only a potential threat, the soldiers who continued to serve in the French Army in FWA posed a real and immediate threat. This was borne out by the attempted rebellion that occurred in the *tirailleurs'* unit in Côte d'Ivoire on 13 February 1941. After a European sergeant slapped the face of an African sergeant during an argument, twenty-seven African *tirailleurs* stormed off the base with their weapons. The incident ended without casualties after an official from the colonial staff succeeded in locating the *tirailleurs* and persuading them to give him their weapons and return to their unit. The military commander of the subdivision of southern Côte d'Ivoire in fact referred to the incident as banal, but the governor's secretary-general did not agree and called it a strong reaction to injustice. In a report of 15 February by the commander of the battalion in which the incident occurred, he called the European sergeant's act an "unfortunate reflex" and said significant steps had been taken against him because he had lost his composure and slapped an African of the same rank.[51] It is worth noting that these steps were taken only against the European sergeant (not against any of the African soldiers), reflecting the regime's desire to appease the Africans and avoid feelings of bitterness and injustice among them.

It is interesting, though, that the soldiers' revolt that so concerned the Vichy authorities actually erupted after the Vichy regime in FWA had come to an end and De Gaulle's Free French forces had taken over the federation. In contrast to the appeasement attempts that quelled the Kindia revolt, this uprising, which occurred at Camp de Thiaroye, near Dakar, on 1 December 1944, was brutally repressed by the French.

After long periods of imprisonment in German camps 1,280 African soldiers returned to Dakar and were installed in a camp some ten miles from the city. The poor conditions in the camp, combined with the refusal of their French commanders to give them their due payments, led the soldiers to revolt. The French, who could not support the idea of armed soldiers contesting French colonial authority so close to the federal capital, opened fire on the soldiers, killing thirty-five of them, according to French official records, and wounding many more. The tragic events in Thiaroye were depicted in Outhmane Sembene's film *Camp de Thiaroye*, in which he likened the facility to a German camp and compared French colonial violence, be it under Vichy or the Free French, to Nazi violence and cruelty.[52]

When I talked with African informants about their own memories from the war, some of them spoke of the Thiaroye episode as one of the most significant. The interesting point here is that two of them, who were otherwise very knowledgeable about the chronology of war events, attributed the repression of the revolt to the Vichy regime.[53] When I reminded one man that this event actually happened after the Vichy period was over both in FWA and in metropolitan France, he was surprised but soon responded: "Well, it was the spirit of Vichy" (Alors, c'était l'ésprit de Vichy).[54] This fascinating mistake reflects the harshness and racism that characterized the Vichy regime in general. However, the regime's policy toward soldiers was careful, and there was an attempt to avoid at all costs any recourse to violence.

This gentle approach toward soldiers was also evidenced in an attempt to tend to their physical and spiritual needs—by opening two brothels in Thiès and Bamako with supervision of the workers' health and by appointing a military chaplain for Christian and Muslim soldiers who were far from home.[55] The Ministry of the Colonies also took care to maintain contact with soldiers who had been wounded and hospitalized in France. In a letter of 4 September 1941 the minister of the colonies informed the minister of defense that he intended to send an official from the colonial administration who knew the Bambara language to visit wounded African soldiers in hospitals in Marseille.[56]

The Ministry of the Colonies was also prepared to see to it that the colonial soldiers' feelings were not hurt. This concern was inspired by a report published by the Ministry of Defense on 31 January 1941, which noted that the European salutation on military correspondence was sometimes also addressed to soldiers from the colonies who were not of European stock. The report said this situation created confusion and suggested specifying when "colored Frenchmen" were being addressed.[57] In response Gratien Candace, a member of the Senate and the vice-president of the Chambre des Députés, wrote to the minister of the colonies calling on him to change this address since it was likely to offend black soldiers. It was suggested, then, that they instead be called "overseas Frenchmen" (*Français d'outre-mer*) or "Frenchmen from the empire" (*Français de l'empire*), so they would not feel they were being differentiated from the other soldiers on the basis of their skin color.[58]

In another case a letter was sent by the Supreme Command of the Ground, Air, and Naval Forces of FWA to the minister of the colonies, expressing deep concern about damage to the morale of the soldiers in French West Africa. The letter claimed this damage was caused by reading articles in the newspaper *Gringoire*. It was difficult for the soldiers to understand the newspaper's enthusiastic words of praise for the victories of the Axis forces. In addition articles that spoke of the defeat that "the newspaper had long foreseen" seemed to cast doubt on the message that was being conveyed to the soldiers about France's recovery and unification. The writer warned that if articles of this kind were not censored, he would forbid his soldiers to read the newspaper.[59]

The policy of both the colonial administration in FWA and the Ministry of the Colonies in Vichy was in fact dictated by deep fear, often expressed in official correspondence, of the potential destructive force represented by the soldiers who had served in France, seen its downfall and the triumph of its enemies, and were witness to the dissension within its army's ranks and the continuation of the war by the British. These soldiers, who had returned to their villages or would do so in the future, could tell their families, friends, and neighbors stories that the colonial administration preferred were not told. They were also likely to expect extra privileges because they had risked their lives for France, and, most worrisome of all, they had experience in the use of weapons and perhaps still even possessed weapons.

Indeed, most of the colonial regime's fears had some basis. The large number of violent incidents involving discharged soldiers, and the circumstances of these incidents, testify to soldiers' disappointment with France and their unwillingness to cooperate with the lower levels of the colonial administration—the village and canton chiefs, whom they regarded as inferior because they had not served in the army or been in Europe.

Reports of soldiers' declarations that the French no longer had authority and that they preferred the British caused consternation in the colonial regime, which sought to put a stop to such trends and feared their possible influence on the morale of the public, which at the same time was being exposed to Anglo-Gaullist propaganda.

The fear of hostile reactions to the colonial administration among discharged soldiers was not new. After World War I there were cases in which African soldiers who had participated in the war refused to accept the chiefs' authority. Many administrative reports from the 1920s and 1930s expressed concern about the behavior of the discharged soldiers and the bad example they set.[60] In the Vichy period, however, these fears gained a new dimension. There was now also a danger that the British and the Gaullists in the bordering colonies would exploit the soldiers' ill will to stir up disturbances. The regime took two kinds of measures to cope with this problem. First, it tried to persuade the soldiers who had witnessed the fall of France that France would, notwithstanding, continue to be strong and that there had been good reason for signing the armistice with Germany. At the same time the colonial regime and the Ministry of the Colonies tried to tend, as much as possible, to the soldiers' welfare.

When the soldiers returned to their villages, their neighbors were eager to hear their stories recounting experiences of war and faraway places. The colonial administration had to be sure that France would not be portrayed embarrassingly and that these stories would have no undesirable consequences. To do so it tried to employ a "language" that was familiar to the soldiers and to the African rural population—the language of Islam. Islamic messages, however, were not to be transmitted directly, as French administrators could hardly pretend to be "authentic" voices representing Islam. The mediator conscripted for this purpose was a prominent Islamic leader—Sheik Seidou Nourou Tall.[61]

Seidou Nourou Tall became a messenger of the French colonial administration after the death of his father-in-law, El-Haj Malick Sy, the leading Tijani marabout in Senegal. Tall traveled all over FWA, encouraging the cultivation of cash crops and urging loyalty to France.[62] Often referred to by the French as the "marabout of African soldiers," Tall was asked to speak to African soldiers who were about to depart for the front after the outbreak of World War II. He continued in this role during the Vichy period and after.[63] French colonial officials often reported on Tall's speeches, their value, and the effect they had on soldiers. These reports summarize the speeches from the beginning of the war through the Vichy period and give us an idea of the tenets the colonial regime hoped to convey to the rural population through the voices of African soldiers.

The main theme of Tall's speeches at the beginning of the war was denunciation of German colonialism. Germany was depicted as the black man's nightmare. The charismatic marabout called on the soldiers to sacrifice their lives for France and praised Britain for fighting alongside the "beloved fatherland."[64] The change of rhetoric in Tall's speeches following France's defeat by Germany was gradual. He continued to denounce Germany and denied the defeat well into July 1940.[65] This denial could not, of course, last long. When Tall finally admitted that France had signed the armistice agreement, he explained that this was the way Marshal Pétain had chosen to save France and make it stronger. He stressed to the soldiers that what was most required of them now was discipline: "I was a soldier myself. I know what it is to be a soldier. A soldier is a person who is disciplined, not semidisciplined, but absolutely. . . . When mobilization came, a large number of you responded to the call; the Marshal, to avoid a massacre, asked for an armistice. He has faith in you. Have faith in him and in our leaders whom you must obey totally, at all times and under all circumstances, according to the wish of the Marshal, premier French soldier, and according to the rule of 'Discipline.' "[66]

Tall asked the soldiers to remain obedient and respectful of the French and to observe the values of the National Revolution when they returned to their villages—meaning to work hard and spend time with their families.[67] He noted that the National Revolution values of "Work, Family, and Fatherland" had been discussed in the Quran and the Hadith long before they were endorsed by the Vichy regime. He quoted a Hadith attributed to the Prophet Mohammed: "The love of the Fatherland stems from faith" (in Arabic, "Hubb al-watan min al-īmān").[68] According to a British intelligence report Tall encouraged the soldiers to boost their agricultural activity and cautioned them against suggesting that France had been defeated by Germany.[69] In his later speeches to soldiers Tall no longer mentioned Germany but spoke mainly of Pétain and described him in emotional terms as a loving father.[70]

By modifying his speeches to match the changes of colonial regime in FWA, Tall continued to help the Vichy regime transmit its messages to the soldiers. These messages concentrated on achieving what the authorities wanted most from the soldiers and eventually from the African population as a whole: respect, obedience, and calm. During this period African soldiers were not expected to die for France; they were just asked not to cause any problems. They also received rather detailed explanations of the principles of Vichy ideology and were told that these values were compatible with Islam. It was hoped that these notions would reach the ears of villagers through the soldiers and limit the effects of any embarrassing stories the soldiers might tell.

Seidou Nourou Tall is an example of a distinguished and charismatic Islamic leader who chose to accommodate the French colonial regime, then later adapted to the establishment of the Vichy regime in FWA and again to the reestablishment of republican colonialism. He represents one of the attitudes of the important marabouts, who maintained the same type of relations with the new colonial administration as they had with its predecessors. But this was only one Muslim approach toward the Vichy colonial regime. Let us now examine the wide spectrum of Muslim positions, as well as Vichy policy toward the Muslim elite, which was vital for the maintenance of effective colonial rule.

The Vichy Regime and the Muslims

When the French were attempting to conquer the vast territory that was later to become FWA, they encountered diverse and numerous Muslim societies that were eventually added to the already vast Muslim population they ruled in Algeria. By the early twentieth century, according to David Robinson, France saw itself as a "Muslim power," meaning an imperial power with Muslim subjects who were under its protection, and therefore was trying to forge an "Islamic policy." During the process of colonization the French tried to understand local Muslim societies, divide them into various categories, find potential allies, and isolate enemies.[71]

West African Islam is mostly influenced by Sufi orders. These orders appealed to their audiences by emphasizing feelings rather than practice and by making the rigid laws of Islam more flexible. Sufi orders also generally accepted pre-Islamic faiths and thus made Islam easier to absorb. The leaders of the branches of the different orders were called caliphs or "great marabouts." In the areas that the French took over in West Africa the main orders were the Quadiriyya, the Tijaniyya, and the Muridiyya, which grew within the Quadiriyya.[72]

The French Republic feared Islam because of the historical hostility between this religion and Christianity, as well its own hostility toward religion in general. The French perceived the first Sufi orders that they encountered in Algeria as secret societies with destructive potential against the colonial order. Initially, as a written culture, Islam was seen as something halfway between barbarity and progress. While in the Maghreb the French viewed Islam as an obstacle to progress, in sub-Saharan Africa it was viewed in a more complex way. On the one hand it was perceived as lagging far behind Western civilization; on the other the French believed that it could advance African societies. After World War I, however, fear of an international Islamic conspiracy overshadowed all other considerations. French Islamic experts, such as Paul Marty, began to warn against the view that Islam was a necessary evolutionary step toward Western civilization, preferring non-Muslim African societies to Muslim ones in the name of an ostensible African authenticity.[73]

The French tended to differentiate between "fanatic" and "tolerant" Muslim groups and attempted to limit the influence of those they perceived as belonging to the first category. The figure of Haj Umar, an Islamic leader who led a jihad during the French in the nineteenth century, and the Tijaniyya order to which he belonged symbolized for them Islamic fanaticism and militancy. This stereotype persisted well after Umar's movement had been subdued. Relations between the French colonial regime and the Tijaniyya order began to improve only when Malick Sy became the order's leader in Senegal. Seidou Nourou Tall completed this transformation by becoming a mediator between the French and African Muslims. After World War I the Murids, who were earlier considered by the French as fanatic Tijanis (although they had nothing to do with the Tijaniyya order), began to be integrated into Senegal's groundnut industry, and their relations with the French improved as well. As for the third order, the Quadiriyya, the French saw it as tolerant and cooperative from the outset.

During the 1920s, then, the French colonial regime and African Islamic leaders reached a rapprochement. The leaders of the Sufi orders adapted to the colonial reality and learned to take advantage of it. The climax of good relations between them and the French was under the Popular Front, when Governor-General Marcel De Coppet began subsidizing the construction of mosques and participated in Muslim festivals.[74]

As already noted, it would be a severe oversimplification to regard the attitude of African Muslim leaders to French colonial rule as shifting from resistance to collaboration. In the introduction to *Le temps des marabouts* Jean-Louis Triaud notes the problematic nature of using the terms *collaboration* and *resistance* in discussing the Muslim elite's attitudes toward the colonial regime. He stresses that these terms are especially problematic in the French context because of their connotations in the French memory of the World War II period. (This is all the more true when discussing Muslim elites' attitudes toward the Vichy regime.) Triaud maintains that using these terms does not leave room for the wide variety of reactions between those two extremes. The term he proposes in regard to the approaches of the different Muslim figures is *accommodation*, which encompasses all the different modes of accommodating the new balance of power without necessarily leading to ideological cooperation.[75] David Robinson also criticizes the "resistance" literature that often divides colonial subjects into resistors and collaborators. He examines the great marabouts of the first decades of colonization and demonstrates the paths of accommodation they chose.[76]

There was, however, an exception to this general trend of accommodation in the form of an Islamic movement that split from the Tijaniyya order the moment the order began to find its place within the colonial setting. This was the Hamalliyya movement, named for its leader, Sheikh Hamallah. This specific movement is extremely important to the evaluation of relations between the Vichy colonial regime and Islam. Although it began to emerge around World War I and became influential in the 1920s, its major clash with French colonial rule and its subsequent repression occurred under Vichy rule.

Passive Resistance: Sheikh Hamallah and the Vichy Colonial Regime

Sheikh Hamallah adopted the practice of the Algerian marabout Al-Akhdar of repeating one of the prayers of the Tijaniyya eleven times instead of twelve, and as a result the colonial administration called him and his disciples the "Tijaniyya of the eleven beads" (referring to the prayer chain), as distinct from the orthodox Tijaniyya, who were called the "Tijaniyya of the twelve beads." Al-Akhdar himself had in fact already broken from the central stream of the Tijaniyya, but the movement was named for his disciple Hamallah.

Hamallah's main criticism of the Tijani leaders concerned their attitude toward French colonial rule, which was beginning to change at the time, and their deviation from the teachings of Haj Umar. So long as Malick Sy was alive, Hamallah was not especially active; however, with the death of the Tijaniyya leader, he began trying to attract important religious figures from the movement's central stream and other orders and criticizing marabouts who cooperated with the "French infidels." According to oral testimonies he once declared: "France considers the marabout as a candle: once it is used it is good for nothing." He opposed marabouts who chose to work with the French and said that "the marabout is like a lamp that, in order to give better light, should avoid getting dirty."[77] His own strategy was to ignore the French as much as he could but not disobey them directly. In this way he hoped to avoid giving them any excuse to act against him. During the 1920s French administrators complained that he came to see them only when he was formally invited and never attended

French celebrations like other Islamic leaders. They also resented the fact that Hamallah refused to declare his loyalty to French colonial rule, even during World War I.[78]

Whereas the Tijaniyya order was popular among the educated classes in Senegal and French Sudan, the Hamalliyya movement had greater appeal for the poorer populations of Mauritania and Sudan. Its emergence as a strong movement in the mid-1920s posed a problem for the French administration because the other Tijanis, still greater in number, regarded the Hamalliyya movement as heretical and tried to suppress it. The French feared the movement because of its declared hostility to non-Muslims. In 1924 a series of incidents between the Hamallists and their Tijani opponents came to a head in a conflict that erupted in Nioro, in French Sudan. Subsequently a number of violent incidents occurred, and the fact that Sheikh Hamallah did nothing to try to restore order led the French to imprison him in December 1925. He remained in jail for ten years in West Africa and was then exiled to France for two years. The exile greatly enhanced his prestige, and the number of his supporters only grew.

When he returned to Africa, the authorities tried to lure him over to their side via the mediation of Seidou Nourou Tall. And indeed, in September 1937 a reconciliation was achieved between him and the other Tijanis when Hamallah agreed to waive his demand that the prayers be recited eleven times rather than twelve.[79] However, this reconciliation did not last long. Hamallah was unable to prevent further violence from erupting in 1938 in the region of Nioro. His eldest son in particular had been humiliated by a hostile Moorish tribe and was determined to demand his revenge. He began to make clandestine preparations for an attack on his enemies, which he hid even from his father. His efforts culminated in a bloody battle in Mouchgag, a village in Nioro, in which around four hundred people were killed. The timing of this attack on the enemies of the Hamalliyya was not a coincidence. It took place about a month after the debacle, on 24 July 1940. News of the defeat of France had given the Hammallists the impression that such an attack on their enemies would be easy because the Vichy colonial regime would be occupied by other, more pressing matters. This belief was mistaken, of course, as the Vichy regime could not afford to ignore any form of disorder, even when it was not aimed directly at the colonial regime. In fact the timing of the attack even convinced some colonial administrators that the Hamallists were ready to massacre French people, although there was no evidence that this confrontation was directed against or intended to undermine French authority.[80]

Following the incidents in Nioro the governor of French Sudan requested, on 9 September 1940, that it be determined whether the Hamallist movement had been involved; he also called for keeping Sheikh Hamallah under close surveillance while not taking any measures against him.
About a month later the governor of Senegal, G. Parisot, sent the commandant of the circle of Thiès the translation of a declaration by Sheikh
Hamallah in which he denied having stirred up the riots. The governor
said the sheikh's son had exploited his father's prestige to lure his supporters into slaughter and robbery at a moment when France's defeat
in Europe suggested it had been weakened in FWA.[81] However, Boisson
himself was not convinced of Sheikh Hamallah's innocence. In February
1941 he suggested to the governor of French Sudan that he demand that
Hamallah publicly condemn the violent acts that had been committed—
that is, that he declare his allegiance to the French order or "reveal his
true face." Boisson also told the governor to take measures to uncover
the Hamallist sources of the outbreak and thus to be critical of Sheikh
Hamallah in public, thereby discouraging the subversive elements.[82]

Although Boisson was highly suspicious of Hamallah and not at all
convinced that he had nothing to do with the violent incidents of July
1940, it took him almost a year to act against him. This delay in action
can be explained by colonial hesitation in acting against an Islamic leader
who had many supporters in parts of the federation that were considered
"difficult to control." Eventually, however, Boisson chose to arrest the
Islamic leader and his supporters to avoid further troubles. On 19 June
1941, a day later termed by the Hamallists "Terrible Thursday," the Vichy
authorities arrested Hamallah. This was done very early in the morning
both to try to surprise Hamallah and to avoid attracting too much attention. Along with him about eight hundred of his supporters were arrested
as well. They were divided into three categories: the very influential, who
were sentenced to ten years in prison; the less influential, who were sentenced to five years; and the moderate, mainly old people, women, and
children, who were released after twenty-four hours. In October thirty
people who were considered close to Hamallah were sentenced to death.[83]
Sheikh Hamallah himself was banished to Algeria and later to France,
where he died in a hospital in January 1943.

But this was not the end of the Hamallah affair. Even after his ban-
ishment the French continued to be concerned about the activities of
his supporters and the danger they posed. The authorities were particularly worried by the spread of rumors about the sheikh's expected return
to Africa.[84] They knew, for example, that followers of Hamallah were

spreading the word that he had not been imprisoned at all but rather had been taken by the Angel Gabriel and would reappear at the right moment to draw the "sword of the believers." The sheikh's family did not mourn his two sons who had been executed because they refused to believe they were not among the living.[85] These rumors made the colonial regime monitor carefully the remnants of the Hamalliyya movement and attribute to it almost every Muslim-instigated disturbance or violent act.

In fact one of the most violent incidents under Vichy, the "massacre" of Bobo-Dioulasso, was attributed to Hamallah's supporters even though no clear evidence was found for such a linkage. A year after the Hamallist riots a group of Muslims in Bobo-Dioulasso, in Côte d'Ivoire (in an area that belonged to Upper Volta before being annexed to Côte d'Ivoire in 1932), murdered some Europeans who were sitting in the coffeehouse of the Dallet Hotel. The killing, which the colonial authorities later termed "the massacre of Bobo-Dioulasso," occurred on 3 August 1941. It was later learned that the attack had been planned for about five months, inspired by the announcement of a man named Sheikh Amadou, who presented himself as a guardian of the tomb of the Prophet in Mecca and called for holy war against the Europeans. The day and the place had been carefully chosen: Sunday, the Europeans' day of rest, and a coffeehouse where they would habitually spend this day. Before the attack a mass prayer service was conducted that lent it the guise of a holy war. Twenty-five armed Muslims perpetrated the attack, killing five French citizens and wounding eight. It was not long before a declaration was made linking the massacre to Hamallist activity, but in fact no such connection had been proven.[86]

The colonial administration immediately took a series of severe punitive measures. In addition to imprisoning the attackers, it imposed sanctions on chiefs and the city's religious leaders because they had not reported to the administration the presence of "fanatic Muslims," most of whom had come from outside the city or even from outside the circle. Likewise collective punishments were imposed on the residents of the quarter from which the attackers had come. Houses in or near the location of meetings the conspirators had held were destroyed, and a fine of ten thousand francs, which was the annual tax collected from all residents of the city, was imposed on all the residents of the quarter.

In September 1941 the administrator of Upper Côte d'Ivoire sent a report on the investigation of the incident to the governor. The report concluded that this was a local episode with neither an international connection nor links to other internal groups. The leaders of the conspiracy belonged to the Tijaniyya of the eleven beads and had received their inspiration from marabouts in the Nioro area. The administrator claimed that the events in Bobo-Dioulasso could be explained in terms of Muslim fanaticism that had been encouraged by rumors about the defeat of France and did not require inspiration from outside. He did not believe the murderers had been encouraged by the Gaullists because in secret directives about establishing Gaullist cells, it was recommended not to call in any way for a revolt by "natives."[87]

Two days later Boisson reported on the episode to the minister of the colonies. He wrote that it was a case of an eruption of Muslim fanaticism among some "visionaries" and that there was reason to believe this fanaticism could not have come solely from a local source. Boisson explained that the main conspirator, Outhmane Traoré, appeared to be a small-minded fanatic who did not know how to read French or Arabic and thus could not be assumed to have influence on any important Muslim order. In Boisson's opinion he belonged to one of the many Hamallist or Yacoubist sects whose members more or less had emancipated themselves from the rules of Muslim orthodoxy.[88] At the same time Boisson did not discount the possibility that this was a movement seeking to create problems in the French territory and noted that he had been informed that Lieutenant L. A. M. Blondel, who was in charge of propaganda for the task force of Free France in the Gold Coast, had spoken of a German presence in the Côte d'Ivoire.[89]

The Hamallah movement represents the extreme end of the spectrum of Vichy-Muslim relations. It seems, though, that the extreme character of these relations was more a result of Vichy colonial fears than of the real intentions of Hamallah and his followers. It is obvious that the Hamallists took advantage of the new circumstances and what seemed to them French weakness. But in fact their actions were directed against their African Tijani enemies and not against the French. The French did not establish a clear relation between Hamallah and the Bobo-Dioulasso killings, but the sheikh's refusal to cooperate with or even accommodate them, and his insistence on ignoring French colonial rule, convinced colonial authorities that he was dangerous and therefore should be dealt with harshly. The greatest fear of the Vichy colonial regime was that such ostensible Islamic militants, or even more moderate Muslim elements, would join forces with the Gaullists' networks across the border.

Muslim Leaders and Gaullist Espionage Networks
Suspicion of a link between Muslim elements and the British and Gaullists

who operated from the British West African colonies arose both from the Hamallist riots and from the Bobo-Dioulasso episode. In the former case suspicion was directed at the French lieutenant Jean Montezer, who had allegedly passed information to Sharif Hamallah on the situation in Europe. A check into Montezer's tour of the region in fact revealed that this suspicion was unfounded; nevertheless, the figure of Montezer well illustrates the colonial administration's apprehensions of the dangers of such a connection.[90]

In the course of his service the French officer had developed a special interest in African Islam and had even forged ties with Muslim religious figures. In a way Montezer could be presented as a French mediator between the colonial administration and the African Muslim orders. He was different from most French ethnographers and Islamists in that he wished to become close to his African informants, to the point of friendship. In 1939 he published a booklet, *Afrique et l'Islam* (Africa and Islam), that passed the inspection of the Directorate of Political and Administrative Affairs. Subsequently the head of the directorate announced to the General Security Service that the booklet clearly summarized basic data that would undoubtedly prove helpful to those in the colonial administration and the army who had a connection with Islamic circles in FWA. At the same time he noted that the booklet's conciseness was likely to lead to mistaken conclusions. For example, in regard to Sheikh Hamallah, Montezer did not mention his militant doctrine and did not question his loyalty to France. The official added that there were a number of items in the booklet that should not be disseminated among "native" circles. As an example he cited the chapter on German Islamic policy, which contained details that were likely to be interpreted in an undesirable fashion by the "natives" and result in the Germans gaining sympathy they did not deserve. Montezer indeed called into question the honesty of German Islamic policy, but this was not enough to neutralize the danger. The report also noted that Montezer had received his information about Islam from a Tijani with certain interests, who therefore had done everything he could to present a case for the Tijaniyya and against the Quadiriyya.[91]

In November 1940 Montezer crossed the border to Gambia and joined the Free French forces that operated from its capital, Bathurst. He was made responsible for disseminating Anglo-Gaullist propaganda in FWA. Montezer appealed particularly to Muslim circles but also to other groups such as black soldiers, distributing such general proclamations as the following, which was intercepted in Dakar in January 1941: "One justice. 'Republican France was rotten,' the people of Vichy repeat again and again. Lords Pétain, Weygand, Laval, and Darlan, were you not, just a few months ago, important people in this unfortunate republic? What did you say then? Nothing! What did you do then? Nothing! Your place is with Daladier and all the rest. If they are guilty, you too are guilty."[92]

This propaganda network succeeded in severely unsettling the Vichy regime, which took all measures to eliminate it. A report by the head of the Special Police and Security Service on the imprisonment of one of Montezer's emissaries revealed the great effectiveness and wide scope of this network. The emissary who was captured said that all the Senegalese members of the Dyula who were in Bathurst, numbering about a hundred, had been sent by the French officer on different missions. He explained that the job of emissary was very tempting. His friend who was captured with him had received two thousand francs for each journey. He refused to admit how much money he had himself received, but the writer of the report said that judging from the amount of goods he had purchased, it apparently came to thousands of francs.[93] Apart from arresting those suspected of being in Montezer's service, the colonial administration took security measures to prevent the dissemination of propaganda announcements. In Dakar and its environs barriers were set up at the railroad stations and main roads, and travelers' parcels were scrutinized by customs officials. Outside this area roadblocks were set up to check vehicles and their passengers.[94]

Montezer's network had representatives in Dakar, Saint Louis, Kaolack, Thiès, and Diourbel and extensions in Mauritania, Niger, and French Sudan. Most agents knew each other, so the arrests of some of them in 1940–41 brought about the fall of the network. One of its main activists, Abdel Kader Diagne, who later wrote a booklet on the resistance in Senegal, was imprisoned for two years in France. Upon his release in 1942 he reorganized the network, which then numbered 220 members, of whom 107 were Africans.[95] In addition other large and small networks operated all over FWA.[96]

Montezer's move to Gambia and the espionage and propaganda networks that he established were even more worrying to the colonial administration in light of his many ties with Muslim leaders in FWA. On 13 November 1940 the head of the General Security Service alerted the head of the Directorate of Administrative and Political Affairs of the immediate need to undermine Montezer's authority among the Muslims in the Dakar region. He expressed apprehension that in case of a further attempted attack by De Gaulle's forces, Montezer would succeed in putting Africans who naively believed he held an official position in the "service of treason." Boisson also wrote to the commander of the Army of French Africa (Général de corps d'armée, commandant supérieur des troupes de l'Afrique française) that Montezer's move to Gambia necessitated certain measures of caution and security. He requested that he be told precisely which local groups had connections with Montezer and the level of his influence among them.[97]

From the reports on the many investigations that were conducted on the Montezer affair it emerged that the French officer did indeed have ties with Muslims of quite important standing in FWA. A list that the head of the General Security Service sent to his counterpart at the Directorate of Administrative and Political Affairs on 2 December 1940 included the names of the nine main individuals who were in contact with Montezer. All of them held positions connected to the Islamic religion: Abdel Kader Diagne, notary and founder of the Muslim Brotherhood (La fraternité musulmane); Khali Jibril Diagne, chief of the N'Garaff-Médina neighborhood; Haj Ibrahima Kane, marabout of Medina; Haj M'Baye Diagne, imam of the Great Mosque of Medina; Sheikh Touré, representative of the Murids in Dakar; Abd al-Aziz Sy, son of Haj Malik Sy; Kamil Fale, representative of the Maurs in Dakar; Amadou Mustafa M'Backe, caliph of the Murids and son of Amadou Bamba, founder of the Muridiyya; and Sheikh Anta M'Backe, a great marabout.[98] Some of the Muslim figures who appear on this list were regarded by the colonial regime as highly important leaders of the Muslims in Senegal or were relatives of such leaders.[99] Hence, although the colonial administration was quite certain that these people and others were connected in one way or another to Montezer's activity, it was careful not to take overly strong steps against them.

The special treatment such people received is evident in the orders that the head of the General Security Service conveyed to the commandant of the circle of Baol (Senegal) on the steps to be taken regarding Bassirou M'Backe, brother of the great Murid Mamadou Mustafa (and son of Amadou Bamba), who, according to some investigations, had received at his house in Kaolack many of Montezer's emissaries: "We must request of the commandant of the circle of Baol to draw the attention of M'Backe to the discomfort likely to be caused to his well-being and religious prestige as a result of a not overly passive approach regarding the subversive activities of some of his co-religionists. Investigations that will be necessary as a result of these activities are likely to cost him police interventions that up to now have been avoided."[100]

Apparently this won the marabout's attention, and he hastened to write to Boisson in February 1941 to refute the accusations that had been leveled at him. He averred that the nature of the relations between marabouts and their disciples was exclusively religious. The disciples turned to the marabout only on religious questions, and he did not know about other activities. He added that this was especially so when students transgressed the laws of Islam and, out of fear of the marabout, tried to keep this from him. M'Backe wrote that when the ties between France and England were severed, he had assembled his disciples in the mosque of Kaolack and ordered them to put an end to the trade between Senegal and Gambia and be content with trade within their country of origin. In May 1940 he had left his house in Kaolack and now returned there only sometimes to check his agricultural crops. He believed his disciples had heeded his advice. He himself had always been honest, and he had no intention of defending a disciple who had erred, even if it was his own son. As for Montezer, he admitted that he had met him once when one of his disciples introduced them. However, he had refused to provide him with a guide who would take him to Bathurst because he knew this was not a fitting role for a marabout. At the end of the letter M'Backe expressed his sorrow at the fact that the administration suspected him and mentioned that his father and brothers had been legionnaires and that he too was loyal to France and would even be prepared to give his life for it.

Boisson was not entirely persuaded by this letter, but the response that he asked the governor of Senegal to convey to M'Backe was quite delicate. Boisson requested that the governor emphasize to M'Backe that his personal prestige and religious authority gave him a special obligation to guide his disciples from a moral standpoint. Boisson acknowledged that M'Backe was not responsible for everything his disciples did, but he noted that he had an overall responsibility for them, and intentional or unintentional ignorance of their deeds was not sufficient to exonerate him of all blame.[101] Such delicate treatment, as reflected in letters concerning marabouts who were suspected of collaborating with the Gaullists, a transgression that was considered extremely grave, points to the colonial regime's cautious attitude toward Muslim religious leaders.

As we have seen, these leaders, who usually had great influence over substantial portions of the population, took different approaches to the colonial regime. There were some, such as Seidou Nourou Tall, who served as mediators between the administration and the populace and some who chose the path of Sheikh Hamallah—that is, total disconnection from the colonial administration, a disconnection that generally was interpreted by the French as hostility and opposition to their rule even though that was not always the intent. The French feared the potential danger posed by the great influence of the marabouts and tried, on the one hand, to conciliate them by inviting them to important ceremonies and providing tokens of honor and financial gifts to mosques and, on the other, to neutralize this influence or make it work to their advantage.[102] On 26 May 1941 the governor of Senegal sent a note to his circle commandants, who monitored the activity of the marabouts. He called for restricting the movement of those who conducted tours in Senegal and sending them back to their home villages: "A situation has emerged in which too many marabouts are wandering with their disciples and propagating messages orally or in writing. You must request of the marabouts and their disciples to set an example and remain in their villages. You must impose punishments on the basis of the *indigénat* on those who do not report an address change and put an end, with the help of counsel or personal influence, to these unnecessary and sometimes even dangerous movements. If that does not help, you must deprive the traveling marabouts of their authorization for free movement."[103]

The French also feared the phenomenon of "prophets" who warned of all manner of catastrophes and thus induced anxieties in the Muslim population that elements hostile to the regime were liable to exploit. In September 1941, in the area of the circle of Thiès, a letter was disseminated in Arabic that purportedly had come from Mecca and described a host of calamities that would befall those who did not repent religiously within three months. The governor of Senegal noted that this was a recurring phenomenon and requested of the circle commandant that he take a number of measures: (1) speak with the religious leaders and explain to them that such propaganda could have an influence on the Muslim population during this difficult period; (2) placate the population in every possible way, whether via the marabouts or directly; (3) view and quarantine every document of this kind; and (4) report any reaction by the population to the governor without delay. In another case the 1940 annual report of the governor of Senegal spoke of Muslims who came to Christian villages and said the Germans in the occupied zone of France were shooting priests and soon would also come to Senegal. The Muslims explained to the Christians that their only way to escape a similar fate was to convert to Islam.[104]

Thus, the French treatment of marabouts was delicate yet also forceful. They strove not to offend the honor of suspicious marabouts and avoided arresting them as far as possible, apparently because they feared a harsh reaction from believers. They were also aware of the marabouts' great importance as mediators between the colonial regime and the Muslim population in calm periods and even more so in such unstable times.

More "Carrots" than "Sticks": A Cautious Islamic Policy

In September 1941 one of the missionaries of the White Fathers (Pères blancs) who was living in the Upper Volta area described the colonial administration's policy toward the Muslims.[105] He characterized it as extremely sympathetic—indeed, he claimed, too sympathetic. The missionary wrote that he and his friends were facing enormous difficulties, such as disease and death, but the gravest difficulty was Islam and the colonial administration's blindness toward it. The administration was treating all the villages as Muslim, on the pretext that most of their population was Muslim, and all the circles as Muslim, on the pretext that most of the important districts were Muslim. The missionary noted that he understood that France needed to relate respectfully to the "religion of the Arabs," but the preference for Islam over Catholic and Protestant Christianity was, in his view, an injustice. Furthermore the systematic proliferation of Islam even in non-Muslim areas, together with the establishment of mosques in these areas, was a grave crime against France. He claimed that the attack in Bobo-Dioulasso was a consequence of this policy. The colonial administration applied exactly the same policy in regions where there was a Muslim majority as in regions where there were almost none. This had fostered a situation where chiefs in non-Muslim areas were beginning to convert to Islam. The officials of the administration were not wasting any opportunity to guarantee Islam the esteem of France, an esteem that was exclusive. He concluded by writing that it was no wonder that one could find almost no one but Muslims among the administration workers— bureaucrats, translators, mechanics, and guards—in a country that was almost completely "fetishistic."[106]

One must, to be sure, consider with a certain skepticism this description of colonial policy toward Islam because it comes from a missionary who by the nature of his work regarded Islam as an obstacle. Nevertheless, there is additional testimony that the colonial administration did indeed demonstrate a sympathetic attitude toward Muslim elements so long as they were not considered dangerous. For example, in a letter from the imam of the Great Mosque of Medina (a neighborhood in Dakar), dated March 1941, the imam thanked the governor of Dakar and its surroundings for a donation of one thousand francs to the Tijaniyya order, which had been given at the initiative of General Maxime Weygand.[107] In October 1942 the minister of the colonies suggested establishing a mosque in

Marseille. Such a plan had first surfaced in 1936 in response to a request by Muslims from southern France but was not executed because of the authorities' lack of interest. In 1941 the idea again arose, this time with a view to constructing the mosque in Nice. However, it was quickly resolved that "this beautiful resort city is not designed for mosques to be built in it," and it was again decided to establish the mosque in Marseille, where there were more Muslims.[108]

A further example is Vichy policy on the issue of pilgrimage to Mecca. Whereas during World War I the colonial regime had prohibited the pilgrimage on the grounds that the Muslims who made it would be influenced by elements hostile to France, it was decided, with the outbreak of World War II, not to reinstate this policy. The French government thereby sought to demonstrate that France remained the country that protected Islam and to thus win Muslim support. The Vichy regime did not change this decision, and after a small decrease in the number of pilgrims in 1941, their number gradually increased until 1945.[109]

In general the colonial regime's policy toward Islam in the Vichy period was in many ways a direct continuation of French Islamic policy prior to World War II. The regime's ambivalent attitude toward Islam, manifested at once through fear and suspicion and a desire to exploit Islam so as to facilitate control, continued throughout the Vichy period. The colonial administration closely monitored the activity of different Islamic groups and sought to prevent marabouts from wandering from place to place. On the other hand the regime exploited Muslim religious figures such as Seidou Nourou Tall to disseminate its propaganda among the African population and to maintain Muslim loyalty to the colonial administration. The French strove not to annoy important Muslim religious figures so as not to arouse unrest among their followers and avoided taking drastic measures against marabouts who were suspected of "anti-French" activity, notwithstanding the wartime circumstances that exacerbated tensions in the colonies.

The French did become somewhat less friendly toward Islam than in the period of the Popular Front, when amicable relations reached a peak under Governor Marcel de Coppet. For example, the practice that began during the rule of the Popular Front of having administration officials take part in Muslim celebrations was stopped during the Vichy period and renewed only in 1944.[110] Yet during the Vichy period as well the colonial regime continued to make gestures toward Muslims such as donations to mosques. Moreover, the decision to build a mosque in Marseille, an idea that had first arisen in 1936, was finally reached only during the Vichy period. Donations for the construction of religious monuments also helped establish the colonial regime's legitimacy in the eyes of the federation's Islamic population. Thus the Vichy colonial regime tried to continue the general lines of the Islamic policy that had emerged prior the war. Sometimes, however, it was forced to take a harsher approach and more closely monitor the activities of Muslim groups because of the wartime circumstances and the activity of the Anglo-Gaullists, who were also trying to reach out to Muslim elements.

For its part the Muslim establishment in FWA, generally speaking, did not change its attitude to the colonial administration during the Vichy period and continued to follow the path of accommodation, although some marabouts cautiously assisted Gaullists or at least maintained relations with them. The main problems the colonial regime encountered originated with marginal Muslim groups or with groups that had broken off from the central stream of the Tijaniyya and whose main conflict was with this Islamic order. Violent eruptions in Muslim areas were not a new phenomenon. As noted, violent incidents connected to the activity of the Hamallists, for example, had occasionally occurred in French Sudan since the beginning of the twentieth century. At the same time wartime conditions and Anglo-Gaullist activity encouraged such attacks and intensified the colonial regime's wariness of them, a wariness that led to thorough investigations of possible links between Muslims and the English and the Gaullists across the border.

8.

Vichy Colonialism and African Society

Change and Continuity

This examination of the ways in which the Vichy colonial regime inter-acted with the "modern" and "traditional" elites of FWA tends to reflect a large measure of continuity. In fact many of the ideas introduced by Vichy colonial theoreticians regarding the policies toward "old" and "new" elites existed before Vichy in the form of the policy of "association." This was considered the best policy toward both kinds of elites. Was Vichy policy then just another form of the doctrine of association? A positive answer to this question might easily explain the continuity in the regime's colonial policies in FWA. In general terms one could argue that the new regime simply embraced association and rejected the notion of assimilation and thus continued an already existing tendency in French colonial theory in the interwar era.

However, I would claim that it is too simplistic to view Vichy colonial policy as a mere continuation of the policy of association. As I mention at the beginning of part III, even when association replaced assimilation, the latter continued to exist in the French colonial mind, even if in a rather limited way. This is especially true with regard to the four communes of Senegal. The great change in Vichy colonial policy then was the total and decisive rejection of this idea. For the Vichy regime no African—nor anyone else without French blood running in his or her veins, for that matter—could be considered French. For Vichy colonial theoreticians assimilation was a disastrous idea that could never have worked and that undermined French sovereignty in the colonies. Therefore the term had to be erased from the colonial vocabulary. This idea was reflected in a colonial policy in FWA that no longer distinguished between Africans who held French citizenship and those who did not, instead drawing the line according to race.

Another change that Vichy colonialism brought was the support the ideas of "association" received in the regime's metropolitan policies and ideology—the enforced admiration of hierarchy; the respect for traditional and agricultural elements of society; the rejection of the idea of equality and homogeneity within French society; and the idea that French citizenship was the right of those who were "truly" French, not culturally but racially. Vichy colonialism, then, erased any remnant of the ideas that had permitted the accordance of French citizenship to Africans in the first place—meaning the belief in equality, at least potentially, among all humans.

Other distinctions of the Vichy colonial regime were related more to the circumstances of France's defeat than to ideology. Differences in colonial policy toward citizens, évolués, chiefs, soldiers, and Islamic leaders often stemmed from the special circumstances of World War II. To the difficulties the French colonial regime had already experienced during the first global conflict, the division between the Free French and the Vichyites, and the readiness of the British to stir up trouble in FWA, added new and complex challenges. The administration was thus forced to be especially vigilant in its relations with all of these groups.

The humiliation of the metropolitan power, the accentuated racism felt in both urban and rural areas, and the harsh economic circumstances of the war all created an atmosphere that changed African concepts about the colonial power. As one of my informants stated, decolonization was bound to occur anyhow, but Vichy colonial rule precipitated it by raising the consciousness of Africans regarding the real nature of colonialism.

If we take into consideration the combination of the unfavorable conditions for the regime and its harshness, the fact that acts of violent resistance to it were rare points to the relative success of the regime's policy toward various African sectors. In fact the attack on Europeans in Bobo-Dioulasso and the rice rebellion in Casamanse, both discussed earlier, were the only major violent expressions of discontent among the African population during the Vichy period.

At the beginning of part III it is suggested that recent literature on the Vichy period in France has seen a growing tendency to probe beyond the limited categories of "collaboration" and "resistance." Resistance thus is not defined only as organized activities of networks or movements but as varied actions of men and women in their everyday lives that expressed discontent with the existing reality of occupation and authoritarian rule.

Similar attitudes toward the concept of "resistance" in general have developed in other, quite different contexts. In a book about the black working class in the United States, for example, Robin Kelley claims that in order to understand the ways in which black workers rebelled against discrimination and repression during and following World War II, one must dig beyond the surface of trade unions, political institutions, and social movements into the everyday lives, cultures, and communities of these "race rebels."[1] He describes, for instance, black spectators in the cinema who, forced to sit in a segregated balcony, used the cover of darkness in the cinema hall to throw popcorn on the heads of the Whites sitting below "in cushioned chairs, secure they thought in their power."[2] Kelley emphasizes the important role of public space, such as the cinema or public transportation, as grounds on which many Blacks rebelled against discrimination by simple acts of defiance, such as refusing to evacuate their seats for white people. Thus for black workers public space embodied the most violent and repressive elements of racism but ironically also provided many opportunities to rebel by allowing a certain anonymity that made policing more difficult.[3]

A consideration of Africans' everyday cultural and political acts of protest within the colonial public space under Vichy is most useful in acquiring a fuller picture of nonorganized and subtler forms of resistance to the new regime. In between quiet acceptance of or collaboration with the Vichy regime and open violent resistance to it, most Africans used various strategies to overcome the problem of food shortages, evade recruitment for forced labor, and sometimes express their resentment of the regime's racism. Bara Diouf recalled that, while in the first year of the regime people somehow ignored the situation, in the second year they began to react. In the street where he lived African youngsters often quarreled with French sailors and soldiers. On Ponty (today Pompidou) Avenue fights occurred all the time. The policy of segregation was also met with protests from young Africans. In the cinemas Africans were compelled to sit in the front rows, while Europeans sat in the back, where the view was better. On one occasion a group of young Africans bought tickets, then went and sat in their places in the front, donning top hats so that the Whites in the back could not see a thing.[4] Another quiet act of resistance, this time by an old African veteran, was his refusal to accept his pension, claiming that it was German money.[5]

Catherine Atlan discusses other intriguing forms of resistance in Saint Louis and Dakar. In Saint Louis two hairstyles for women appeared simultaneously during the war. One was in honor of De Gaulle, and the other was called a "boos," as a reference to *boches* (a derogatory name for Germans), and resembled a Prussian hat (*casque*). One interpretation of these coiffures is that through them the women of Saint Louis expressed both their openness to the world and their relative indifference toward the conflict.

The same spirit of indifference was expressed in popular songs that circulated in the streets of Dakar during the war. One of these songs referred to the Anglo-Gaullist attack on Dakar in 1940:

> Richelieu ak Barham
> Du ma tere ñew
> Falong Falong

> (The *Richelieu* and the *Barham*
> Do not scare me
> Falong Falong)[6]

The *Richelieu* was the warship of Vichy, and the *Barham* belonged to the British Navy, which had attacked the city. This song is a rejection of the war of the Whites, who were all menacing the Blacks.[7]

In the rural areas of Senegal a popular resistance movement developed in the region of Basse-Casamance that took several forms. In 1942 a charismatic female prophet by the name of Alin Sitouë Diatta succeeded in attracting many followers. Her religious message associated ancient myths and local rites with personal "visions" integrating contemporary elements. The prophet predicted not only the arrival of rain and the dispositions of divine forces but also the departure of the Whites. According to rumors she recommended disobeying the Europeans, refusing to do military service, and abandoning the cultivation of the white rice that had been introduced by the Portuguese in favor of the local "red rice." She was finally arrested on 31 January 1943, but the myth surrounding her personality continued to develop, and her spiritual influence became even stronger. Her uncle, Benjamin Diatta, was a local notable in Ziguinchor. Before the war he was a province chief and a member of the colonial council. The Vichy authorities dismissed him in 1941, accusing him of showing ill will in organizing military conscription in the region of the Diola. He later became a symbol of Vichy colonial repression for the local *évolués* and other inhabitants of the region.[8]

Acts of protest also occurred after the Vichy period was over. When the French Army paraded through the streets of Dakar in 1944, many Africans did not salute the tricolor flag. A fight then broke out when a

Frenchman started hitting dissenting Africans. According to A.D.M., this was the motive for De Gaulle's Brazzaville speech. He wanted to appease the Africans because he knew that the atmosphere had changed.[9] Diouf also reported that his sense of revolt was radicalized during the Vichy period. After the war he was drafted into the French Army. While he was serving as a sergeant, his commanders wished to send him to officers' training so that he could serve in Indochina. He refused because he knew that Africans were being used as cannon fodder.[10]

Open violent revolt against the wrongs of colonial rule was rare in FWA even in times of relative calm. During the war, under an especially repressive colonial regime that was more alert than usual to the possibility of revolt and more than ready to repress it with all its might, this kind of overt resistance was almost impossible. That does not mean, however, that the bluntly racist policies of the Vichy regime were accepted with no protest. Africans used public space, especially where racial segregation existed, as a means of showing their discontent with the new regime. They used cultural means, such as hairstyles, to demonstrate their indifference to the colonizer "family" disputes, and they resorted to religious and social movements or economic strategies such as smuggling to survive their everyday hardships. These subtle forms of resistance probably contributed to the development of an anticolonial consciousness in the years that followed, especially among urban Africans, who were no longer willing to accept colonial injustices. In the next and concluding part of this book the Vichy period in FWA is examined in a comparative context and linked to the historical events in FWA that led to decolonization.

PART IV

The Long-Term Significance of the Vichy Period for West African History

In French collective memory the Vichy period is undoubtedly one of the most traumatic and controversial. According to Éric Conan and Henry Rousso those four dark years—1940–44—occupy for the French a place that is disproportionate with respect to the context of their country's history. They see the presence of this past (*un passé qui ne passe pas*) both as a symptom of unfinished mourning and as a warning signal for the future of French identity and the strength of its universalistic values.[1]

This is hardly the case for FWA. This federation was a colony whose destiny was determined in France. The people of FWA had no say regarding the decision to support Pétain in 1940 and little freedom to choose whether to accept his policies or not. True, the changes in colonial policy from the republican era were not dramatic, and a large degree of continuity was maintained, as shown in parts II and III; nevertheless, one can certainly not dismiss the Vichy period in FWA as insignificant to the historical processes that began after the war. Something did change under Vichy: most particularly, new political options appeared that had not existed before. The change of regime was also highly significant for the small but politically important Western-educated elite that discovered for the first time the real nature of colonial rule and the deadlock it presented for them. Part IV addresses the ways in which the Vichy era influenced the decolonization of FWA.

To better appreciate this influence it is vital to first examine the Vichy period in a comparative colonial perspective. In chapter 9 I first discuss Free French policy in the parallel years in the neighboring federation of FEA. The comparison of the two colonial regimes, which were rivals in their ideologies, will help us to isolate the elements of Vichy policy that were part of an inherent ideology from those that emerged from the circumstances of the war. I then compare the main characteristics of Vichy policy in FWA to policy in other parts of the Vichy-controlled empire, especially those that were void of any significant German influence. In chapter 10 I evaluate the significance of this period in FWA for the postwar decolonization process. I then discuss the role of the Vichy legacy in the political developments in FWA and its imprint on the discourses used by various African actors during the postwar anticolonial struggle.

9.

Vichy Colonialism

A Comparative Perspective

Vociferous opponents of the idea of assimilation often argued that the French empire covered a huge area replete with a range of cultures and peoples at different stages of evolution. Therefore it was totally illogical to implement the same policy and export the same metropolitan institutions to every corner of the empire. This argument was sometimes also perceived as valid for France itself. In fact it was Vichy ideology that continued such ideas as the need to maintain diversity and to reject the "false" equality upon which the Republic's values were based. Nevertheless, in spite of these beliefs the Vichy regime implemented the same ideology and social organizations in all of the colonies it was able to retain. The National Revolution, as opposed to republican values, was equally applicable, according to the regime, in FWA as it was in Guadeloupe, Madagascar, or Indochina. This is not to say that its implementation was identical in all of the Vichy-ruled colonies, but as we shall see, the similarities were greater than the differences. The real difference lay, in fact, in the impact the Vichy period had on the various colonies, and this dissimilarity stemmed from the divergence of the historical, social, cultural, and political situations in these colonies more than from variances in Vichy colonial policy.

In order to place the period discussed here in a wider context, the basic elements of Vichy colonial policy and the responses to it at the time and after the war will be compared in several French colonies. The bulk of the discussion will concentrate on colonies that, like FWA, had no German presence or direct influence: Madagascar, Guadeloupe, and Indochina. Reference will also be made to the French colonies of North Africa, which played an important role in the events of World War II. But first I will compare the Vichy experience in FWA to French colonial rule in the neighboring federation of FEA, which was under Free French control. This examination of the similarities and differences in colonial policies in the two federations will enable us to isolate those that were influenced by war conditions and to better understand the nature of the Vichy brand of colonialism.

Free French Colonial Policy in FEA

The federation of FEA, established in 1910, was often called the "Cinderella of the French empire," as it had many fewer resources and was less developed than its neighbor FWA.[1] It consisted of four territories, Chad, Gabon, Ubangui-Chari (today the Central African Republic), and French Congo (today Congo-Brazzaville), and the mandate of Cameroon. Despite its perceived limitations and its reduced strategic importance, Charles De Gaulle attributed tremendous significance to his success in gaining control over this territory in 1940. Possessing FEA gave De Gaulle what he missed the most—territory.[2] In October 1940 he visited the federation and defined the main steps the colonial administration should take during the war. He clarified that Free France should not only protect the territories that joined its ranks but also maintain order and support their economic efforts.

Félix Eboué, a black administrator from French Guyana who declared his alliance to De Gaulle while serving as the governor of Chad, outlined an independent colonial policy as the governor-general of FEA. He often refused to take instructions from De Gaulle's representatives who came to visit the federation and even threatened to resign several times. Eboué took care to tour the colonies personally, with the intent of uplifting the people's spirit and encouraging economic efforts.[3]

Born in 1884 in Guyana, an old French colony inhabited at the time by around twenty thousand people, Eboué enjoyed the status of French citizen. He had won a scholarship to study at a high school in Bordeaux, where he excelled in his studies. In 1905 he moved to Paris and a year later entered the École coloniale. When he graduated in 1908 he was sent to Madagascar for his first overseas post.[4] Obviously his own status as an assimilated colonial citizen influenced his decision to reject the Vichy regime. Nevertheless, as we shall see, it did not make him support the policy of assimilation in the territories under his sway.

Eboué's policy can be evaluated through circulars he distributed to his governors at the time. He believed that in spite of "the mistakes of the past," the French presence in Africa remained vital and should not tolerate any criticism or resistance from Africans.[5] While he proclaimed his belief in the fundamental values of the French Revolution and the Third Republic, he rejected the notion of assimilation. It was not possible, he stated, to turn the African into a Parisian worker or a farmer from Normandy, nor should French civilization destroy the different lifestyles that had long existed in Africa.[6]

Eboué's main reproach of French colonial policy regarded its attitude toward traditional chiefs. He objected to the system of appointing chiefs who actually served as colonial officials but lacked legitimacy among the local population and tried rather to uphold the status of traditional chiefs whose rule was legitimate in the eyes of the local population. Eboué was deeply concerned about the disintegration of traditional society and the emergence of a new African elite of pétits bourgeois and merchants living in the cities. Of these two elites Eboué certainly preferred the traditional one.[7]

To prevent the disintegration of traditional society Eboué introduced two reforms in FEA: he defined the new status of *notables évolués*, and he established autonomous administrative units called *communes indigènes*.[8] Eboué explained that citizenship in FEA should not be perceived in the same way as citizenship in France. The aim of the new status was not to re-create the African as a Frenchman but to turn him into a citizen of FEA by teaching him to rule his people without oppressing them. It was accorded to African men and women who had lived in the colony for at least ten years; knew how to speak, read, and write French fluently; had an occupation that benefited the colony; had fulfilled their military obligations; and were "decent."[9] *Notables évolués* could not acquire French citizenship, though they did receive some privileges, such as the right to organize in social and political frameworks, the right to be elected to the municipal councils of the *communes indigènes*, exemptions from forced labor, tax breaks, and so on.[10]

The second reform, of the *communes indigènes*, was related to the first. These autonomous administrative units were put under the control of a French official. They served as municipal councils and consisted of Africans who held the status of *notables évolués*. They were responsible for urbanization, road maintenance, sports, and professional education for the community.

Ultimately these reforms were not influential. Only 485 Africans out of 3.5 million in the federation were granted the new status, and even those few could easily lose it if a local colonial official so decided. The governors of the territories were not keen to implement Eboué's reforms. Instead forced labor continued and even increased due to the need for gold, timber, and rubber for the war. The *indigénat* remained in force (with certain signs of relief in 1943–44), and the tax burden increased.[11] In fact the Free French determination to bring the few colonies they possessed into the war effort—be it for military service abroad or building public works at home—heavily increased the burden on the African population in FEA. During the war ten thousand soldiers and civilians were recruited in the federation for wartime purposes.[12]

Free French policy at this time also extended to matters of agriculture— one of the pillars of local subsistence. The agricultural policy was based on three principles: (1) the colonies should supply their own food; (2) they should contribute as much produce as possible to the war effort; and (3) their economic situation must improve during the war.[13] These principles were difficult enough to uphold in times of peace; during the war it was impossible to do so. Nevertheless, the attempt to enforce them increased the pressure on the colonized population to invest more efforts in agricultural production and grow specific crops that were needed in France.

In spite of his clear preference for the traditional elite, Eboué did not neglect young educated Africans. He made efforts, for example, to integrate Africans into positions that had previously been reserved exclusively for Europeans. He encouraged them to set up sports clubs, literary societies, and discussion groups. Some of these organizations were transformed after the war into political parties.[14] Eboué also worked to advance the education of young Africans so that they could join the colonial apparatus. On 13 April 1942 he decided to establish in each of the federation's four territories an *école primaire supérieure*. These schools aimed to train Africans to serve in the colonial administrative and commercial subaltern staff and to prepare candidates for the *école supérieure*, which had been founded in the capital, Brazzaville, in 1935.[15]

Like the Vichy regime in FWA the Free French saw propaganda as vital in the new precarious circumstances brought on by the war. They too had to explain to their colonial subjects that in spite of its defeat France was still a powerful colonizer. Belonging to the camp of those who pursued the struggle against Nazi Germany made it easier for the Free French, as they did not have to justify the armistice, but explaining why they were also fighting against the official regime in France necessitated a great deal of persuasion. In Free French propaganda a special place was reserved for the figure of De Gaulle. He was presented to Africans as a giant who refused to accept the defeat to the Germans and thus had rallied forth to save France. Due to the small number of Africans who owned radio sets, propaganda was disseminated mainly through engaging photographs of De Gaulle. These pictures, accompanied by his famous quotation "La France a perdu une bataille, elle n'a pas perdu la guerre," reached even the most remote areas of FEA.[16] The presentation of De Gaulle as a loving and protective father who was the personification of France resembled that of Pétain in Vichy-ruled FWA. And indeed it was De Gaulle who filled the empty space left in post-Vichy FWA as well.

The hardships that the people of FEA endured during the war were not unlike those experienced in FWA. In both federations forced labor increased, and the pressure to boost production due to shortages caused by the war was strong. The ability of FEA to export further exacerbated this pressure. The economic situation in both colonies was dire and made Africans look for ways to survive. Some aspects of Eboué's policy do not seem unlike Vichy's, especially his preference for the African traditional elite and his rejection of assimilation. Even his idea of initiating a new status would have, most likely, been acceptable to Vichy colonial policy-makers.

Nevertheless, there are some major differences that can shed light on the specific nature of Vichy colonialism. First, the increased and manifested racism that existed in FWA under Vichy made the hardships caused by the war almost unbearable. Second, while Eboué did not like to encourage assimilation, he did allow some privileges to a small number of Africans that were totally unheard of in the neighboring federation. It is also important to bear in mind that the status of *originaires* did not exist in FEA before the war; therefore Eboué's idea of a new status should be seen as a step forward for Western-educated Africans and not a step backward. In other words, while the physical conditions in the two federations during the war were similar, the atmosphere was different. Vichy colonialism had its own character, and as we shall now see, this character was not unique to FWA.

Vichy in North Africa, Madagascar, Indochina, and Guadeloupe

The French colonies of North Africa, especially Algeria, were seen more as a direct extension of metropolitan France than overseas territories. The reasons for this were their relative proximity to France and their large number of European settlers (around one million in Algeria; 240,000 in Tunisia; and 440,000 in Morocco on the eve of World War II). North Africa in general and Algeria in particular were the subjects of a heated argument when France was defeated. In June 1940 the colonial administration in North Africa intended to continue the struggle against Germany. Pétain objected because he believed this would only lead to harsher armistice conditions and to German occupation of the empire. Eventually, a few weeks later, the colonies of North Africa dedicated themselves fully to Pétain's "cult."[17]

Just like in France and FWA most of the colonial officials in North Africa were not replaced. Even newly appointed officials were recruited from among the same milieus as their predecessors. In Morocco Governor-General André Noguès retained his position in spite of his initial objection to the armistice. His counterpart in Tunisia, Governor Marcel Peyrouton, who had served for many years under the Third Republic, was appointed interior minister of the Vichy government. Admiral Jean Pierre Estéva replaced him as governor on 25 July 1940. The governor-general of Algeria, Admiral Jean Abrial, was replaced after one year by the last chief of staff before the defeat, Maxime Weygand, who had been stationed in Algeria since October 1940 as the general representative of the Vichy government. He was replaced in November 1941 by Yves Châtel, who had served the republic for many years in Indochina.[18]

The ideology of the Vichy regime was enthusiastically accepted in the political atmosphere that prevailed among the large population of European settlers in Algeria. The mass organization of the regime, the French Legion of Combatants (Légion français de combattants), was extremely popular. In June 1941 it included 107,000 members—64,000 Europeans and 43,000 Muslims.[19] Most of the European population of Algeria supported the National Revolution and the abolition of the 1871 Cremieux Decree that had accorded French citizenship to the Jews of Algeria.[20]

As Michel Abitbol, Jacques Cantier, and Christine Levisse-Touzé demonstrate in their respective studies, the Vichy ideology was imported to Algeria. This was expressed not only in the persecution of the enemies of the regime but also in the thorough implementation of the principles of the National Revolution. The General Education reforms were implemented in Algerian schools, and the colonial regime took care to organize ceremonies and parades in the Vichy style.[21]

As in FWA the Vichy regime in Algeria was concerned about Anglo-Gaullist propaganda, but the great difference between the two lay in the threat German propaganda posed to the French colonial authority. A few weeks after the armistice the Germans fully resumed the dissemination of propaganda among the Muslim population of North Africa through the radio and the press. They also helped to subsidize a few small extremist groups. The radio broadcasts were in French, Arabic, and the Kabyle language. They attacked French colonial policy and presented Hitler as the liberator of Algeria from French oppression. While refraining from inciting revolt, the German propaganda spoke of the approaching victory of the Third Reich and presented the Jews and the British as the common enemies of Germany and the Arab-Islamic world. These messages fell on fertile ground and fostered hope among many Algerians that the end of French colonial rule was near. Under the influence of German propaganda many popular songs were written that described Hitler as "victorious and generous," as a "lion" who had arrived to liberate the oppressed peoples of North Africa.[22]

The German propaganda attracted North African nationalists, such as members of the Algerian Partie du peuple Algérien (PPA), members of the political movements Destour and Néo-Destour in Tunisia, and some members of the close entourage of the Sultan of Morocco.[23] The Germans also edited an Arabic review in Paris, entitled *Al-duniā al-Jadīda* (The New World), that was directed at the North African political elite. In addition to the political parties, whose leaders saw Nazi Germany mainly as an anticolonial weapon, there were some real pro-Nazi elements among the local population—for example, the Comité Musulman de l'Afrique du Nord, founded by the Algerian Muhammad al-Maadi Lakhdar.[24]

German activity and attempts to influence the local population in North Africa made the regime most concerned about the possible eruption of revolts among Algerians. It thus initiated preventive arrests of those considered potential troublemakers. The regime's fear proved to be realistic. As early as 10 August 1940 riots between Muslims and Europeans in a quarter of Algiers erupted, and resentment against European settlers gradually increased. On 25 January 1941 soldiers stationed in the city's center declared a mutiny. The leader of the anticolonial movement L'Étoile Nord-Africaine (The North African Star), Massali Hadj, was accused of organizing this revolt and sentenced to sixteen years' hard labor.[25] In Tunisia the population remained calm at first, but gradually the Néo-Destour party adopted a more anti-French tone and began to demand independence.[26]

Vichy rule in North Africa officially ended in November 1942, when the Allies landed there. However, its influence was not easily effaced, and its legislation remained in force at least until May 1943, when De Gaulle arrived. The National Revolution found it could flourish in Algeria. French colonialism in this colony even before Vichy had been much harsher than in FWA, and far less flexible, mainly due to the vast European settlement and the special status of Algeria as a French *département*. Nevertheless, the Vichy regime accentuated the already racist colonial system and contributed in its harshness to the violent nature of the anticolonial movement after the war. The first shot in the Algerian war was fired, in fact, in May 1945, in the Setif riots. The violent repression that followed only managed to postpone the anticolonial war by nine years.

When we compare the Algerian case to other French colonies that were located at a much greater distance from France, we can clearly see that the German presence had no bearing on the way the National Revolution was implemented. The cases of Madagascar, Indochina, and Guadeloupe, studied by Eric Jennings, demonstrate this point well and help us locate the case of Vichy rule in FWA in a wider colonial context.

Of the three colonies there is some similarity between Madagascar and Indochina, while Guadeloupe is essentially different. The French colonized the island of Madagascar in 1895, at about the same time they consolidated their rule over most of FWA. Unlike FWA, however, Madagascar attracted French settlers, although in much smaller numbers than did the colonies of North Africa. About 23,000 Europeans, mostly French, lived on the island on the eve of World War II, alongside a population of 3.6 million Malagasy and 10,500 Asians and other Africans.[27] Like Madagascar, Indochina had some French settlers—between 25,000 and 39,000 in 1940, about 0.2 percent of the overall population. These settlers were mainly rightist and antirepublican and therefore, like their counterparts in Madagascar and Algeria, enthusiastically welcomed the Vichy regime.[28] Indochina was to a large extent an invented composite that included Laos, Cambodia, Tonkin, Annam, and Cochin-China (the last three constitute Vietnam today). French colonial rule there up to the 1930s was repressive. Under the Popular Front some reforms were introduced, but these were much more superficial than in other colonies. For example, unlike in FWA, trade unions in Indochina did not gain formal recognition under the Popular Front.[29]

Madagascar's remoteness from metropolitan France and its proximity to British East Africa notwithstanding, the colonial authorities of the island opted in July 1940 to support the Vichy regime and adopted its ideology. But Vichy rule ended in September 1942 with the British military invasion.[30] In Indochina, despite the Japanese presence between 1940 and 1945, the Vichy regime controlled most official activities, such as the police force, education system, tax levying, banking, and governmental decisions.[31]

Just as in FWA, in both colonies the ideology of the National Revolution was introduced into the colonial sphere, and much effort was invested in propagating Pétain's ideas to the local population. Indeed, the regime's usual scapegoats—Jews, Communists, and Freemasons—were persecuted in Madagascar and Indochina, despite their tiny number. At the same time the colonial regime actively encouraged Malagasy and Vietnamese boys and girls to participate in sports and set up a special school for physical education.[32]

Other similarities to Vichy-ruled FWA can be found in the presentation of the figure of Pétain and the positive attitude toward tradition. In Madagascar Pétain was called, in Malagasy, Ray-Aman-Dreny (Father and Mother), mirroring his portrayal in FWA as a loving and caring father. However, there was an additional element to this presentation in Madagascar, where he was also shown as a local traditional ruler, thus justifying the fact that the Malagasy people had to pay "tribute" and were recruited to work for him. In Madagascar, then, there was a real attempt to revive the folklore of the Merina monarchy and reconstruct its ceremonies—with Pétain replacing the traditional monarch.[33] In FWA such attempts at reconstruction were not found, perhaps due to the complex precolonial reality there.

In Indochina the Vichy regime invested special efforts in the attempt to demonstrate the resemblance of its ideology to the local traditional cultures. In this domain it went further than in any of the other Vichy-controlled colonies discussed here. According to the regime the Annamite people were more ready for the National Revolution than any other people in the French empire because Vichy philosophy was perfectly compatible with their tradition. The Vichy colonial administration in Indochina even went so far as to find parallels between Pétain's ideology and Confucianism.

The repressive Vichy rule in Madagascar contributed to the emergence of a national movement on the island that demanded independence after the war. One of the national parties, the Democratic Movement for Malagasy Renovation (Partie démocratique du renovation Malagache), evoked the Vichy period in its demand for independence by associating the liberation of France from Vichy rule and German occupation to the liberation of the Malagasy people from the French and Madagascar's demand for independence. The party's leader stated in a 1946 speech that just as the people of Paris had risen against the Germans, so did the Malagasy people wish to be liberated from the French. Another political movement, PANAMA (Parti National Socialiste Malagache), was founded clandestinely in 1941 as a response to harsh Vichy policy. This movement later paved the way for the insurrection of 1947. Vichy colonial policy in

Madagascar thus contributed to the development of national aspirations, which eventually led to a violent process of decolonization.[34]

Violence also dominated the decolonization process in Indochina. The attempts to revive old traditions only contributed to the development of nationalistic feelings among the various peoples of Indochina. The Vichy regime thus unintentionally helped to inspire anticolonial ideas and even provided their adherents with a framework in which to act by encouraging the establishment of youth movements. Some of these movements took a different course from that intended. The king of Cambodia, for example, established a youth movement in 1941 whose aim was to mold young Cambodians in a military spirit. This group adopted fascist elements and encouraged Khmer nationalism. After the war such groups provided a useful framework for anticolonial activities.[35]

According to Jennings the specific nature and history of French colonial rule in Guadeloupe made the effect of the Vichy period on this colony and other similar ones (Martinique, Réunion, and French Guyana) quite different from its effect in Madagascar and Indochina. On 1 July 1940 Constant Sorin, Guadeloupe's governor, unexpectedly declared his support for Vichy, despite his leftist political inclinations and his marriage to a British woman believed to be Jewish. The main elected assembly of the island tried to reverse this decision, but to no avail. All representative bodies were suspended, and politicians who resisted the support for Vichy were arrested.[36]

In 1940 304,329 people inhabited Guadeloupe. It was one of the "old colonies" (anciens colonies) and before World War II enjoyed the special status shared by Martinique, Réunion, French Guyana, and the four communes of Senegal. The law courts acted according to metropolitan judicial principles. Although these rights sometimes seemed precarious, and the pre–World War II period saw several political crises, Guadeloupe was considered the success story of the Third Republic and the policy of assimilation. The changes the Vichy regime introduced there, then, were much more radical and significant than in FWA, Madagascar, or Indochina.[37]

The general Vichy policy in Guadeloupe was similar in many respects to that in other Vichy-ruled colonies. The regime put massive pressure on the local population to grow agricultural crops and backed this pressure with the Pétainist ideology of a "return to the soil."[38] The educational reform that took place in France was also implemented in Guadeloupe. Training in manual work and agriculture increased at the expense of training in other fields, and the children spent most of their school hours singing songs of praise for the Marshal and participating in ceremonies.[39] It seems that the educational reform in Guadeloupe was more significant than in FWA, where the same subjects encouraged by Vichy had prevailed in the colonial educational system before the war.

As in FWA the rise of racism in Guadeloupe during the Vichy period contributed to feelings of resentment among the local population, and again this was manifested in popular resistance. Some resisters to Vichy rule opted to move to the neighboring island of Dominica, which was under British control. This form of resistance existed in FWA as well and was even easier there, as no boat was required for the trip. Vichy propaganda did win some hearts, however, as some Blacks who were hostile to the Republic supported the new regime.[40]

It has already been noted that resistance to Vichy had different results in Guadeloupe than in Madagascar and Indochina. The crushing of political rights under Vichy made their assurance in the future vital. The demand in Guadeloupe was not for independence but for the enforcement of these rights so that they could not be revoked again. And indeed, after the end of Vichy rule in these Caribbean islands in June 1943, all citizens' rights were immediately restored. After the war, on 19 March 1946, Guadeloupe, along with Martinique and Guyana, received the status of a full-fledged French *département*. This status was presented as a prize for the efforts of its people during the war and their help in achieving victory.[41]

As we can see from comparing FWA to the other colonies that were under Vichy control, the similarity in the implementation of the National Revolution in parts of the empire that varied greatly politically and culturally is striking. There is no doubt that the Vichy regime insisted on adapting its ideology to every corner of the French empire. The differences that did exist were related more to the direct ramifications of Vichy policy for local populations and to the pre-Vichy colonial reality in the various colonies.

If we now look again at the case of FWA, we can see that in spite of its many similarities to other colonies, Vichy rule there was distinctive. In fact FWA may be situated between Madagascar and Indochina (and to some degree Algeria), on the one hand, and Guadeloupe, Martinique, and Guyana, on the other. In the first group the Vichy period caused already existing anticolonial feelings to flare, which in turn led to a violent decolonization process after the war. French colonial rule in these colonies was repressive and inflexible, especially due to the presence of white settlers. Even the liberal reforms of the Popular Front did not have much effect on colonial rule in these three colonies. The Vichy regime only accentuated, then, an already racist and harsh colonial policy. In the second group the loss of republican rights only enforced the will of the local inhabitants to tighten the bond between them and the "true" republican France so that their rights would be guaranteed. These *anciens colonies*, with their relatively small populations and long traditions of political participation, did not present a menace to metropolitan France, which was prepared in the years following the war to turn them into French *départements d'outre-mer*. The Vichy period, with its denial of political rights, only reinforced the will of the local elites to be absorbed into France. On the French side Vichy repression was perceived as something that should be redressed, and the best way to do so was by the departmentalization of these colonies.

FWA fits between these two extremes. Although the Africans who had the same benefits as the inhabitants of Guadeloupe, Martinique, and Guyana were only a tiny percentage of the federation's entire population, their political influence far exceeded their numbers. On the other hand general colonial policy, although repressive, was more flexible than in Algeria, Madagascar, or Indochina. The implementation of significant political reforms under the Popular Front proves this point. African political leaders after the war hoped to achieve equality within the colonial system, but the French were not interested in absorbing this vast territory in which most inhabitants were devoid of any political rights.

When African political leaders realized that full assimilation was impossible, their aim became achieving some kind of autonomy within a French framework. As we shall see, only when it was clear that such a solution was not possible did independence become a political aim. Even then most African political leaders sought some kind of close cooperation with France. The nature of the decolonization process in FWA was influenced by this search for continued relations with France. Unlike the process in Madagascar, Indochina, and Algeria, the separation from France was relatively peaceful and far from complete. The next and final chapter discusses the effects of the Vichy period on postwar political developments in FWA.

10.

Vichy's Postwar Impact

Decolonization in FWA

Although assimilation never worked in FWA because, as Immanuel Wallerstein suggests, it was never tried, it remained a feature of French colonial
discourse from the moment the French set foot in the region, in theory
at least.[1] Even after World War II assimilation was still needed to justify
colonial rule, despite its impracticality and, indeed, danger for colonial
administrators.

From the metropolitan perspective Vichy colonial policy, despite its
clear link to what came before, was presented as an aberration, just as it
was presented in the metropolitan context. French republican colonialism
continued to be presented after the war as progressive and modernizing, a
kind of dominion that would eventually lead all Africans to equality and
prosperity. From the African perspective postwar political discourse relied
heavily on the same ideas, and the demands presented to the colonizer
were in line with the concept of assimilation. African political leaders
invoked "republican liberties" to press their demand for equality and assimilation. The common theme of all political demands was the rejection
of "Vichy-style" racial discrimination.[2]

Unlike the decolonization of Algeria, Madagascar, and Indochina, that
of FWA has not received much attention from researchers until recently.
The reason for this is the relative absence of violence in the process and
its somewhat less "dramatic" character. But it is precisely this ostensibly
calm character that makes decolonization in FWA so interesting.

In contrast to Britain, France had no intention of leaving its colonies
after the war ended. The British of course had not expected that independence would arrive so soon, but they did have this goal in mind. The
main aim of the Congress of Brazzaville, which the French organized in

December 1944, was to maintain the empire and prevent decolonization. The dominant political aim of the Africans corresponded with these ideas. They demanded full equality within the French framework, not political independence. (There was no single voice here, of course. Other elements that will be discussed later, such as youth and student organizations, did call for independence at an early stage.) By 1956, however, it was clear that the concept of assimilation was dead and that the only way for Africans to achieve equality was by gaining political independence. The independence of Tunisia and Morocco, and that of Ghana (the Gold Coast before independence) a year later, as well as the ongoing fighting in Algeria, influenced both French and African politicians and reshaped their ideas about their common future. The French were relieved that no violence had erupted in FWA but were concerned that if no reforms were introduced the relatively peaceful political atmosphere in the federation might change.[3] The Loi-cadre, passed in 1956, which gave semiautonomy to the eight territories of FWA, actually put an end to the goal of assimilation and paved the way for political independence. It liberalized and decentralized the colonial administration, introduced universal suffrage, extended the authority of the territorial assemblies, and provided each of them with a ministerial council that actually served as a shadow cabinet. African politicians, such as Léopold Sédar Senghor, were not enthusiastic about the new law because it accorded power to the territories at the expense of the federation. Others claimed that the changes were too little, too late because they did not ensure political equality.[4]

When De Gaulle returned to power in 1958, his options with regard to FWA were rather limited. Within one year, between 1956 and 1957, the word *independence* entered the vocabulary of African politics, not as a necessity but as a possibility. The federal party the Rassemblement Démocratique Africain (RDA), established by Félix Houphouët-Boigny in 1946 and to be discussed further later, mentioned the right to independence but did not speak about it as inevitable. The hesitancy of most African political leaders to demand independence stemmed from economic concerns. De Gaulle came up with the idea of a Franco-African community in which France would still hold authority over foreign and security affairs. The new constitution of 1958 and the African vote in favor of De Gaulle's community (with the exception of the people of Guinea, who voted against the idea and gained immediate independence) were an attempt to avoid complete independence and create a political framework that would preserve FWA within a greater France. However, soon enough the French renounced this idea and realized that colonial relations with FWA could be maintained after the independence of these territories at a much lower cost. Guinea's independence, Senghor's attempts to establish a federation with some of the other territories, and the lack of coordination and common interests among the territories of FWA all contributed to the rapid disappearance of the community, which in fact turned into a short transitional period leading to independence.[5]

As noted in the introduction, World War II is considered the trigger of the process of decolonization, a sort of point of no return from which the road to independence was inevitable. In this chapter I intend to explore this assumption with regard to the Vichy period in FWA. To do so I will examine several elements of African society that influenced the process of decolonization after the war to determine whether it is possible to trace any Vichy influence in their discourse and modes of action. I will first discuss those who led most of the West African territories to independence: the African Western-educated elite. I will then move on to the trade unions; the African planters in Côte d'Ivoire; and finally to the element considered the most radical in FWA, the youth and student movements.

On 1 July 1945 the Senegalese poet and politician Léopold Sédar Senghor published an article entitled "Défence de l'Afrique noire" in the journal *Esprit*, in which he wrote: "We are sick of nice speech—of derogative sympathy. What we need are actions. . . . We are not separatists, but we want equality. We insist: Equality."[6]

After Vichy, then, words were no longer sufficient. African politicians wanted to see positive action to support the rhetoric of republican values. The Senegalese politician and the leader of the French Socialist party's section in Senegal, Lamine Guèye, reflected this approach when he expressed in a parliamentary debate in Paris in March 1946 his anger at the fact that Vichy legislation had not yet been abrogated in Dakar. He opened by recounting Vichy acts in Dakar. He mentioned the decree against the Jews that also indirectly harmed Africans, who suddenly had to prove they were not Jewish. He continued by describing the Vichy policy of segregation that still existed in Dakar—for example, separate lines for Blacks and Whites. Senghor interrupted Guèye at this point to recall an incident in which he was denied service at a French company, during the Vichy period, because he was not Aryan. Guèye added that at the same company he was sent to stand in the line designated for Africans. This kind of policy still continued, he claimed, in 1946. "In Dakar," he emphasized, "I do not speak of the *brousse*." But here Guèye raised the claim that in fact this racist legislation was not only a "leftover" from the Vichy period but had to some extent been passed after Boisson left

FWA, meaning under the Free French—for example, discrimination in allocations for black and white colonial officials. He also referred to the massacre at Thiaroye (discussed in chapter 7) and to the soldiers who were still in prison. [7] Guèye's and Senghor's presentation of their arguments demonstrates that African politicians, already at this stage, did not see the Vichy period as a "parenthesis" in the history of French colonial rule in West Africa, as it was viewed in France at the same time. It was considered more as a climax of racism that was inherent in colonial rule. The Vichy period allowed latent racist policies to go wild, and after it was over the French had to prove that republican France was indeed different from Vichy France.

It is also quite obvious that such discourse was extremely effective in the postwar years. It is interesting that Vichy racism did not provoke a militant kind of anticolonialism in FWA. Although the concept of assimilation had been formally and totally denied in the Vichy period, after the war the fight for assimilation and equality became even fiercer. There is some ambivalence here. On the one hand African politicians realized that the Vichy period proved that their privileges were not guaranteed and that Vichy colonial policy was in fact only a facet of French colonialism, which actually continued to exist even after the Vichy period was officially over. On the other hand they saw the Vichy episode as an opportunity to increase their demands for equality on the grounds that if the Fourth Republic wished to disassociate itself from Vichy France it had to firmly guarantee African rights under colonial rule.

This rhetoric of the "two Frances"—the "true" one and the "other" one—also prevailed in the establishment of new organizations of évolués in the colonies after the war. Several African organizations of "Vichy victims," for instance, employed the idea of the two Frances in their attempts to achieve certain goals after the war. In a long and detailed letter members of the Section indigène du groupe combat de Guinée (Native Section of the Combat Group of Guinea) recounted their numerous complaints about colonial rule in their territory to Mr. Lecompte-Boynet, a delegate of the Consultative Assembly in Conakry. They opened by presenting themselves as members of the resistance movement who had never despaired for France. They went on to describe their actions under Vichy and named some of their comrades who had been executed by the Vichy authorities. They then raised a similar claim to the one made by Guèye: although the Vichy government was dead, some of its zealous supporters were still around, carrying on with their lives as if nothing had changed. They added that they felt hatred toward no one but reckoned that the "new France" would best be rebuilt by dignified people. Those who swam and fished in stormy waters, according to the writers, should be banished from the "new France." They then listed various domains in which they called for improvements or changes of policy. They noted, for example, the poor living conditions of most of the inhabitants of Guinea, which had not really improved since the establishment of colonial rule. They lamented the colony's inferior medical conditions and asked for more services; they pointed to the small percentage of African children who attended schools; and they demanded equal treatment for equal merit, meaning ending privileges for Africans who were French citizens. All évolués, according to them, should be considered a bridge between the French and the "primitive" mentalities.[8]

A similar organization was the Amicale des condamnés, internes et victimes de Vichy du Sénégal et de la Mauritanie (Association of Convicts, Internees, and Victims of Vichy in Senegal and Mauritania), which, like others, was established toward the end of the war. The main political goal of this organization was to demand the purge of Vichy elements in the colonies and the extension of the democratic regime to the overseas territories. Its leaders sent letters to French officials, such as the governor-general and even De Gaulle, presenting various demands. They asked, for example, for a thorough investigation of the cases of Vichy victims and for recognition of the existence of an African resistance in the colonies. The organization listed the victims, dead and living, whom it aimed to represent. This list is interesting as it includes both individuals who were persecuted for their support for the Free French and Africans who were simply recruited for forced labor. These people could have easily been defined as "victims of colonialism." However, describing them as victims of Vichy was apparently much more useful, as it put the colonial regime in a position in which it had to denounce any Vichy policy, even if it was no different from a previous republican one. The activity of the organization was successful, at least to some degree. The colonial administration agreed to appoint special commissions to examine the claims of those who saw themselves as victims of Vichy.[9]

Apart from organizations that specifically defined themselves as representing victims of the Vichy regime in a certain colony, other bodies used the same rhetoric to attain their goals. Such was the Senegal Teachers' Trade Union (Amicale des instituteurs du Sénégal), whose leader, Mar Diop, was appointed to one of the commissions assigned to examine the cases of victims of Vichy. This was one of the first cohesive trade unions in FWA. It was established in 1930, mainly by William Ponty School graduates. [10] Diop's credentials for the post were based on a copy of a letter from 19 June 1940 in which he had stated: "We refuse to envisage even for a moment an eventual Nazi domination. If France decides to live, we shall live with it. If France has to perish, let us renounce life. In short, Senegal shall remain with France or shall cease to exist." [11]

The idea of the "two Frances," and its use to achieve political goals, were not unique to the Western-educated African elite. One of the most dramatic events in the postwar decolonization process in FWA was the months-long railway strike in 1947–48 that served as the basis for Outhmane Sembene's novel God's Little Bits of Wood. Frederick Cooper maintains that the goal of this strike was not anticolonial in its character, as Sembene describes it, but rather assimiliationist. I would like to suggest that Vichy repression had a great impact on the discourse of the strike leaders, as well as on the capacity of the French administration to react firmly against them. Ibrahima Sarr, the strike leader, used the rhetoric of the "two Frances" in his first formal speech. He called for "the abolition of antiquated colonial methods condemned even by the *new and true France*, which wishes that all its children, at whatever latitude they may live, be equal in duties and rights and that the recompense of labor be a function solely of merit and capacity" (emphasis added). [12]

According to Cooper, although the railway strike was later interpreted as part of an anticolonial struggle against France, it was in fact more the demand of a certain sector of African society that they be granted rights on a par with the parallel sector in French society. The struggle, then, was not "national" but professional. The strikers' goal was to achieve equality with railway men from metropolitan France and thus to link their life chances to a structure separated from the rest of African life. This goal was precisely what made it so difficult for the French colonial authorities to repress the movement. In other words, it was much harder to reject a call for equality based on French republican ideals than to fight against a nationalist call for independence. The colonial regime found it difficult to return to old-style colonial methods. As Robert Delavignette explained, "The strong style directed at the strikers will not itself resolve the problem . . . if the government gives the impression of going back, after a detour, on trade union freedom and on the abolition of forced labor." [13]

The Vichy period had a major impact on the later avoidance of repression. If it was difficult before the war to reconcile French republican rhetoric with harsh colonial policies, after Vichy it became almost impossible. Every act of repression immediately led to an embarrassing comparison with Vichy racism. In the postwar years, when French political discourse presented the Vichy years as an almost inexplicable deviation from the French republican tradition, such a comparison was something to be totally avoided.

In the case of the railway strike the strikers employed Vichy repression to enhance their demands for equality with their French counterparts. In the case of the African planters in Côte d'Ivoire Vichy racism actually widened the scope of their political goals. The harsh discrimination in the allocation of forced laborers and the recruitment of African planters as workers on European plantations led Houphouët-Boigny to reform his concepts regarding equality with European planters. Instead of continuing his campaign for equal distribution of forced laborers, after the war he attempted to abolish forced labor altogether. African planters, meanwhile, also struggled for their own interests. In 1944 Houphouët-Boigny established the Syndicat Agricole Africain, whose aims were to put an end to forced labor and to fight against the colonial economic discrimination against African planters. This discrimination, which reached its peak under Vichy, included stringent quality control, which sometimes ended in the destruction of crops, as well as the practice of paying less for African produce than for European.

The SAA expanded quickly to over twenty thousand members and in 1946 became the nucleus of Côte d'Ivoire's first political party, the Partie Démocratique de la Côte d'Ivoire.[14] This important and influential political party functioned to an extent like a trade union for the African planters as well as Ivoirian peasants. The rise to power of the PDCI brought with it the eventual fall of European planters in Côte d'Ivoire. The influence of this party went beyond the borders of Côte d'Ivoire, as its leader, Houphuët-Boigny, also led the RDA, which had branches all over FWA. During the PDCI's early years a crisis emerged in its relationship with the French administration that brought about a series of violent incidents, the most serious in FWA. At the beginning of the 1950s, however, both sides changed their approach, and the PDCI adopted a policy of cooperation with France. Unlike most branches of the RDA, which shared an attitude of militant anticolonialism, the PDCI did not emphasize independence but rather the economic advantages of staying under French protection.[15]

The "radical" element in the anticolonial struggle in FWA, found in youth and student movements, also reflects an explicit relation to the Vichy period. As we have seen, Vichy policy in France and the colonies saw youth as the most important element of society. While youth movements, especially the Scouts and Catholic organizations, had existed be-

fore Vichy, the new colonial regime gave a real boost to their proliferation, mainly in the urban centers of the colonies. The Vichy regime also
expanded the idea of the youth organization to include youth centers and
work camps. Although the motive behind the organization of youth was
to turn this energetic population sector into a mouthpiece of the regime
and to mold it according to the values of the National Revolution, youth
groups actually provided a framework into which other ideas and goals
could eventually be injected.

Organizations of all sorts, including youth movements, were in fact
the basis of the anticolonial struggle in FWA, as well as in many other
colonies. While the Vichy government suspended most African organizations, it still allowed some to function as long as they professed the goals
of the National Revolution, were loyal to the regime, and were closely
supervised. Following the war the colonial administration encouraged
the establishment of organizations in Africa modeled on those in Europe.
But as far as the colonial administration was concerned, these groups
were useful only as long as they served as its auxiliaries. As soon as they
offered a framework within which social and political protest could be
developed, they were viewed as dangerous. And indeed, these organizations did serve as a basis for political action, as they trained their members
in political language and tools. They also created alternative channels to
those of the administration and linked African organizations with similar
international bodies. Even associations that were ostensibly nonpolitical,
such as youth groups or sports clubs, soon became politicized as a result
of these new channels of communication.[16]

In the upsurge of associational activity in FWA after the war, the student
and youth movements were especially active. From 1955 onward they
expressed much more radical demands than most African politicians. In
fact they were the first to demand full independence for the colonies of
FWA. They totally rejected the idea of assimilation and expressed their
wish to disassociate themselves from France. As we have seen, youth had
represented a threat to the French colonial regime both before and under
Vichy. The colonial administrations in both cases had endeavored to channel youthful energy to their own benefit. The French colonial regime after
the war set the same goal. In 1952 colonial authorities established *conseils
de la jeunesse* (youth councils) in most territories of FWA, with the aim
of officially sponsoring youth movements in the federation. But despite
colonial attempts to control these movements, they soon became a focus
for radical opposition not only to French colonialism but also to African
political leaders, whom they saw as accomplices of the colonial order.

Another way the French administration tried to control what they called African youth's *esprit revendicatif* was in fact very similar to a method used by Vichy—creating supervised spaces in which young people could meet and engage in a harmless kind of cultural activity. By the end of 1956 colonial authorities had established 157 cultural centers throughout FWA at the cost of 257 million francs. The main aim of these centers was to divert youth attention and energy from the political domain to cultural activities, such as theater and drama. Authorities also intended to create a meeting place for young educated Africans and French people. They believed that such direct contact was becoming increasingly scarce and that French colonial rule was now too formalized and bureaucratic and much less personal than in the prewar era. This was in fact seen as the main reason for the alienation of African educated youth. The project, however, failed, mainly because from the outset it encountered fierce opposition from its target audience—African young people. The administration soon realized that policies that had worked under and before Vichy were no longer practicable. Soon after the centers were established, the governor of Senegal pointed out to the governor-general that they had become the opposite of what was intended; they were now a focal point of opposition to French colonial rule. He suggested that the whole project be abandoned, as it was clear that African youth did not want anything to do with it.

In fact African young people did not object to the idea of having organized meeting places, but they refused to be supervised by colonial authorities. They longed for venues where they could get together and talk freely, even about politics, without being watched by "big brother."[17] The name they gave to such places was *maisons des jeunes*. Interestingly enough this was the same term the Vichy regime had used for its own very different brand of youth centers.[18] The choice of the name may demonstrate the effect that Vichy policy toward youth had on African young people. While the idea of Vichy's *maisons des jeunes* was totally different from that of young Africans at the end of the 1950s, the use of the same term indicates perhaps that expanded youth activity under Vichy had left a mark on African youth. They, however, took the idea of meeting places for young people in a completely different direction from that intended by the Vichy colonial regime and those that followed.

Colonialism in FWA after Vichy was not the same as before. The colonizer's option of resorting to repression in times of crisis was extremely limited. Of course one can argue that fear of being equated with the Vichy regime did not prevent the French from using massive force in other parts of their empire. However, it is important to bear in mind that the struggle in FWA was mostly nonviolent and the demands posed to the colonizer tended to focus on equal rights and not on independence.

The Vichy period had, then, two kinds of effects on postwar political developments and discourses in FWA. The first was the idea of "two Frances," which did not exist before Vichy. Most African politicians saw Vichy colonialism more as an extremely racist version of the old republican colonialism than as a distinctive kind of colonialism. Nevertheless, they knew how to employ the myth of "good" and "bad" colonialism to attain their political goal, which, at least in the immediate postwar years, was still assimilation. The second effect this period had on the decolonization process in FWA was the framework it provided for anticolonial struggle. Such a framework was also found in other Vichy-ruled colonies. But while in Algeria, Madagascar, and Indochina the Vichy period fostered national feelings and precipitated the "ugly divorce" from the colonizer, in FWA it was used by most African political leaders as an instrument to tighten a bond with the "true" France that would be based on Liberty, Equality, and Fraternity.

Conclusions

Ah! Seigneur, éloigne de ma mémoire la France qui n'est
Pas la France, ce masque de petitesse et de haine sur le
Visage de la France
Ce masque de petitesse et de haine pour qui je n'ai que haine
—mais je peux bien haïr le Mal
Car j'ai une grande faiblesse pour la France

Léopold Sédar Senghor

In this extract from a 1945 poem entitled "Prière de paix" (A Prayer for Peace) Senghor, according to the Nigerian author Wole Soyinka, places himself as God and offers mercy and forgiveness to the colonizer-sinner. Soyinka even goes as far as to describe the poem as the confession of a "strange—one would almost say perverse—love affair."[1] Without probing the nature of Senghor's personal relations with France, this poem and especially the quoted extract reflect a more general issue that is at the basis of this book. When the Vichy period was over, the Free French who took over FWA continued to assert to the Africans (as they did when they diffused their propaganda from the British colonies) that the Vichy regime represented a false face of France—a repressive, racist, and authoritarian face that was in fact a mask covering France's real visage: the republican, egalitarian, and democratic one.

But in fact for the Western-educated elite in FWA it was not so clear after the war which of these two faces was the mask. For many the Vichy period actually exposed the real face of France and the fact that colonialism was necessarily racist. But as Senghor declared in his poem, he was greatly fond of France and thus preferred to see the cruelty of colonial rule as something that was alien to the "true" French spirit. As we saw earlier (see chapter 10), this was indeed the discourse adopted by African political leaders when they tried to reach equality within the framework of French colonialism. But in fact colonial rule represented this ostensible "other face" of France long before the Vichy period. In spite of the rhetoric and the limited practice of the theory of assimilation, French colonial rule in FWA was mostly repressive and had many racist elements, like any other kind of colonial rule. The Vichy period, though, radicalized these racist elements and turned them against an elite that had not suffered so much in the past from the injustices of colonialism. The important turning point was that now this "other face" of France was also exposed in the *métropole*. France was now authoritarian, officially racist, and repressive at home, not only in the colonies. The Vichy experience, then, encouraged some leading African politicians to believe that if France wanted to eliminate its "Vichy face" it must start treating its colonial subjects differently.

Before Vichy there was only one France and one form of colonialism for the Africans. World War II and the division of France into two ideological camps, each asking for legitimacy from the colonized, opened for Africans numerous unprecedented options. For the *originaires* and the *évolués* the Vichy period was indeed decisive in their attitude toward the colonizer. Under Vichy colonial rule the republican rhetoric that covered up the repressive nature of colonialism disappeared, leaving a pure racist colonialism that officially rejected all ideas of equality and assimilation and made no distinctions among the colonized population. Viewed from this perspective the Vichy era in FWA was indeed a watershed in the history of the region. The African politicians who emerged after the war from the ranks of this African elite would no longer settle for republican rhetoric. They demanded action. They no longer accepted French colonialism at face value but endeavored to change its nature by invoking Vichy's dark past. It was the failure of this endeavor that eventually led African political leaders to the only alternative left to them—independence.

The study of the Vichy period in FWA is vital, then, to understanding the history of this region, but what about the history of France, the colonizer? What conclusions can be drawn from the Vichy experience in FWA about the relevance of France's colonial adventure to its metropolitan history? The case of the Vichy years in FWA demonstrates well, and in several ways, the importance of linking France's colonial history to its metropolitan one in order to better understand the latter.

First, without the colonial aspect the full picture of the Vichy episode in French history cannot be revealed. The study of Vichy in the colonies reinforces some of the statements that historians such as Robert Paxton and Henri Michel have made about Vichy France and even adds some vigor to them. The meticulous implementation of Vichy ideology, including the persecution of the regime's enemies—Jews, Communists, and Freemasons—in faraway colonies where their number was so negligible and where practically no Germans had set foot, emphasizes the fact that the Vichy regime's policy was not a result of Nazi pressure but was implemented freely and enthusiastically, stemming from internal ideology.

The colonial side of the story also helps to explain the Vichy regime's relations with Britain. After all, in the colonial sphere Britain, not Germany, was France's number-one rival. The fear of a British invasion of the colonies influenced Vichy policy in relation to its former ally.

Close observation of the French empire is vital to understanding the efforts of the Vichy regime to persuade the French public of the necessity of signing the armistice. The colonies played a major role in the attempt to restore France's lost honor and in providing the defeated *métropole* with a dignified status in the new world that was to arise after the war.

Vichy's accentuated racism in the colonies emphasizes the role of race and racist thinking in France during the twentieth century. Racism was indeed not invented by Vichy. It flourished in France during the nineteenth and twentieth centuries and was related to the colonial conquests in Africa in several ways. According to so-called scientific racism Africans were classified as the most inferior race, but this led to opposing conclusions. Some racist theoreticians of the nineteenth century, such as Arthur de Gobineau and Gustave Le Bon, believed that colonization of these "inferior races" posed a danger to Western civilization, as the encounter with them could lead to "contamination" of the white race. Others believed that the ostensible superiority of the white race obliged it to colonize the inferior races and to exploit the resources that they were not intelligent enough to exploit themselves.[2] In both cases, however, assimilation that was based on a belief in equality among all humans (at least in their potential) was absolutely rejected. When Jules Ferry formulated his "colonial theory" he declared: "The superior races have a right because they have a duty. They have the duty to civilize the inferior races."[3] Racist theories, then, were at the basis of colonization.

Just as the development of racist thinking served as justification for colonial expansion, the colonial reality fertilized racism in metropolitan France during the first half of the twentieth century. Colonial wars and conquests and later the need to control huge populations encouraged racist images of colonial subjects in metropolitan France. These images were produced in colonial expositions, cinema, literature, and commercials advertising colonial products. Colonial exhibitions, which attempted to bring the colonies to the French people's doorsteps, presented Africans as exotic animals or as colonial products.[4] While during the period of colonization Africans were usually presented to the European public as half animals or scary savages that had to be subdued, in the interwar era, when colonial rule was established, the African was presented as a child or a tamed savage who was no longer frightening but still had a long way to go before becoming civilized. A good example is the image of the *tirailleurs sénégalais*, as reflected in a commercial for cornflakes called "Banania": a grinning African soldier says in inarticulate French, "Y'a bon Banania."[5]

Colonialism encouraged such racist attitudes in France well before Vichy. The new regime, however, gave racism a legitimacy it did not have previously. In metropolitan France, though, racism was expressed especially against the Jews, while the inhabitants of the empire were presented as France's loyal and beloved children. In the empire racist thinking that had existed all along manifested itself in the attitudes of colonial officials toward their subjects and in formal colonial policy.

The French encounter with the colonies and the peoples they conquered in the late nineteenth century, and their need to justify this conquest, encouraged racist ideas and images in France during the first half of the twentieth century. Vichy France, then, had a long history of racist thinking to rely on when it attempted to spread its ideology among the French people.

The colonial sphere is also important to understanding the ideological struggle between Vichy ideology and that of republican France. In fact it was one of the battlegrounds for this ideological tussle. Some of the most significant points of disagreement between the two ideologies were reflected in the colonial perceptions on both sides. The Vichy regime argued that its ideology's superiority was manifested in its ability to adjust itself not only to different regions and cultures of France but also all over the empire. Criticisms of the Third Republic's colonial policy pertained mainly to its inflexibility and its inability to accommodate a diversity it basically denied. According to Vichy theoreticians, the values of the Republic contradicted the political, social, and cultural realities in the colonies. Furthermore republican colonialism, in their view, made no distinction among various and distanced regions within the empire. This criticism was not really accurate. The republican idea of the civilizing mission and especially of assimilation had been tried in a very limited scope and only in the *anciens colonies*. As we have seen, for most of the French empire's colonial subjects Vichy ideology was not that different from the ideology that preceded it. However, in the ideological domain the struggle between the perceptions of how the colonies should be ruled highlights some of the basic principles the Vichy regime tried to promote.

In spite of the criticisms of republican colonialism the colonies themselves and the first colonizers were seen by Vichy as parts of an ideal society possessing the "right" values. The new regime actually conceived of the empire as terrain on which its ideas and values had already been implemented for years. This view reinforces arguments such as those raised by Hannah Arendt and Aimé Césaire about colonialism as a preparatory stage for totalitarianism, fascism, and Nazism in Europe. In his *Discours sur le colonialisme* Césaire claims that colonialism brought about the decivilization of Europe. The horrors that were performed in its name caused a universal regression. The members of the European bourgeoisie, so he claims, were awakened by the horrible shock of Nazism and refused to see the truth—that before they were the victims of this supreme barbarity they were its accomplices; before they experienced this barbarity they legitimized it because it had been directed until then only toward non-European peoples. According to Césaire the origins of Nazi racism lay in Western humanism. French colonizers such as Albert Sarraut expressed contempt toward non-European peoples and claimed that they were lazy and savage and that therefore their resources must be exploited for them. None of the cultural or religious elite of Europe came to the defense of these peoples. The colonial conquest was based upon this racism, which served as its justification. It transformed the colonizers and dehumanized them. They became accustomed to seeing other people as animals and thus turned into animals themselves. Césaire believed that the Western civilization that performed and justified colonialism was a sick civilization and that Hitler in fact was its punishment.[6]

Arendt also saw the colonial expansion of 1884–1914 as an introductory stage for later catastrophes, perceiving a great deal of resemblance between some of the basic elements of colonial rule and the totalitarian phenomena of the twentieth century. The imperialist administrators, she said, refused to govern in accordance with the general standards of justice and liberty in their own countries. Racism was the state doctrine only in Nazi Germany during the 1930s, but in fact it had a powerful hold over public opinion everywhere in Europe. The racist thought that had originated in the eighteenth century developed all over the West during the nineteenth century. It was certainly the ideology of the imperialist states in the twentieth century. Arendt suggested that this racism was strongest in relation to Africa. It provided a kind of emergency explanation for people whose humanity scared Europeans so much that they were not interested in belonging to the same human race as them. Race and bureaucracy were the two means through which the colonial powers ruled the non-Western world. While racism had always attracted the worst elements within Western civilization, the colonial bureaucracy was composed of administrators who ruled through decrees and reports and lived according to the ideals of a modern knight in shining armor who had come to the rescue of primitive and helpless peoples. Arendt claimed that when these administrators no longer believed in the universal validity of the law, when the European masses discovered the virtue of white skin in Africa, when bureaucrats in India suggested "administrative massacres," and when officials in Africa declared that no ethical considerations would be allowed to stand in the way of white rule—it was then that the stage was set for every possible horror. Under everyone's nose lay many of the elements that, when assembled, could create a totalitarian government based on racism.[7]

The Vichy regime's view of the French colonizers as "heroes" supports the notion that in the French case, at least, the colonial experience was a preparatory field for the establishment of an authoritarian regime in France. Indeed, most of the ideas promoted by Vichy ideology were not new in the colonial sphere. For Vichy the colonies provided an example of the "true" French spirit that the National Revolution tried to promote. This was good terrain for young and courageous Frenchmen, like the engineer who came to the Sahara desert to build a railway among its dunes under the blazing sun (see chapter 5). It was far enough from the "decadent" cafés of Paris that the French living there were not affected by the ailments of the *métropole*. With French settlers seen as the precursors of the "right" French ideology, it is not surprising that they received Vichy ideology so enthusiastically. The regime perceived the colonies as such fertile soil for its values that, amazingly, even some colonized aspects of culture, such as the importance of the family and the reliance on agriculture, were seen as compatible with ideals of the National Revolution. It was no coincidence that the National Revolution adapted so well to the colonial reality. Vichy authoritarianism and its rejection of parliamentary democracy had been practiced in the colonies before Vichy. The colonies were thus fertile ground for the flourishing of antirepublican and antidemocratic values. Even the most fervent republican colonial officers found it extremely difficult, if not impossible, to implement the values they believed in without undermining colonial stability. Indeed, it can be argued that French antirepublicanism found a training field in the colonies long before the outbreak of World War II. Although it is difficult to prove, colonial practices might even have had some effect on the *métropole*. After all there were vast territories, officially a part of France, where parliamentary democracy had never been implemented.

The importance of the Vichy years in FWA and the other French colonies to understanding this period in French metropolitan history highlights the weight of France's colonial experience in general. This is an inseparable part of France's history. Ignoring it leaves an important and fascinating part of the story untold.

Notes

Introduction
1. Bara Diouf, b. 1931, interview, Dakar, 14 Feb. 2001.
2. Jennings, *Vichy in the Tropics.*
3. Cantier, *L'Algérie*; Levisse-Touzé, *L'Afrique du Nord*; Akpo-Vaché, *L'AOF.* Michel Abitbol discusses North Africa under Vichy in relation to the Jewish population; see *Les juifs.*
4. Only recently a special issue of *Outre-mers* was entitled "Vichy and Its Colonies." Two articles in this volume deal with FWA, but both limit themselves to specific issues: Pierre Ramognino dwells upon the tools of repression used by the regime in West Africa, especially against the French enemies of the National Revolution, and Vincent Joly discusses the military effort in French Sudan between 1940 and 1942. See Ramognino, "Le pétainisme"; Joly, " 'Se defender contre quiconque?' "
5. Akpo-Vaché, *L'AOF*, 156–57.
6. Conklin, *A Mission to Civilize.*
7. Ten people were interviewed. Most of them belonged to the Western-educated elite, although none was a French citizen. All except one lived in Dakar during the war.

Part 1. FWA and Its Place in the Vichy Colonial Idea
1. Qtd. in *La Légion*, Aug. 1940.

1. Setting the Stage for Vichy
1. For an overview of the variety of peoples and cultures in this vast region, see Conklin, *A Mission to Civilize*, 25–30.
2. The colonial council in 1920 replaced the general council (*conseil général*), which included twenty members chosen by the African citizens of the four communes of Senegal. The colonial council included forty-four members; eighteen of them represented the citizens, and twenty-six were chosen by canton or province chiefs who were not citizens. The chiefs received precise orders from the colonial administration with regard to their voting, and thus the administration could control the council. See Morgenthau, *Political Parties*, 127.
3. During the Vichy period Upper Volta was part of Côte d'Ivoire. It became a separate territory again in 1946.
4. Morgenthau, *Political Parties*, 1.
5. Johnson, "African Political Activity," 542.
6. Morgenthau, *Political Parties*, 125.
7. Cohen, "Colonial Policy of the Popular Front," 368.
8. Lydon, "Women, Children," 171.

9. Coquery-Vidrovitch, "The Popular Front," 155.

10. Coquery-Vidrovitch, "The Popular Front," 157–58.

11. This project, which aimed to prepare the land of the Niger Delta for the cultivation of rice and cotton, is discussed in detail in chapter 5.

12. Lydon, "Women, Children," 171–73.

13. Lydon, "Women, Children," 182.

14. Coquery-Vidrovitch, "The Popular Front," 163.

15. Lydon, "Women, Children," 183.

16. Person, "Le front populaire au Sénégal," 93.

17. Person, "Le front populaire au Sénégal," 90–92.

18. This congress, further discussed in chapter 10, was assembled by De Gaulle with the aim of planning reforms in the colonial system that would allow the empire to stay intact.

19. Echenberg, *Colonial Conscripts*, 88. For an example of the methods by which Africans were recruited at the beginning of the war, see Joly, "La mobilisation au Soudan." On the propaganda used to recruit soldiers, see Echenberg, "Morts pour la France," 365–68.

20. Akpo-Vaché, *L'AOF*, 24.

21. Crowder, *Colonial West Africa*, 272.

22. Crowder, *Colonial West Africa*, 28–33.

23. Hitchcock, "Pierre Boisson," 309–10.

24. Paxton, *Vichy France*, 43.

25. Hitchcock, "Pierre Boisson," 317.

26. Lanne, "Chad, the Chadians," 312; Thomas, *The French Empire at War*, 49–65.

27. Suret-Canale, *Afrique noire*, 577. On the deterioration of Anglo-French relations in this period, see Thomas, "The Anglo-French Divorce."

28. Diouf, interview.

29. Boubacar Ly, b. 1936, interview, Dakar, 16 Feb. 2001. Bara Diouf also mentioned seeing the plane that was shot down by the battleship *Richelieu*.

30. Loucou, "La deuxième guerre mondiale," 184.

31. Hitchcock, "Pierre Boisson," 318.

2. "A Source of Pride and Greatness"

1. Ageron, "Vichy, les Français et l'empire," 132.

2. Viard, *L'empire et nos destins*, 12–13.

3. Viard, *L'empire et nos destins*, 6–9.

4. Viard, *L'empire et nos destins*, 13.

5. Delavignette, *Petite histoire*, 61.

6. Coudray, "L'empire colonial français," 56; Quinzaine Impériale, *L'empire, notre meilleure chance*, 3; Rivière, *A travers*, 9–11

7. Viard, *L'empire et nos destins*, 17–37.

8. Viard, *L'empire et nos destins*, 52.

9. Maunier, "L'empire français," 3–4.

10. Viard, *L'empire et nos destins*, 52–53.

11. Leblond, "La littérature coloniale," 28.

12. Demaison, *Destins de l'Afrique*, 6.

13. Quinzaine Impériale, *L'empire, notre meilleure chance*, 4.

14. Delavignette, *Petite histoire*, 62. Robert Delavignette joined the colonial administration in 1919. He served for six years in French West Africa (Niger and Upper Volta). Between 1937 and 1946 he served as the director of the École nationale de la France d'outre-mer. On his career and attitudes to his colonial mission, see Mouralis and Piriou, *Robert Delavignette, savant et politique*.

15. Delavignette, *Petite histoire*, 62.

16. Cohen, "Robert Delavignette et les responsabilités," 129–30.

17. Viard, *L'empire et nos destins*, 57.

18. Viard, *L'empire et nos destins*, 53.

19. Pinardel, *La France*; Bachelier, *Géographie*.

20. Rivière, *A travers*, 9–11; Ricord, *Au service de l'empire*, 8. Ricord's book was published after the war but, according to its introduction, written during the war.

21. On propaganda in Vichy France, see Gervereau and Peschanski, *La propagande*; Rossignol, *Histoire de la propagande*.

22. Ageron, "Vichy, les Français et l'empire," 128.

23. Gervereau and Peschanski, *La propagande*, 205.

24. Gervereau and Peschanski, *La propagande*, 112.

25. *La France coloniale: Les 50 premières causeries de Radio-Paris*, "Dakar, Métropole française de l'Atlantique," 27 Mar. 1942, 20:45–21:00; "Notre production africaine de cacao," 18 Aug. 1942, 19:30–19:45; "Méditerranée-Niger, acte de foi française," 12 June 1942, 21:30–21:45; "La piste coloniale no 1," 4 Aug. 1942, 19:30–19:45.

26. *La France coloniale*, "Un centenaire en exil: Le Gabon," 24 Apr. 1942, 21:30–21:45; "L'Afrique équatoriale française," 8 Sept. 1942, 17:00–17:15.

27. *L'illustration*, 11 May 1940, 24 Aug. 1940, 5 Oct. 1940, 2 Nov. 1940; *Gringoire*, "Menaces sur notre empire," 26 Sept. 1940.

28. These are two cities along the Niger river in French Sudan (now Mali).

29. See *La Légion*, Aug. 1941, Sept. 1941.

30. *La Légion*, Aug. 1941.

31. *La Légion*, Sept. 1941.

32. *La Légion*, Aug. 1941, Nov. 1941.

33. *Gringoire*, "Menaces sur notre empire," 26 Sept. 1940; "Mauvais coup de Dakar et offensive diplomatique," 3 Oct. 1940; "Prisonnier des gaullists—Je reviens du Gabon," 9 May 1941; "Le Transsaharien," 13 June 1941; "L'empire devant la dissidence," 25 July 1941; "Bataillons noirs," 26 Sept. 1941; "Djibouti, capital de la fidélité," 23 Jan. 1942; "L'AOF—Carte maîtresse du jeu français," 1 May 1942; "À la gloire de notre empire," 29 May 1942; "Alert sur l'empire," 30

Oct. 1942. For the fiction see "Mort du prince impérial," 5 Sept. 1940; "Fête au palais de Makoko," 27 Feb. 1941; "Ilô Samori," 13 Mar. 1941; "L'empereur du Tchad," 30 May 1941; "Fachoda," 22 Aug. 1941.

34. Leblond, "La littérature coloniale," 20.

35. On the colonial exhibitions in France between the wars, see Ezra, *The Colonial Unconscious*, 21–46.

36. Agence économique des colonies, *Vous voulez aller aux colonies?*

37. Agence économique des colonies, *Les colonies aux expositions*, 4–5.

38. Blanchard and Boëtsch, "Races et propagande coloniale," 552–53.

39. Bowles, "Newsreels," 430–31.

40. Akpo-Vaché, *L'AOF*, 49, 55.

41. Ageron, "Vichy, les Français et l'empire," 124; Cohen, *Rulers of Empire*, 161–62.

Part 2. The National Revolution in FWA

1. See, e.g., the implementation of anti-Jewish laws in FWA: Ginio, "La politique antijuive."

2. Jennings, *Vichy in the Tropics*, 17–19.

3. Vichy Settles In

1. Akpo-Vaché, *L'AOF*, 53–54. Immediately after the armistice was signed, a German named Dr. Klaube traveled to Dakar. This was not an official visit though. Klaube was an agent for Lufthansa based in Gambia, and the purpose of his visit was to organize the repatriation of a number of German civilians who were in Dakar when the war broke out. See Hitchcock, "Pierre Boisson," 327.

2. Lawler, *Soldiers, Airmen*, 21–22.

3. Archives Nationales, Paris (hereafter AN), 268mi/1.

4. Blanchard and Boëtsch, "La France de Pétain," 27–28.

5. AN, 268mi/1.

6. Cohen, *Rulers of Empire*, 115.

7. Boisson's colonial career began after World War I, during which he was wounded and lost a leg. After graduating from the École coloniale he was sent to Brazzaville, the capital of FEA, and served in various positions for the next thirty years. His last position before moving to Dakar was as the governor-general of FEA, as noted in chapter 1. See *Hommes et destins*, 4: 81–87.

8. Hitchcock, "Pierre Boisson," 334.

9. Cohen, *Rulers of Empire*, 158.

10. Hitchcock, "Pierre Boisson," 322.

11. George Rey belonged to the colonial administration and continued to serve as administrator after the war. In the 1950s he supported the French government's reforms in the colonies. Hubert Deschamps began his colonial career after World War I. He was a socialist and assimilationist and served in Léon Blum's

government in the 1930s. See Cohen, *Rulers of Empire*, 133, 187. Also see Lawler, *Soldiers, Airmen*, 6.

12. Akpo-Vaché, *L'AOF*, 283–84.

13. Akpo-Vaché, *L'AOF*, 57.

14. Lawler, *Soldiers, Airmen*, 11.

15. Lawler, *Soldats d'infortune*, 130.

16. On Geismar's case, as well as the implementation of anti-Jewish laws in FWA, see Ginio, "La politique antijuive," 109–18.

17. Archives Nationales du Sénégal (hereafter ANS), 17G/396 (126). One of the subaltern officers involved in this case, Jacquemin-Verguet, later became an enthusiastic Vichy supporter. After the war, when he was put on trial for his support, he used this accusation against him to clear his name, explaining that his support for Vichy was only an act meant to enable him to keep his post. See ANS, 17G/23 (1).

18. Cohen, *Rulers of Empire*, 160.

19. Hitchcock, "Pierre Boisson," 323.

20. ANS, O516 (31).

21. Cohen, *Rulers of Empire*, 68; Asiwaju, "Control through Coercion," 41–43.

22. Asiwaju, "Control through Coercion," 51–53.

23. Cohen, *Rulers of Empire*, 119.

24. Archives Nationales, Centre des archives d'outre-mer, Aix-en-Provence (hereafter CAOM), Affaires politiques, 883/5, 9 Feb. 1942.

25. ANS, 17G/97 (17), 3 May 1941.

26. ANS, 17G/104 (17).

27. Marty, "La politique indigène," 8.

28. Cohen, *Rulers of Empire*, 122.

29. CAOM, Affaires politiques, 635/11, 25 Mar. 1941. This is a circular from the governor of Senegal to the *commandants de cercles*.

30. Akpo-Vaché, *L'AOF*, 127–28; Zucarelli, *La vie politique*, 18; Cohen, *Rulers of Empire*, 159.

31. Cointet-Labrousse, *Vichy et le fascisme*, 44–47.

32. CAOM, Affaires politiques, 635/6, 639/17; AN, 2G40/1 (200mi/1815), "Dakar et dépendances, Rapport politique annuel," 1940.

33. A more detailed account of the evolution of Vichy historiography since the end of World War II will be provided in part III.

4. Spreading the National Revolution in FWA

1. CAOM, Affaires politiques, 883/20, "Propagande et information aux colonies," 31 Aug. 1940.

2. On the tensions between Britain and Vichy-ruled FWA, see Thomas, "The Anglo-French Divorce."

3. ANS, 11D1/869, "Propagande dissidente ou britannique," 20 Dec. 1940.

4. The Nas el Kitab were usually termed Ahal el Kitab—the "People of the Book," meaning adherents of the three monotheistic religions: Judaism, Christianity, and Islam.

5. Lawler, *Soldiers, Airmen,* 176–78.

6. ANS, 13G/15 (17), 3 Jan. 1941.

7. ANS, 17G/412 (126), "Note au sujet de l'organisation de l'information au Haut-commissariat de l'Afrique française," Apr. 1942.

8. ANS 13G/101 (180), 12 Feb. 1942.

9. The Legion of Black Africa was an extension of the Légion français des combattants, which had been established in Vichy France on 29 Aug. 1940. More on this organization can be found in Akpo-Vaché, *L'AOF,* 73–79. Also see *Paris Dakar,* "La France et l'empire ont célébré la fête nationale de Jeanne d'Arc," 12–13 May 1941.

10. *Paris Dakar,* "Pourquoi et comment fut signé l'armistice," 3 Aug. 1940.

11. ANS, 0/169 (31), Maurice Montrat, *Quand le Maréchal parlait aux indigènes—AOF,* Jan. 1925 (Rufisque, 1942), 5.

12. Montrat, *Quand le Maréchal,* 6–12.

13. ANS, 13G/101 (180), "Télégramme—Administrateur Richaud, commandant cercle Diourbel à Monsieur le Gouverneur, Sénégal," 23 Sept. 1941.

14. Ramognino, "Le pétainisme," 67.

15. ANS 17G412 (126), 10 Feb. 1942.

16. ANS, 17G/412 (126), "Note au sujet de l'organisation," Apr. 1942.

17. ANS, 13G/101 (180), "L'agent N'Diaye Amadou à M. le commissaire de police à Saint-Louis," 9 Apr. 1942.

18. ANS, 13G/101 (180), "L'agent N'Diaye Amadou," 9 Apr. 1942.

19. Hodge, *Radio Wars,* 1–3.

20. Holbrook, "British Propaganda," 351.

21. ANS, 17G/412 (126), "Note au sujet de l'organisation," Apr. 1942.

22. ANS, 17G/412 (126), "Note au sujet de l'organisation," Apr. 1942. See also Akpo-Vaché, *L'AOF,* 81.

23. ANS, 17G/412 (126), Apr. 1942. On the reports of Radio Dakar on the Allied landings in North Africa, see Kingston, "A Study in Radio Propaganda."

24. The two letters are cited in the preface of the third edition of the texts of Monod's broadcasts as they were aired on Radio Dakar: Monod, *L'hippopotame,* 11–12.

25. Wells, "Dustbins, Democracy and Defence," 64. On British film propaganda during World War II, see Chapman, *The British at War.*

26. Taylor, *Film Propaganda,* 15–16.

27. ANS, 17G/412 (126), "Note au sujet de l'organisation," Apr. 1942.

28. Bowles, "Newsreels," 433–35.

29. ANS, 11D/662, "Correspondances—Le Commissaire de police de Saint-Louis à l'Administrateur en chef commandant et à Madame Philipp," Apr.–June 1942.

30. ANS, 11D/662, "Le Commissaire de police de Saint-Louis à Monsieur l'Administrateur commandant le cercle Bas-Sénégal," 3 Aug. 1942.

31. ANS, 17G/412 (126), "Censure cinématographique," 21 Feb. 1942, 3 Mar. 1942, 14 Mar. 1942, 25 May 1942, 22 Dec. 1942, 12 Jan. 1942.

32. Akpo-Vaché, L'AOF, 82.

33. Holbrook, "British Propaganda," 353.

34. ANS, 17G/412 (126), "Censure cinématographique," 21 Feb.1942. See also Akpo-Vaché, L'AOF, 82.

35. Raulin, L'utilisation des colonies, 34–35. On propaganda in films produced by the Vichy regime in France, see Strebel, "Vichy Cinema and Propaganda."

36. On the evolution of the myth of Joan of Arc, see Warner, Joan of Arc, 189–270.

37. Jennings, "Reinventing Jeanne," 713.

38. Rossignol, Histoire de la propagande, 84–85.

39. CAOM, Affaires politiques, 636/1, "Propagande gouvernementale."

40. ANS, O/31 (31), "Des manifestations de la semaine impériale," 1 Sept. 1941. In free translation: "Marshal Pétain, we, the schoolchildren of Dahomey, salute you—we salute you today. . . . In order to accomplish the mission that was started, to save France, we will work with zeal and confidence, and you will be proud of us, our Marshal Pétain, our Papa."

41. ANS, O/125 (31), "Circulaire—Gouverneurs de Dahomey aux commandants des cercles," 1941.

42. According to Christopher Harrison, it was Governor-General De Coppet who introduced the practice of attending Muslim celebrations. In 1940 the governor-general did not attend, but the administration was strongly represented. French participation ceased under Vichy and was resumed only in 1944. See Harrison, France and Islam, 187.

43. There are several examples of such gestures. In March 1941 the imam of the Medina Mosque in Dakar thanked General Weygand for a donation of one thousand francs to the Tijaniyya Order. In the same year the minister of the colonies asked that it be publicized in colonies with a large Muslim presence the Vichy government's project to build a mosque in Marseilles. See CAOM, Affaires politiques, 639/5; CAOM, Affaires politiques, 639/1. As opposed to French colonial policy during World War I, the Vichy administration allowed pilgrimage to Mecca. See Joly, "Un aspect de la politique musulmane," 39, 44.

44. Ranger, "The Invention of Tradition," 211–12.

45. On the establishment of the colonial education system, see Bouche, L'enseignement dans les territoires; Chafer, "Teaching Africans."

46. Hardy, Une conquête morale, 196–98.

47. Le Bon, Lois psychologiques, 32–37.

48. Kelly, French Colonial Education, 189–208.

49. Hardy, Nos grands problèmes, 99.

50. Atkin, "Reshaping the Past," 7.

51. Giolitto, *Histoire de la jeunesse*, 82–83.

52. Halls, *The Youth of Vichy France*, 186; Giolitto, *Histoire de la jeunesse*, 181, 184, 192–93, 197.

53. Atkin, "Reshaping the Past," 7–12.

54. ANS, 0624 (31), "Rapport de M. Barbieri, directeur de l'École normale d'enseignement rural de Sevare," 1941.

55. ANS, 0516 (31), "Service de la jeunesse de l'Afrique Noire—Instructions générales aux chefs locaux," 1942.

56. AN, 2G41/82 (200mi/2687), AOF, "Inspection générale de l'enseignement, année scolaire," 1940–41.

57. ANS, 13G/116 (180), Sept. 1942.

58. ANS, 0/140 (31).

59. Deville-Danthu, *Le sport en noir et blanc*. For a detailed account of Vichy sports policy in FWA, see esp. 127–217.

60. A.D.M., b. 1924, interview, Dakar, 17 Feb. 2001.

61. ANS, 18G/118.

62. ANS 0/176 (31).

63. AN, 2G43/59 (200mi.1850), AOF, "Direction générale de l'instruction publique," Jan. 1944.

64. Rossignol, *Histoire de la propagande*, 31–33.

65. Amouroux, *Quarante millions*, 244–45.

66. Guillon, "La Légion française," 5–6.

67. Amouroux, *Quarante millions*, 247.

68. Amouroux, *Quarante millions*, 254.

69. AN, 2G41/19.

70. Akpo-Vaché, *L'AOF*, 78.

71. Hitchcock, "Pierre Boisson," 324.

72. Loucou, "La deuxième guerre mondiale," 185.

73. CAOM, Affaires politiques, 886/2, 21 Sept. 1940.

74. CAOM, Affaires politiques, 883/20.

75. AN, 2G41/22 (200mi/1829), "Côte d'Ivoire—Rapport politique et social," 1941; ANS, 13G/101 (180).

76. AN, 2G41/22 (200mi/1829), "Côte d'Ivoire—Rapport politique et social," 1941.

77. Zucarelli, *La vie politique*, 20–21.

78. Hitchcock, "Pierre Boisson," 324.

79. Rossignol, *Histoire de la propagande*, 33–34.

80. Akpo-Vaché, *L'AOF*, 77–79.

81. In 1941, for example, the Vichy colonial administration abolished a metropolitan organization called Groupement de la vigilance française that operated in FWA after deciding it was not fulfilling its mission. See CAOM, Affaires politiques, 929/4, 1941.

82. AN, 2G41/22 (200mi/1829), "Côte d'Ivoire—Rapport politique et social,"
1941.

83. ANS, 18G/117 (17).

84. CAOM, Affaires politiques, 929/4.

85. ANS, 21G/84 (17).

86. ANS, 21G/76 (17).

87. ANS, 21G/84 (17).

88. ANS, 21G/84 (17).

89. This movement will be discussed in detail in chapter 7.

90. Atlan, *Elections et pratiques*, 102–3.

91. ANS, 21G/76 (17).

92. ANS, 21G/76 (17).

93. ANS, O516 (31), "Service de la jeunesse," 1942.

94. Saliou Samba Malaado Kandji, b. 1924, interview, Dakar, 18 Feb. 2001.

95. A.D.M., interview.

5. "Thinking Big"

1. Kuisel, *Capitalism and the State*, 128–47.

2. Cooper, *Decolonization and African Society*, 141–42.

3. Ly, interview.

4. Undisclosed subject, b. 1924, interview, Dakar, 16 Feb. 2001.

5. M.K., interview, Dakar, 16 Feb. 2004.

6. I.D., b. 1933, interview, Dakar, 16 Feb. 2001.

7. Echenberg, *Black Death*, 218.

8. Boone, *Merchant Capital*, 50.

9. AN, 2G40/8 (200mi/1816), "Rapport économique annuel, Côte d'Ivoire,"
1940.

10. AN, 2G41/22 (200mi/1829), "Rapport sur la situation économique du
Sénégal," 1941.

11. ANS, O515 (31), 17 Feb. 1941.

12. The colonial administration attempted to encourage the cultivation of rice
in FWA before World War II with the aim of limiting rice imports from Indochina;
see Domergue, "La Côte d'Ivoire," 45.

13. ANS, O515 (31), 20 May 1941.

14. CAOM, 2G40/35 (14mi/1820), "Sénégal—Rapport économique annuel,"
1940; AN, 2G41/19 (200mi/1828), "Dakar et dépendances. Rapport annuel sur le
fonctionnement des différents services de la circonscription"; AN, 2G40/8
(200mi/1816), "Rapport économique annuel, Côte d'Ivoire," 1940.

15. CAOM, Affaires politiques, 929bis/3, May 1941.

16. A.D.M., interview.

17. AN, 21G/25 (200mi/3025).

18. Giblin, "A Colonial State in Crisis," 333–34.

19. Akpo-Vaché, *L'AOF*, 124.

20. Lawler, *Soldiers, Airmen*, 146–49.

21. CAOM, Affaires politiques, 635/1.

22. Akpo-Vaché, *L'AOF*, 137.

23. Gellar, *Structural Changes*.

24. Marseille, *Empire colonial*, 334.

25. Marseille, *Empire colonial*, 335.

26. Boone, *Merchant Capital*, 37–48.

27. Gellar, *Structural Changes*, 22.

28. Coquery-Vidrovitch, "Vichy et l'industrialisation," 71–72, 80.

29. Marseille, *Empire colonial*, 339–40.

30. ANS, 17G/395 (126), 31 Dec. 1941.

31. Marseille, *Empire colonial*, 340.

32. Boisson, *Contribution à l'oeuvre*, 99.

33. AN, AJ72/1877, "La vie industrielle," 16 May 1941.

34. Rossignol, *Histoire de la propagande*, 158–66.

35. CAOM, Affaires économiques, 54/6, 30 Mar. 1942.

36. AN, 2G41/19 (200mi/1828), "Dakar et dépendances. Rapport annuel sur le fonctionnement des différents services de la circonscription," 1941.

37. AN, 2G41/22 (200mi/1829), "Rapport sur la situation économique du Sénégal," 1941.

38. AN, 2G40/8 (200mi/1816), "Rapport économique annuel, Côte d'Ivoire," 1940.

39. CAOM, Affaires économiques, 146/A.

40. CAOM, Affaires économiques, 146/A, 6 Oct. 1942; Affaires politiques, 635/8, 19 Mar. 1941; AN, 2G40/8 (200mi/1816), "Rapport économique annuel, Côte d'Ivoire," 1940; 2G40/1 (200mi/1815), "Dakar et dépendances—Rapport politique annuel," 1940.

41. CAOM, Affaires politiques, 882/1, Mar. 1942.

42. Coquery-Vidrovitch, "Vichy et l'industrialisation," 71.

43. On the symbolism of trains in Victorian England, see Freeman, *Railways and the Victorian Imagination*.

44. Saint-Exupéry, *Le petit prince*, 11.

45. Daniel R. Headrick, *The Tools of Empire*, 200.

46. Daniel R. Headrick, *The Tools of Empire*, 200–201.

47. Sénat, année 1928, "Projet de loi ayant pour objet d'approuver la création d'un office des études du chemin de fer transsaharien"; CAOM, "Affaires politiques," 544/4.

48. CAOM, "Affaires politiques," 544/4.

49. Abitbol, *Les juifs*, 102.

50. ANS, 17G/395 (126).

51. AN, AJ 72/1877, Jean Marguet, "62 ans après le premier projet. . . . On va enfin construire le Transsaharien," *Cri du people*, 8 Mar. 1941.

52. AN, AJ 72/1877, Stephane Lauzanne, "Et M. Berthelot en inaugure au-

jourd'hui le premier tronçon." On this point the British agreed. When discussing the possibility of a Vichy invasion of the British colonies in West Africa, Brigadier F.-A.-S. Clarke from the Gold Coast stated, "It was fortunate, perhaps, that the Trans-Sahara railway had remained only a planned project." See Lawler, *Soldiers, Airmen*, 19.

53. Marcel Jouanique, "Le Transsaharien—voie impériale de demain," *La Loire*, 1 Nov. 1941.

54. Marguet, "62 ans après le premier projet."

55. AN, AJ/1877, "Un véritable acte de foi: Le 'Méditerranée-Niger,'" *Les Nouveaux temps*, 26 Aug. 1942.

56. AN, AJ/1877, "Un véritable acte de foi."

57. Jouanique, "Le Transsaharien."

58. "Le Transsaharien . . . Ce pourrait être une première occasion de collaboration eurafricaine," *OEuvre*, 20 Mar. 1941.

59. Jennings, *Vichy in the Tropics*, 186.

60. ANS, 17G/395 (126).

61. CAOM, Affaires politiques, 882/1.

62. Coudray, "L'empire colonial français," 59.

63. "Transsaharien," *Révolution*, 12 Oct. 1941.

64. Thompson and Adloff, "French Economic Policy," 131.

65. Suret-Canale, *Afrique noire*, 354–60.

66. van Beusekom, "Disjuncture in Theory and Practice," 81–84; Echenberg and Filipovich, "African Military Labour."

67. Conklin, *A Mission to Civilize*, 212–13.

68. Morgenthau, *Political Parties*, 1–2.

69. Fall, *Le travail forcé*, 17–18.

70. On the plantations economy in Côte d'Ivoire during the colonial period, see Chauveau and Dozon, "Colonisation."

71. Morgenthau, *Political Parties*, 3–5.

72. ANS, 17G/396 (126), 10 Sept. 1941.

73. ANS, 17G/396 (126), July 1942.

74. A.D.M., interview. M.K. also mentioned in his interview that Africans were recruited for forced labor in the hinterlands and some were brought to Dakar.

75. Diouf, interview.

76. Kipre, "La place des centres urbains," 97.

77. Rapley, *Ivoirien Capitalism*, 19–21; Zolberg, *One-Party Government*, 57–58.

78. Demaison, *Destins de l'Afrique*, 34–35.

79. ANS, 17G/395 (126), 17 Aug. 1942.

80. Boisson, *Contribution à l'oeuvre*, 92–93.

81. Cooper, *Decolonization and African Society*, 148–49.

82. Conklin, *A Mission to Civilize*, 235–45.

83. Morgenthau, *Political Parties*, 167–70.

84. AN, 2G41/22 (200mi/1829), "Côte d'Ivoire—Rapport politique et social," 1941.

85. Zolberg, *One-Party Government*, 61.

Part 3. Vichy Encounters with African Society

1. Translation: "The France of camping will win over the France of aperitifs and congresses."

2. Paxton, *Vichy France*, 201–8.

3. Guillon, "La philosophie politique," 167–68; Lebovics, *True France*, 171–76.

4. Sternhell, *Ni droite, ni gauche*, 361–62.

5. Jackson, *France*, 7–12.

6. Fishman et al., *France at War*, 4.

7. Jackson, *France*, 12–14.

8. Jackson, *France*, 19–20.

9. Kedward, "Rural France," 126–27.

10. Veillon, "The Resistance and Vichy," 161.

11. Laborie, "1940–1944."

12. See, e.g., Robinson, *Paths of Accommodation*; Stoler and Cooper, "Between Metropole and Colony."

6. Vichy and the "Products" of Assimilation

1. Ageron, *France coloniale*, 189–90.

2. Ageron, *France coloniale*, 195.

3. Ageron, *France coloniale*, 67–68.

4. Betts, *Assimilation and Association*. An influential source, e.g., was Léopold de Saussure's 1899 book, *Psychologie de la colonisation française dans ses rapports avec les sociétés indigènes*, in which he systematically presented all the arguments against assimilation.

5. Betts, *Assimilation and Association*, 34.

6. Betts, *Assimilation and Association*, 36–46.

7. Betts, *Assimilation and Association*, 120–23.

8. Jennings, *Vichy in the Tropics*, 24.

9. Johnson, "Les élites au Sénégal," 25.

10. Until then any African who had lived in the four communes for more than five years could vote.

11. Atlan, *Elections et pratiques*, 56–59.

12. Atlan, *Elections et pratiques*, 51–54.

13. In the other colonies of FWA education had been transferred from the missionaries to secular colonial schools.

14. Leroy, *Raisons et bases*, 5.

15. Maunier, "La politique coloniale," 127–28.

16. Maunier, "La politique coloniale," 124.

17. The legal term *sleeping embryo* was accepted in the Maliki school (one of the four schools of Islam) and reflected a synthesis with the customary law. It was based on the assumption that a pregnancy could last more than nine months when the embryo had "fallen asleep." The aim of this term was to legitimize extramarital pregnancies during a husband's long absence. See Layish, *Divorce in the Libyan Family*, 186.

18. According to William Cohen, the Académie des sciences d'outre-mer attempted to implement this idea in 1942 and put forth a plan for imperial citizenship, but the project was later aborted. See Cohen, *Rulers of Empire*, 161–62.

19. Maunier, "Une citoyenneté d'empire," 5–6.

20. Paillard, *L'empire français de demain*, 41, 28–29. Cited in Jennings, *Vichy in the Tropics*, 28.

21. Abitbol, *Les juifs*, 63–66.

22. Atlan, *Elections et pratiques*, 85.

23. Coquery-Vidrovitch, "Nationalité et citoyenneté," 295.

24. See, e.g., Ousmane Socé, "L'évolution culturelle de l'AOF," *Dakar-jeunes*, 29 Jan. 1942; Mamadou Dia, "Pour ou contre une culture africaine," *Dakar-jeunes*, 12 Mar. 1942; Ouezzin Coulibaly, "La colonisation française vue par un évolué indigène," *Dakar-jeunes*, 4 June 1942. Coulibaly became a deputy of the Rassemblement démocratique africaine, a federal African party headed by Félix Houphouët-Boigny, and Dia was Senegal's first prime minister.

25. Outhmane Socé Diop was born in 1911 and graduated from the William Ponty School. He studied in Paris in the 1930s and wrote his first novel, *Karim*, in 1935. After World War II he became active in the political life of Senegal.

26. Socé, "L'évolution culturelle" ; Vaillant, *Black, French, and African*, 186–87.

27. Joseph Baye, "Le métissage culturel ne doit pas être un but mais un moyen," *Dakar-jeunes*, 26 Mar. 1942.

28. Mamadou Dia became the first prime minister of Senegal after independence. He was arrested by Senghor in 1962 after being accused of trying to overthrow him.

29. Dia, "Pour ou contre."

30. Emile Zinsou, "L'évolution culturelle en AOF—une opinion de Cotonou," *Dakar-jeunes*, 14 May 1942.

31. Charles Béart, "À propos d'une littérature indigène d'expression française," *Dakar-jeunes*, 18 June 1942.

32. ANS, O/31 (31).

33. In 1923 the colonial administration in FWA issued a decree according to which all missionary teachers had to be graduates of French institutions and teach in French, Latin, or an African language. This decree actually closed FWA to British and American Protestant missionaries, so that the only Protestant missionaries who were active in the federation were French. See Thompson and Adloff, *French West Africa*, 582.

34. ANS, 17G/123 (17), 31 Aug. 1941.

35. Marrus and Paxton, *Vichy France and the Jews*, 203–4.

36. Marrus, "French Churches," 314.

37. Marrus and Paxton, *Vichy France and the Jews*, 204.

38. CAOM, Affaires politiques, 883/11, 30 June 1941.

39. CAOM, Affaires politiques, 883/11, 19 June 1941.

40. AN, 21G/143 (200mi/3071), "Questions indigènes (1928–1942)."

41. Marrus and Paxton, *Vichy France and the Jews*, 197–98.

42. Halls, *Politics, Society, and Christianity*, 233. On the Catholic Church in France during the Vichy period, see Renée Bédarida, "La hiérarchie catholique"; Duquesne, *Les Catholiques français*; Mayeur, "Les églises devant."

43. ANS, 17G/123 (17), 22 July 1941.

44. ANS, 17G/123 (17), 31 Aug. 1941.

45. See the answers of the governors of Dakar and of Dahomey, Senegal, Togo, and Mauritania: ANS, 17G/123 (17), 26 Nov. 1941, 21 Dec. 1941, 17 Jan. 1942.

46. Diouf, interview.

47. A.D.M., interview.

48. Sabatier, "Did Africans Really Learn?" 179–80.

49. A.D.M., interview.

50. On the use of sports in the colonies as a means of propaganda, see Gay-Lecost, "La propagande par le sport," 56–60.

51. Kaziende, *Souvenirs d'un enfant*, 10; Konaté, *Le cri du mange-mil*, 57. Kaziende was born around 1912 in Kaya (Burkina Faso). During the war he worked as a teacher in the regional school of Niamey and in the school in Filingué (Niger). After independence he served as a minister in Niger until the coup of 15 Apr. 1974. Konaté was born in 1931 in Saint Louis, Senegal. After independence he served as a *préfet* in various regions of Senegal.

52. Kaziende, *Souvenirs d'un enfant*, 13. Kaziende tells his life story through the character of Sadio. He describes the discussions Sadio has with his friend in which he asserts that the Axis powers are going to win the war. He begins to doubt only after the Allied landings in North Africa.

53. Lemoine, *Douta Seck*, 28–29 (my translation). I would like to thank Catherine Atlan for providing me with this reference.

54. ANS, O512 (31).

55. Laborie, *L'opinion française*, 34–35.

56. CAOM, Affaires politiques, 929bis/3, May 1941, 929bis/4, July 1941.

57. Bara Diouf also presented this beach as an example of Vichy racism, while Boubacar Ly said that the beach was often referred to after the war as a clear expression of racism.

58. Ly, interview.

59. A.D.M., interview.

60. Goerg, "From Hill Station," 11–12.

61. Diouf, interview.

62. Kandji, interview.

63. Johnson, "Les élites au Sénégal," 28–29.

64. *Paris-Soir*, 22 Apr. 1940, qtd. in Atlan, *Elections et pratiques*, 89.

65. CAOM, Affaires politiques, 638/13, 24 Sept. 1940.

66. CAOM, Affaires politiques, 638/13, 30 June 1941.

67. CAOM, Affaires politiques, 638/13, 6 June 1941.

68. CAOM, Affaires politiques, 638/13, 6 June 1941.

69. Johnson, "Les élites au Sénégal," 29.

7. The "Traditional" Elements of African Society

1. African chiefs were usually appointed at the level of the canton or the village. Occasionally an African would be called a "superior chief" and control a larger area. Such a chief was sometimes called a king; he was usually a precolonial local ruler whom the French decided for various reasons not to discard. In 1946 the administrative hierarchy included around fifty thousand African chiefs. See Delavignette, *Freedom and Authority*, 71–72, 79. On French colonial policy with regard to chiefs before World War II and the definition of their status, see Alexandre, "The Problems of Chieftaincies"; Cohen, *Rulers of Empire*, 74–79; and Rouveroy, "Chef coutumier."

2. Geschiere, "Chiefs and Colonial Rule," 154–55.

3. There are quite a lot of such cases. To cite a few examples: A request was made by a former canton chief from Séguéla circle in Côte d'Ivoire, who lost his job before Vichy, to be reappointed; AN, 21G/87 (200mi/3047), 10 Dec. 1940. A canton chief was appointed and was supposed to receive a lower salary than in his previous post. The colonial administration agreed not to reduce his salary and instead withdrew certain perks he was supposed to receive; CAOM, 2G42/3 (14mi/1835), "Soudan-Rapport politique," 1942.

4. Skinner, "The Changing Status," 99–100.

5. Skinner, "The Changing Status, 100–109.

6. AN, 19G/3 (200mi/2837).

7. AN, 5G/11 (200mi/2116), "Réorganisation du Commandement indigène en Côte d'Ivoire, (1936–1948)."

8. Skinner, "The Changing Status," 110.

9. Lawler, *Soldiers, Airmen*, 118–11; Skinner, "The Changing Status," 110.

10. CAOM, 17G/8 (14mi/2289), "Le Moro Naba, Chef du Peuple Mossi à M. le Chef de la Mission Militaire de la France Combattante en Afrique Occidentale Britannique," 9 July 1943.

11. CAOM, 14mi/2289, 17G/8, "Pierre Cournarie à M. Moro-Naba Saghane, Ouagadougou," 13 Aug. 1943.

12. Lawler, "The Crossing of the Gyaman," 57.

13. ANS, 5G/31 (17).

14. Lawler, "The Crossing of the Gyaman," 58.

15. ANS, 5G/31 (17).

16. ANS, 17G/119 (17).

17. ANS, 13G/22 (17), 1941.

18. Echenberg, *Colonial Conscripts*, 88.

19. Azéma, *De Munich*, 44.

20. After the armistice the number of African soldiers in FWA was reduced from 118,000 to 25,000. See Lawler, *Soldiers, Airmen*, 3.

21. ANS, 17G/119 (17).

22. Lawler, *Soldats d'infortune*, 131–32.

23. CAOM, Affaires politiques, 638/6. Also see Echenberg, "Tragedy at Thiaroye," 113.

24. ANS, 11D1/869. The soldiers were supposed to receive upon their demobilization the sum of five hundred francs and at a later stage an additional four hundred francs.

25. AN, 2G40/2 (200mi/1815), "Sénégal—Rapport politique annuel," 1940.

26. ANS, 2D/29 (28).

27. ANS, 2D/29 (28).

28. CAOM, Affaires économiques, 69/1.

29. CAOM, Affaires politiques, 639/15.

30. Rita Headrick, "African Soldiers," 519.

31. ANS, 17G/83 (17).

32. ANS, 2D/29 (28).

33. AN, 2G40/2 (200mi/1815), "Sénégal—Rapport politique annuel," 1940.

34. AN, 2G40/4 (200mi/1815), "Côte d'Ivoire—Rapport politique annuel," 1940.

35. Two parallel justice systems existed in FWA: one for Europeans and Africans holding French citizenship and the other for African "subjects." In the European courts cases were judged by French judges according to French law, while in the native courts French administrators ruled with the assistance of African assessors. See Chabas, "La justice française"; Conklin, *A Mission to Civilize*, 86–102.

36. ANS, 2D/29 (28); AN, 2G40/4 (200mi/1815).

37. Haut Commissariat de l'Afrique française, *La justice indigène*, 419–22. This decree annulled that of 22 Aug. 1939, which also accorded this right to members of the Legion of Honor and to those who were entitled to vote for the local assemblies.

38. Echenberg, *Colonial Conscripts*, 88, 96. On the harsh conditions in which African POWs were held in German camps see Echenberg, "Morts pour la France," 371–78.

39. Thomas, "The Vichy Government," 667, 670–71.

40. CAOM, Affaires politiques, 870/1, 31 Jan. 1941.

41. CAOM, Affaires politiques, 920/2, 19 Mar. 1941.

42. *Paris-Soir*, 12 Mar. 1941.

43. Thomas, "The Vichy Government," 666–67.

44. Certain rights applied, e.g., to fathers with numerous children, World War I veterans, and POWs who suffered from physical problems.

45. CAOM, Affaires politiques, 639/15. There is no indication of which authority was responsible for this report.

46. CAOM, Affaires politiques, 639/15.

47. ANS, 4D/68 (89).

48. CAOM, 634/1.

49. CAOM, Affaires politiques, 870/1.

50. ANS, 4D/68 (89).

51. ANS, 2D/29 (28).

52. Outhmane Sembene, dir., *Camp de Thiaroye* (Algeria, Tunisia, Senegal, 1988), 152 min.

53. A.D.M., interview; Diouf, interview.

54. Diouf, interview.

55. CAOM, Affaires politiques, 637/1; CAOM, Affaires politiques, 883/11.

56. CAOM, Affaires politiques, 870/1.

57. CAOM, Affaires politiques, 883/18, 20 June 1941.

58. CAOM, Affaires politiques, 883/11, 15 Feb. 1941.

59. CAOM, Affaires politiques, 929/4, n.d.

60. Cohen, *Rulers of Empire*, 114. On African soldiers during World War I, see Marc Michel, *L'appel à l'Afrique*.

61. Seidou Nourou Tall was the grandson of Haj Umar and the great-grandson of Muhhamad Bello, the caliph of Sokoto. He was the leader of the Tijanniya order. Tall joined the French Army during World War I and returned home an officer. After the war he moved to Saint Louis and lived close to Babacar Sy, the son of Malik Sy, who had been the leader of the Tijanniya before Tall and was a French supporter. After his mentor's death Tall became the "ambassador" of French civilization. During the 1930s he conducted tours all over FWA, accompanied by administrators and governors, to explain French policy to the African population and to serve as a mediator in cases of dispute. For more on Tall, see Garcia, "Al-Haj Seydou Nourou Tall."

62. Harrison, *France and Islam*, 170–71.

63. Although Tall was a Tijani, the Vichy administration counted on him to communicate its messages to all Muslim soldiers. As a rule the colonial authorities did not have separate policies for the different Islamic orders, with the exception of the Hamallist movement, which they viewed as a threat and thus severely repressed. On Sheikh Hamallah, see Harrison, *France and Islam*, 171–82, 187–90; Joly, "La réconciliation de Nioro." On the Vichy attitude toward this movement, see Akpo-Vaché, *L'AOF*, 141–42; ANS, 11D1/49; ANS 11D1/1302.

64. AN, 19G/43 (200mi/2853), "Visites du Grand Marabout El Hadj Seiydu Nourou Tall," 14 June 1940, 16 June 1940.

65. AN, 19G/43 (200mi/2853), 20 June 1940, 25 June 1949, 27 June 1940, 29 June 1940, 4 July 1940.

66. AN, 19G/43 (200mi/2853), 19 Sept. 1942.

67. AN, 19G/43 (200mi/2853), 12 July 1940.

68. ANS 13G/101 (180). The meaning of the word *waṭan* in classical Arabic is "original place of residence." In this context the term appears three times in the Hadith. With the emergence of Ottoman nationalism among the elite in the nineteenth century, the "Young Ottomans" used the term to justify nationalism and endow it with an Islamic meaning. On the use of this Hadith in the Ottoman national ideology, see Hourani, *Arabic Thought*, 101.

69. Public Records Office, London, FO 371/28257, West African Political Intelligence Centre, Bulletin no. 15, 6 Oct. 1941.

70. AN, 19G/43 (200mi/2853), "Visites du Grand Marabout," 14 July 1940, 1 Aug. 1940, 8 Aug. 1940, 23 July 1941, 21 Apr. 1942, 24 July 1942, 10 Sept. 1942, 19 Sept. 1942, 25 Sept. 1942, 29 Sept. 1942, 17 Oct. 1942.

71. Robinson, *Paths of Accommodation*, 75, 85.

72. The first Sufi order to arrive in West Africa was the Quadiriyya, which was established by Abd el-Quadir Al-Jallani (1079–1166) and spread rapidly from the area of Baghdad all over the Middle East. It reached West Africa in the sixteenth century, and in the eighteenth century Timbuktu (now in Mali) became its center. The second order that reached this region was the Tijaniyya, established by Ahmad al-Tijani in Algeria in the eighteenth century. It spread into West Africa during the nineteenth century. The Muridiyya order was established in Senegal by Amadou Bamba (1850–1927) toward the end of the nineteenth century. On the Quadiriyya, see Cruise O'Brien and Coulon, *Charisma and Brotherhood*. On the Tijaniyya, see Kane, "La Tijaniyya," 475–78. On the Mouridiyya, see Cruise O'Brien, *The Mourides of Senegal*.

73. Levtzion and Pouwels, *The History of Islam*, 169–71.

74. Echenberg, *Black Death*, 150.

75. Robinson and Triaud, *Le temps des marabouts*, 13–14.

76. Robinson, *Paths of Accommodation*, 21–25.

77. These quotes from Hamallah's son are cited in Dicko, *Hamallah*, 81.

78. Traoré, *Islam et colonisation*, 119, 246.

79. The motive for shorter prayers was the assumption that Muslims were unsafe among the infidels and therefore should not engage in long prayers as this could compromise their personal security. Short prayers worried the French, as they saw in them a sign of Islamic militancy. On the Nioro reconciliation, see Joly, "La réconciliation de Nioro."

80; Dicko, *Hamallah*, 93–95; Clarke, *West Africa and Islam*, 213; Harrison, *France and Islam*, 179.

81. ANS, 11D1/49.

82. AN, 19G/7 (200mi/2838), Lieutenant Jean Montezer.

83. Dicko, *Hamallah*, 99–104.

84. CAOM, Affaires politiques, 2258/5.

85. ANS, 11D1/49.

86. Akpo-Vaché, *L'AOF*, 141–42.

87. ANS, 5G/34 (17).

88. This is a movement that broke off from the Hamalliyya and was established by and named after one of Hamallah's disciples, Yacoub Sylla. Sylla presented beliefs that were even less acceptable in Islam than those of Hamallah. He claimed, for instance, that there was no need to study the Quran and that saying "There is no God but Allah" was enough to win salvation. The Yacoubists kept their independence from the Hamalliyya, in spite of the common hostility of both sects to the Tijaniyya's central stream. See Abun-Nasr, *The Tijaniyya*, 155–56. For more on the religious and political activities of Sylla and his relations with the Hamalliyya, see Savadogo, "La communauté."

89. ANS, 5G/34 (17).

90. AN, 19G/7 (200mi/2838), Lieutenant Jean Montezer.

91. AN, 19G/7 (200mi/2838), Lieutenant Jean Montezer.

92. AN, 19G/7 (200mi/2838), Lieutenant Jean Montezer, 8 Jan. 1941.

93. AN, 19G/7 (200mi/2838), Lieutenant Jean Montezer, 21 Jan. 1941.

94. AN, 19G/7 (200mi/2838), Lieutenant Jean Montezer, 27 Dec. 1940.

95. Akpo-Vaché, *L'AOF*, 113.

96. On the activities of these networks, see Akpo-Vaché, *L'AOF*, 114–22.

97. AN, 19G/7 (200mi/2838), Lieutenant Jean Montezer.

98. AN, 19G/7 (200mi/2838), Lieutenant Jean Montezer.

99. Falilou Diallo quotes a letter from Boisson to the Vichy government in which he mentions Mustapha M'Backe and Babacar Sy (the brother of Abd el-Aziz Sy, who appears on the list) as two of the three most important Islamic leaders in Senegal. See Diallo, "Vichy et la religion," 155.

100. AN, 19G/7 (200mi/2838), Lieutenant Jean Montezer.

101. AN, 19G/7 (200mi/2838), Lieutenant Jean Montezer.

102. Akpo-Vaché, *L'AOF*, 88–89.

103. ANS, 11D1/1302.

104. AN, 2G40/2 (200mi/1815), "Sénégal—Rapport politique annuel," 1940.

105. The Catholic mission arrived in the area of Upper Volta at the beginning of the twentieth century and ended Islam's five-hundred-year monopoly in this region. Following its arrival a competition began among the Catholic missionaries, the marabouts, and the colonial administration over the control of the region's population. See Kouanda, "Marabouts et missionnaires," 33.

106. CAOM, Affaires politiques, 637/1.

107. CAOM, Affaires politiques, 639/5.

108. CAOM, Affaires politiques, 639/1.

109. Joly, "Un aspect de la politique musulmane," 39, 44.

110. Harrison, *France and Islam*, 186–87.

8. Vichy Colonialism and African Society

1. Kelley, *Race Rebels*, 1–4.

2. Kelley, *Race Rebels*, 35.

3. Kelley, *Race Rebels*, 58–75.

4. Diouf, interview.

5. A.D.M., interview.

6. *Falong* is a lebou word used by traditional fighters at the beginning of a battle.

7. Atlan, *Elections et pratiques*, 117–18.

8. Atlan, *Elections et pratiques*, 104–6.

9. A.D.M., interview.

10. Diouf, interview.

Part 4. The Long-Term Significance of the Vichy Period

1. Conan and Rousso, *Vichy*, 1.

9. Vichy Colonialism

1. M'Bokolo, "French Colonial Policy," 173.

2. On the struggle between Vichy and the Free French over FEA, see chapter 1.

3. Castor and Tarcy, *Félix Eboué*, 109.

4. Castor and Tarcy, *Félix Eboué*, 9, 12–15.

5. M'Bokolo, "French Colonial Policy," 178.

6. Castor and Tarcy, *Félix Eboué*, 119.

7. M'Bokolo, "French Colonial Policy," 180–81.

8. Lanne, "Chad, the Chadians," 319. The idea of *notables évolués* is similar to Maunier's notion of the *mitoyen*, discussed in part III.

9. Castor and Tarcy, *Félix Eboué*, 120–23.

10. M'Bokolo, "French Colonial Policy," 185.

11. M'Bokolo, "French Colonial Policy," 186–89.

12. Lanne, "Chad, the Chadians," 313–15.

13. Castor and Tarcy, *Félix Eboué*, 139.

14. Castor and Tarcy, *Félix Eboué*, 143–44.

15. Lanne, "Chad, the Chadians," 319.

16. Lanne, "Chad, the Chadians, 318. Translation: "France has lost a battle. It has not lost the war."

17. Levisse-Touzé, *L'Afrique du Nord*, 64; Abitbol, *Les juifs*, 51.

18. Abitbol, *Les juifs*, 52–53.

19. Cantier, *L'Algérie*, 58–61.

20. Levisse-Touzé, *L'Afrique du Nord*, 144.

21. Cantier, *L'Algérie*, 117–18, 128–29.

22. Abitbol, *Les juifs*, 56; Levisse-Touzé, *L'Afrique du Nord*, 109; Cantier, *L'Algérie*, 113–14, 145.

23. The Destour (Constitution) party was founded in 1920 by Western-educated Tunisians. In 1934 some of the younger members of this party, under the

leadership of Habib Bourguiba, founded a new party called Néo-Destour. This party led Tunisia to independence after World War II.

24. Abitbol, *Les juifs*, 57.

25. Levisse-Touzé, *L'Afrique du Nord*, 140–41; Cantier,*L'Algérie*, 112.

26. Levisse-Touzé, *L'Afrique du Nord*, 145.

27. Jennings, *Vichy in the Tropics*, 35–36.

28. Jennings, *Vichy in the Tropics*, 136–37.

29. Jennings, *Vichy in the Tropics*, 135–36.

30. Jennings, *Vichy in the Tropics*, 38.

31. Jennings, *Vichy in the Tropics*, 150–51.

32. Jennings, *Vichy in the Tropics*, 42–43, 46–47. On Vichy policy toward youth in Madagascar, see Jennings, "Vichy à Madagascar."

33. Jennings, *Vichy in the Tropics*, 65–71.

34. Jennings, *Vichy in the Tropics*, 76–77.

35. Jennings, *Vichy in the Tropics*, 188–90, 198.

36. Jennings, *Vichy in the Tropics*, 85–88.

37. Jennings, *Vichy in the Tropics*, 80–84.

38. Jennings, *Vichy in the Tropics*, 108.

39. Jennings, *Vichy in the Tropics*, 110–11.

40. Jennings, *Vichy in the Tropics*, 116–25.

41. Jennings, *Vichy in the Tropics*, 127–29.

10. Vichy's Postwar Impact

1. Wallerstein, *Africa*, 50.

2. Chafer, *The End of Empire*, 30, 37, 44, 49.

3. Aldrich, *Greater France*, 301.

4. Betts, *France and Decolonization*, 122–23.

5. Betts, *France and Decolonization*, 125–26.

6. Benot, *Les députés africains*, 38.

7. Benot, *Les députés africains*, 48–49.

8. CAOM, 14mi/2289, 17G/14, "La Section Indigène du Groupe Combat de Guinée à M. Lecompte-Boynet, Membre du CNR Délégué à l'Assemblée Consultative," 8 June 1945.

9. ANS, 10N/234, "Amicale des condamnés de Vichy," 9 Jan. 1945.

10. Person, "Le front populaire au Sénégal," 81.

11. ANS, 10N/302, "Saint-Louis," 19 June 1940; "Commission intégration des agents victimes des instructions de Vichy," 5 Jan. 1944, 4 Mar. 1948.

12. Cooper, *Decolonization and African Society*, 242.

13. Cooper, *Decolonization and African Society*, 241–48.

14. Chafer, *The End of Empire*, 44–45.

15. Morgenthau, *Political Parties*, 166–67.

16. Wallerstein, *Africa*, 54.

17. Chafer, *The End of Empire*, 133–36.

18. These youth centers were supposed to reflect the local community's tradition and diffuse Vichy ideology among African youth. See ANS, 0516 (31).

Conclusions

The epigraph: Senghor, "Prière de paix," 93. As translated in Soyinka, *The Burden of Memory*: "Oh Lord, dismiss from my memory the France that is not France, this mask of pettiness and hate upon the face of France. The mask of pettiness and hate for which I've only hate—but surely I can hate the evil for I am greatly fond of France."

1. Soyinka, *The Burden of Memory*, 115–16.
2. Cohen, *French Encounter with Africans*, 260–61.
3. Palermo, "Identity under Construction," 296.
4. Palermo, "Identity under Construction," 292.
5. Hale, "French Images of Race," 138–45.
6. Césaire, *Discours sur le colonialisme*, 11–18.
7. Arendt, *Origins of Totalitarianism*, 123, 131, 158, 185–86, 221.

Bibliography

Archival Sources

Archives nationales, Centre des archives d'outre-mer, Aix-en-Provence. Affaires politiques, dossiers: 544/4; 634/1; 635/6, 11; 636/1; 637/1; 639/1, 5, 15, 17; 870/1; 883/5, 11, 18, 20; 886/2; 920/2; 929/4; 929bis/3, 4; 2258/5. Affaires économiques, dossier: 146/A. Séries: 2G, 17G.

Archives nationales, Paris. Séries: 268/mi, 2G, AJ72, 5G, 19G, 21G.

Archives nationales du Sénégal, Archives de l'AOF, Dakar. Séries: 5G, 13G, 17G, 18G, 21G, O, 2D, 4D, 11D, 10N.

Public Records Office, London. Series: FO 371

Secondary Sources

Abitbol, Michel. *Les juifs d'Afrique du nord sous Vichy.* Paris: G.-P. Maisonneuve, 1983.

Abun-Nasr, Jamil M. *The Tijaniyya: A Sufi Order in the Modern World.* Oxford: Oxford University Press, 1965.

Académie des sciences d'outre-mer. *Hommes et destins: Dictionnaire biographique d'outre-mer.* 10 vols. Paris: Académie des sciences d'outre-mer, 1977.

Added, Serge. *Le théâtre dans les années Vichy, 1940–1944.* Paris: Editions Ramsay, 1992.

Adler, K. H. "Vichy Specificities: Repositioning the French Past." *Contemporary European History* 9, no. 3 (2000): 475–88.

Agence économique des colonies. *Les colonies aux expositions, foires et manifestations de 1942.* Paris: 1943.

———. *Vous voulez aller aux colonies?* Paris: 1943.

Ageron, Charles-Robert. *France coloniale ou parti colonial?* Paris: PUF, 1978.

——— "Vichy, les Français et l'empire." In *Le régime de Vichy et les Français,* ed. Azéma and Bédarida, 122–34.

Akpo-Vaché, Catherine. *L'AOF pendant la deuxième guerre mondiale.* Paris: Karthala, 1996.

———. "Souviens-toi de Thiaroye! La mutinerie des tirailleurs sénégalais du 1er décembre 1944." *Guerres mondiales et conflits contemporains,* no. 181 (1996): 21–26.

Akpo-Vaché, Catherine, and V. Joly. "Les élites africaines face à l'administration Gaulliste (1943–1946)." In *Les chemins de la décolonisation de l'empire colonial français,* ed. Charles-Robert Ageron, 481–92. Paris: CNRS, 1986.

Aldrich, Robert. *Greater France: A History of French Overseas Expansion.* London: Palgrave, 1996.

Alexandre, Pierre. "The Problems of Chieftaincies in French West Africa." In *West African Chiefs,* ed. Crowder and Ikime, 24–78.

Amon d'Aby, F. J. *La Côte d'Ivoire dans la cité africaine*. Paris: Editions Larose, 1951.

Amouroux, Henri. *Quarante millions de pétainistes*. Paris: Robert Laffont, 1988.

Annet, Armand. *Aux heures troublées de l'Afrique française*. Paris: Edition du conquistador, 1952.

Arendt, Hannah. *The Origins of Totalitarianism*. Cleveland and New York: The World Publishing Company, 1951.

Aron, Robert. *Histoire de Vichy*. Paris: Librairie Arthème Fayard, 1954.

Asiwaju, A. I. "Control through Coercion: A Study of the Indigénat Regime in French West African Administration, 1887–1946." *Bulletin de l'*IFAN, B ser., 41, no. 1 (1979): 36–71.

————. "Migrations as Revolt: The Example of the Ivory Coast and the Upper Volta before 1945." *Journal of African History* 17, no. 4 (1976): 577–94.

Atkin, Nick. "Reshaping the Past: The Teaching of History in Vichy France, 1940–1944." *Modern and Contemporary France* 42 (1990): 7–16.

Atlan, Catherine. "Elections et pratiques électorales au Sénégal (1940–1958): Histoire sociale et culturelle de la décolonisation." Ph.D. diss., Ecole des hautes études en sciences sociales, Paris, 2001.

Azéma, Jean-Pierre. *De Munich à la Libération, 1938–1944*. Paris: Seuil, 1979.

————. "Vichy et la mémoire savante: Quarante-cinq ans d'historiographie." In *Le régime de Vichy et les Français*, ed. Azéma and Bédarida, 23–44.

Azéma, Jean-Pierre, and François Bédarida, eds. *Le régime de Vichy et les Français*. Paris: Fayard, 1992.

Bachelier, Alain François. *Géographie—Classe de troisième—La France et la France d'outre-mer*. Paris: 1943.

Barrès, Maurice. *Le roman de l'énergie nationale: Les déracinés*. Paris: Charpentier, 1897.

Bazin, Jean. *Les Bambara du Segou et du Kaarta*. Paris: G. P. Maisonneuve and Larose, 1976.

Bédarida, François. "Vichy et la crise de la conscience française." In *Le régime de Vichy et les Français*, ed. Azéma and Bédarida, 77–96.

Bédarida, Renée. "La hiérarchie catholique." In *Le régime de Vichy et les Français*, ed. Azéma and Bédarida, 444–62.

Behrman, Lucy C. *Muslim Brotherhoods and Politics in Senegal*. Cambridge: Harvard University Press, 1970.

Benoist, Joseph Roger de. "The Brazzaville Conference; or, Involuntary Decolonization." *Africana Journal* 15 (1990): 39–58.

Benot, Yves. *Les députés africains au Palais Bourbon*. Paris: Chaka, 1989.

Betts, Raymond F. *Assimilation and Association in French Colonial Theory, 1890–1914*. New York and London: Columbia University Press, 1961.

————. *France and Decolonization, 1900–1960*. New York: St. Martin's Press, 1991.

Blanchard, Pascal, and Gilles Boëtsch. "La France de Pétain et l'Afrique: Images et propagandes coloniales." *Canadian Journal of African Studies* 28, no. 1 (1994): 1–31.

———. "Races et propagande coloniale sous le régime de Vichy 1940–1944." *Africa* (Rome) 49, no. 4 (1994): 531–61.

Blum, Charlotte, and Humphrey Fisher. "Love for Three Oranges; or, The Askiya's Dilemma: The Askia, Al-Maghili and Timboktu, c. 1500 AD." *Journal of African History* 34, no. 1, (1993): 65–91.

Boisson, Pierre. *Contribution à l'oeuvre africaine.* Rufisque, Senegal: Imprimerie du Haut Commissariat de l'Afrique noire, 1942.

Bolle, Pierre. "Les Protestants et leurs églises." In *La France et la question juive,* ed. Wellers, Kaspi, and Klarsteld, 171–95.

Boone, Catherine. *Merchant Capital and the Roots of Power in Senegal, 1930–1985.* Cambridge: Cambridge University Press, 1992.

Bouche, Denise. "Autrefois, notre pays s'appelait la Gaule. . . . Remarques sur l'adaptation de l'enseignement au Sénégal de 1817 à 1960." *Cahiers d'études africaines* 8, no. 29 (1968): 110–22.

———. "L'enseignement dans les territoires français de l'Afrique occidentale de 1817 à 1920: Mission civilisatrice ou formation d'une élite?" Ph.D. diss., Lille, 1975.

———. "Le retour de l'Afrique occidentale française dans la lutte contre l'ennemi aux côtés des alliés." *Revue d'histoire de la deuxième guerre mondiale* 29, no. 114 (1979): 41–68.

Bousbina, Said. "Al-Hajj Malik Sy: Sa chaîne spirituelle dans la Tijaniyya et sa position à l'égard de la présence française au Sénégal." In *Le temps des marabouts,* ed. Robinson and Triaud, 181–98.

Bowles, Brett. "Newsreels, Ideology, and Public Opinion under Vichy: The Case of *La France en marche.*" *French Historical Studies* 27, no. 2 (2004): 419–63.

Brenner, Louis. "Concepts of Tariqa in West Africa: The Case of the Quadiriyya." In *Charisma and Brotherhood in African Islam,* ed. Donal Cruise O'Brien and Christian Coulon, 33–52. Oxford: Clarendon Press, 1988.

Brévié, Jules. *Islamisme contre "naturisme" au Soudan français: Essai de psychologie politique coloniale.* Paris: Leroux, 1923.

Brunschwig, Henri. "The Decolonization of French Black Africa." In *The Transfer of Power in Africa: Decolonization, 1940–1960,* ed. Gifford and Louis, 211–24.

———. *Mythes et réalités de l'impérialisme colonial français, 1871–1914.* Paris: A. Colin, 1960.

Burrin, Philippe. *La France à l'heure allemande, 1940–1944.* Paris: Seuil, 1995.

Cantier, Jacques. *L'Algérie sous le régime de Vichy.* Paris: Karthala, 2002.

Capelle, Jean. *L'éducation en Afrique noire à la veille des indépendances (1946–1958).* Paris: Karthala, 1990.

Castor, Elie, and Raymond Tarcy. *Félix Eboué: Gouverneur et philosophe.* Paris: L'Harmattan, 1984.

Cazin, M. *Ecole militaire de l'artillerie: Cours d'histoire.* Montpellier: Causse, Graille, Castelnau, 1942.

Césaire, Aimé. *Discours sur le colonialisme.* Paris and Dakar: Présence africaine, 1989.

Chabas, J. "La justice française en Afrique occidentale française." *Annales africaines* (1955): 79–108.

Chafer, Tony. *The End of Empire in French West Africa: France's Successful Decolonization?* Oxford: Berg, 2002.

———. "Teaching Africans to Be French? France's 'Civilising Mission' and the Establishment of a Public Education System in French West Africa, 1903–1930." *Africa* (Rome) 56, no. 2 (2001): 190–209.

Chafer, Tony, and Amanda Sackur, eds. *French Colonial Empire and the Popular Front: Hope and Disillusion.* London: Macmillan, 1999.

Chapman, James. *The British at War: Cinema, State, and Propaganda.* London and New York: Palgrave Macmillan, 1998.

Charton, A. "L'enseignement et l'éducation en A.O.F." *L'enseignement public* (1939): 193–208.

Chauveau, J.-P., and J.-P Dozon. "Colonisation, économie de plantation et société civile en Côte d'Ivoire." *Cahiers* OSTROM, Sciences humaines ser., 21, no. 1 (1985): 63–80.

Chazan, Naomi. "Politics and Youth Organizations in Ghana and the Ivory Coast." Ph.D. diss., Hebrew University of Jerusalem, 1973.

Clarke, Peter B. *West Africa and Islam.* London: Edward Arnold, 1982.

Cohen, William B. "The Colonial Policy of the Popular Front." *French Historical Studies* 2, no. 3 (1972): 368–93.

———. *The French Encounter with Africans: White Responses to Blacks, 1530–1880.* Bloomington: Indiana University Press, 1980.

———. "Robert Delavignette et les responsabilités de l'administrateur colonial." In *Robert Delavignette savant et politique (1897–1976),* ed. Bernard Mouralis and Anne Piriou, 125–35. Paris: Karthala, 2003.

———. *Rulers of Empire: The French Colonial Service in Africa.* Stanford: Hoover Institution Press, 1971.

Cointet-Labrousse, Michèle. *Vichy et le fascisme: Les hommes, les structures et les pouvoirs.* Paris: Editions complexe, 1987.

Conan, Éric, and Henri Rousso. *Vichy: An Ever-Present Past.* Trans. Nathan Bracher. Hanover and London: University Press of New England, 1998.

Cone, Michele C. *Artists under Vichy: A Case of Prejudice and Persecution.* Princeton: Princeton University Press, 1992.

Conklin, Alice L. *A Mission to Civilize: The Republican Idea of Empire in France and West Africa, 1895–1930.* Stanford: Stanford University Press, 1997.

Cooper, Fredrick. *Decolonization and African Society: The Labor Question in French and British Africa.* Cambridge: Cambridge University Press, 1996.

———. " 'Our Strike': Equality, Anticolonial Politics and the 1947–48 Railway

Strike in French West Africa." *Journal of African History* 37, no. 1 (1996): 81–118.

Coquery-Vidrovitch, Catherine, ed. *L'Afrique occidentale au temps des Français: Colonisateurs et colonisés, c. 1860–1960*. Paris: La Découverte, 1992.

———. "Le financement de la mise en valeur coloniale en Afrique noire, 1900–1945." In *Etudes africaines offertes de H. Brunschwig*, 237–52. Paris: Editions de l'école des hautes études en sciences sociales, 1983.

———. "Nationalité et citoyenneté en Afrique occidentale française: Originaires et citoyens dans le Sénégal colonial." *Journal of African History* 42, no. 2 (2001): 285–305.

———. "La politique économique coloniale." In *L'Afrique occidentale au temps des Français: Colonisateurs et colonisés, c. 1860–1960*, ed. Catherine Coquery-Vidrovitch, 105–40. Paris: La Découverte, 1992.

———. "The Popular Front and the Colonial Question: French West Africa: An Example of Reformist Colonialism." In *French Colonial Empire and the Popular Front: Hope and Disillusion*, ed. Chafer and Sackur, 155–63.

———. "Vichy et l'industrialisation aux colonies." *Revue d'histoire de la deuxième guerre mondiale* 29, no. 114 (1979): 69–94.

Coudray, Lallier du. "L'empire colonial français." *Semaine de la France d'outre-mer: Série de conférences*. Chambre de Commerce, Vichy, 1941.

Crowder, Michael. *Colonial West Africa*. London: Frank Cass, 1978.

———. "The 1939–1945 War and West Africa." In *History of West Africa*, ed. Crowder and Ajayi, 2: 596–621.

———. *West Africa under Colonial Rule*. Evanston: Northwestern University Press, 1968.

Crowder, Michael, and J. F. A. Ajayi, eds. *History of West Africa*. 2d ed. London: Longman, 1987.

Crowder, Michael, and Obaro Ikime. *West African Chiefs*. Ile-Ife, Nigeria: University of Ife Press, 1970.

Cruise O'Brien, Donal. *The Mourides of Senegal: The Political and Economic Organization of an Islamic Brotherhood*. Oxford: Oxford University Press, 1971.

———. *Saints and Politicians*. Cambridge: Cambridge University Press, 1975.

Cruise O'Brien, Donal, and Christian Coulon, eds. *Charisma and Brotherhood in African Islam*. Oxford: Clarendon Press, 1988.

David, Philippe. "Iconographie de l'histoire des transports en Afrique noire: Les cartes postales." In *Les transports en Afrique*, ed. Hélène d'Almeida-Topor, Chantal Chanson-Jabeur, and Monique Lakrour., 55–65. Paris: L'Harmattan, 1992.

De Gaulle, Charles. *Mémoires de guerre, l'unité, 1942–1944*. Paris: Plon, 1956.

Delafosse, Maurice. "L'animisme nègre et sa résistance à l'islamisation en Afrique occidentale." *Revue du monde musulman* 49 (1922): 121–65.

Delavignette, Robert. "La formation professionnelle de l'administrateur colonial." *L'empire français et ses ressources: Conférences d'information organisés en février–mars 1942*. L'école supérieure d'organisation professionnelle, Paris, 1942.

———— *Freedom and Authority in French West Africa*. London: Oxford University Press, 1950.

————. *Petite histoire des colonies françaises*. Paris: PUF, 1941.

Demaison, André. *Destins de l'Afrique*. Clermont-Ferrand: Centre d'expansion française, 1942.

Désalmand, Paul. *Histoire de l'éducation en Côte d'Ivoire*. Vol. 1. Abidjan: Centre d'édition et de diffusion africaines, 1983.

Deschamps, Hubert. *Roi de la brousse: Mémoires d'autres mondes*. Nancy: Berger-Levrault, 1975.

Deville-Danthu, Bernadette. *Le sport en noir et blanc: Du sport colonial au sport africain dans les anciens territoires français d'Afrique occidentale (1920–1965)*. Paris: L'Harmattan, 1997.

Dia, Mamadou. *Mémoires d'un militant du tiers-monde*. Dakar: Publisud, 1985.

Diagne, Abdel Kader. *La résistance française au Sénégal et en AOF pendant la guerre 1939–1945*. Exemplaire ronéotypé, slnd.

Diallo, Falilou. "Vichy et la religion au Sénégal." *Le mois en Afrique*, nos. 241–42 (1986): 151–59.

Dicko, Sëidina Oumar. *Hamallah: Le protégé de Dieu*. Paris: Al-Bustan, 2002.

Domergue, D. "La Côte d'Ivoire de 1912 à 1920: Influence de la première guerre mondiale sur l'évolution politique économique et sociale." *Annales universitaires d'Abidjan*, I ser., 4 (1976): 35–59.

Duquesne, Jacques. *Les Catholiques français sous l'occupation*. Paris: Grasset, 1986.

du Tilly, Hayaux. *L'unité de l'empire français*. Vichy: Clerc SARL, 1944.

Echenberg, Myron. *Black Death, White Medicine: Bubonic Plague and the Politics of Public Health in Colonial Senegal, 1914–1945*. Portsmouth: Heinemann, 2002.

————. *Colonial Conscripts: The Tirailleurs Sénégalais in French West Africa, 1857–1960*. Portsmouth: Heinemann, 1991.

————. "Morts pour la France: The African Soldier in France during the Second World War." *Journal of African History* 26, no. 4 (1985): 363–80.

————. "Tragedy at Thiaroye: The Senegalese Soldiers' Uprising of 1944." In *African Labor History*, ed. Gutkind, Cohen, and Copans, 109–27.

Echenberg, Myron, and Jean Filipovich. "African Military Labour and the Building of the Office du Niger Installations, 1925–1950." *Journal of African History* 27, no. 3 (1986): 533–51.

Ezra, Elizabeth. *The Colonial Unconscious: Race and Culture in Interwar France*. Ithaca: Cornell University Press, 2000.

Fage, J. D. *An Introduction to the History of West Africa*. Cambridge: Cambridge University Press, 1955.

Fall, Babacar. *Le travail forcé en Afrique occidentale française (1900–1945)*. Paris: Karthala, 1993.

Fishman, Sarah, Laura Lee Downs, Ioannis Sinanoghi, Leonard V. Smith, and Robert Zaretsky, eds. *France at War: Vichy and the Historians*. Oxford: Berg, 2000.

Frank, Robert, and Henri Rousso. "Quarante ans après: Les Français et la libération." *L'histoire* 67 (1984): 60–71.

Freeman, Michael. *Railways and the Victorian Imagination*. New Haven: Yale University Press, 1999.

Friedmann, Yohanan. *Prophecy Continuous: Aspects of Ahmadi Religious Thought and Its Medieval Background*. Berkeley: University of California Press, 1989.

Gamble, David Percy. *The Wolof of Senegambia*. London: International African Institute, 1975.

Garcia, Sylvianne. "Al-Haj Seydou Nourou Tall: 'Grand Marabout' Tijani." In *Le temps des marabouts*, ed. Robinson and Triaud, 247–76.

Gay-Lecost, Jean-Louis. "La propagande par le sport: Vichy, la politique sportive de l'état de Vichy dans l'empire, 1940–1944." In *L'empire du sport*, ed. Catalogue de l'exposition organisée au CAOM en mai–juillet 1992, 56–60. Aix-en-Province: AMAROM, 1992.

Gellar, Sheldon. *Structural Changes and Colonial Dependency: Senegal 1885–1945*. Beverly Hills and London: Sage Publications, 1976.

Gervereau, Laurent, and Denis Peschanski. *La propagande sous Vichy, 1940–1944*. Paris: BDIC, 1990.

Geschiere, Peter. "Chiefs and Colonial Rule in Cameroon: Inventing Chieftaincy, French and British Style." *Africa* (London) 63, no. 2 (1993): 151–73.

Giblin, James L. "A Colonial State in Crisis: Vichy Administration in French West Africa." *Africana Journal* 16 (1994): 326–40.

Gifford, Prosser, and Roger Louis, eds. *The Transfer of Power in Africa: Decolonization, 1940–1960*. New Haven: Yale University Press, 1986.

Gifford, Prosser, and Timothy C. Weiskel. "African Education in a Colonial Context: French and British Styles." In *France and Britain in Africa*, ed. Prosser Gifford and Timothy C. Weiskel, 663–711. New Haven and London: Yale University Press, 1971.

Gineste, Roger. "Les débuts de l'enseignement au Sénégal: L'oeuvre de Jean Dard." *Mondes et cultures* 41, no. 3 (1981): 437–53.

Ginio, Ruth. "Les enfants africains de la Révolution nationale: La politique vichyssoise de l'enfance et de la jeunesse dans les colonies de l'AOF (1940–1943)." *Revue d'histoire moderne et contemporaine* 49, no. 4 (2002): 132–53.

————. "French Colonial Reading of Ethnographic Research: The Case of the 'Desertion' of the Abron King and Its Aftermath." *Cahiers d'études africaines* 166 (2002): 337–58.

————. " 'Marshal Pétain Spoke to Schoolchildren': Vichy Propaganda in French West Africa, 1940–1943." *International Journal of African Historical Studies* 33, no. 3 (2000): 201–312.

————. "La politique antijuive de Vichy en Afrique occidentale française." *Archives juives* 36, no. 1 (2003): 109–18.

Giolitto, Pierre. *Histoire de la jeunesse sous Vichy*. Paris: Perrin, 1991.

Girardet, Raoul. *L'idée coloniale en France, 1871–1962*. Paris: La table ronde, 1972.

Goerg, Odile. "From Hill Station (Freetown) to Downtown Conakry (First Ward): Comparing French and British Approaches to Segregation in Colonial Cities at the Beginning of the Twentieth Century." *Canadian Journal of African Studies* 32, no. 1 (1998): 1–31.

Gouilly, Alphonse. *L'Islam dans l'Afrique occidentale française*. Paris: Editions Larose, 1952.

Greene, Nathanael. *From Versailles to Vichy: The Third French Republic, 1919–1940*. New York: T. Y. Crowell, 1970.

Grosser, Alfred. *Le crime et la mémoire*. Paris: Flammarion, 1989.

Gueye, Lamine. *Itinéraire africain*. Paris: Présence africaine, 1966.

Guillon, Jean-Marie. "La Légion française des combattants, ou comment comprendre la France de Vichy." *Annales du midi* 116, no. 245 (2004): 5–24.

————. "La philosophie politique de la Révolution nationale." In *Le régime de Vichy et les Français*, ed. Azéma and Bédarida, 167–83.

Gutkind, Peter, Robin Cohen, and Jean Copans, eds. *African Labor History*. Beverly Hills and London: Sage Publications, 1978.

Hale, Dana S. "French Images of Race on Product Trademarks during the Third Republic." In *The Color of Liberty: Histories of Race in France*, ed. Peabody and Stovall, 131–46.

Halls, W. D. *Politics, Society and Christianity in Vichy France*. Oxford: Berg, 1995.

————. *The Youth of Vichy France*. Oxford: Clarendon Press, 1981.

Hamès, Constant. "Le premier exil de Saikh Hamallah et la mémoire hamalliste." In *Le temps des marabouts*, ed. Robinson and Triaud, 337–60.

Hardy, George. *Une conquête morale: L'enseignement en AOF*. Paris: Armand Collin, 1917.

————. *Nos grands problèmes coloniaux*. Paris: A. Colon, 1929.

Hargreaves, John D. *Decolonization in Africa*. London: Longman, 1988.

Harrison, Christopher. *France and Islam in West Africa, 1860–1960*. Cambridge: Cambridge University Press, 1988.

Haut Commissariat de l'Afrique française. *La justice indigène en AOF*. Rufisque, Senegal: Imprimerie du haut commissariat de l'Afrique noire, 1942.

Headrick, Daniel R. *The Tools of Empire: Technology and European Imperialism in the Nineteenth Century*. Oxford: Oxford University Press, 1981.

Headrick, Rita. "African Soldiers in World War II." *Armed Forces and Society* 4, no. 3 (1978): 501–25.

Hitchcock, William I. "Pierre Boisson, French West Africa, and the Postwar *Epuration*: A Case from the Aix Files." *French Historical Studies* 24, no. 2 (2001): 305–41.

Hodge, Errol. *Radio Wars: Truth, Propaganda and the Struggle for Radio Australia*. Cambridge: Cambridge University Press, 1995.

Hodgkin, Thomas. *Nationalism in Colonial Africa*. London: New York University Press, 1956.

Holbrook, Wendell P. "British Propaganda and the Mobilization of the Gold Coast War Effort, 1939–1945." *Journal of African History* 26, no. 4 (1985): 347–61.

Hourani, Albert. *Arabic Thought in the Liberal Age, 1798–1939*. Cambridge: Cambridge University Press, 1983.

Hunwick, John. "Secular Power and Religious Authority in Muslim Society: The Case of Songhay." *Journal of African History* 37, no. 2 (1996): 175–94.

Institut d'histoire du temps présent. *La mémoire des Français: Quarante ans de commémorations de la seconde guerre mondiale*. Paris: CNRS, 1986.

Jackson, Julian. *France: The Dark Years, 1940–1944*. Oxford: Oxford University Press, 2001.

Janheinz, Jahn. *Who's Who in African Literature*. Tëbingen: H. Erdmann, 1972.

Jennings, Eric T. "Reinventing Jeanne: The Iconology of Joan of Arc in Vichy Schoolbooks, 1940–1944." *Journal of Contemporary History* 29, no. 4 (1994): 711–34.

———. "Vichy à Madagascar: La Révolution nationale, l'enseignement et la jeunesse, 1940–1942." *Revue d'histoire moderne et contemporaine* 46, no. 4 (1999): 729–46.

———. *Vichy in the Tropics: Pétain's National Revolution in Madagascar, Guadeloupe, and Indochina, 1940–1944*. Stanford: Stanford University Press, 2001.

Job, Françoise. *Racisme et répression sous Vichy*. Paris: Messene, 1996.

Johnson, G. Wesley. "African Political Activity in French West Africa, 1900–1945." In *History of West Africa*, ed. Crowder and Ajayi, 2: 542–67.

———. "Les élites au Sénégal pendant la période d'indépendance." In *L'Afrique noire française: L'heure des indépendances*, ed.Charles-Robert Ageron and Marc Michel, 25–30. Paris: CNRS, 1992.

———. "The Senegalese Urban Elite, 1900–1945." In *Africa and the West*, ed. Philip Curtin, 139–87. Madison: University of Wisconsin Press, 1972.

Joly, Vincent. "Un aspect de la politique musulmane de la France: L'administration de l'AOF et le pèlerinage de la Mecque (1930–1950)." *Annales du levant* 5 (1992): 39–58.

———. "La mobilisation au Soudan en 1939–1940." *Revue français d'histoire d'outre-mer* 73, no. 272 (1986): 281–302.

————. "La réconciliation de Nioro (Septembre 1937): Un tournant dans la politique musulmane au Soudan français?" In *Le temps des marabouts*, ed. Robinson and Triaud, 361–72.

————. " 'Se defender contre quiconque?' L'effort militaire au Soudan français, juillet 1940-novembre 1942." *Outre-mers* 91, nos. 342–43 (2004): 83–108.

Kalu, O. U. *The History of Christianity in West Africa*. London: Longman, 1980.

Kane, Ousmane. "La Tidjaniyya." In *Les voies d'Allah: Les ordres mystiques dans l'Islam des origines à aujourd'hui*, ed. Alexandre Popovic and Gilles Veinstein, 475–78. Paris: Fayard, 1996.

Kaziende, Léopold. *Souvenirs d'un enfant de la colonisation*. Vol. 4. Porto-Novo: Assouli, 1998.

Kedward, Harry Roderick. *Resistance in Vichy France: A Study of Ideas and Motivation in the Southern Zone, 1940–1942*. Oxford: Oxford University Press, 1978.

————. "Rural France and Resistance." In *France at War: Vichy and the Historians*, ed. Fishman et al., 125–43.

Kelley, Robin D. G. *Race Rebels: Culture, Politics, and the Black Working Class*. New York: Free Press, 1996.

Kelly, Gail P. "Colonialism, Indigenous Society, and School Practices: French West Africa and Indochina, 1918–1938." In *Education and the Colonial Experience*, ed. Philip G. Altbach and Gail P. Kelly, 9–32. New Brunswick NJ: Transaction Books, 1984.

————. *French Colonial Education: Essays on Vietnam and West Africa*. New York: AMS Press, 2000.

Kent, John. *The Internationalization of Colonialism: Britain, France and Black Africa, 1936–1956*. Oxford: Clarendon Press, 1992.

Kingston, Paul J. "A Study in Radio Propaganda Broadcasts in French from North and West African Radio Stations, 8 November 1942–14 December 1942." *Revue d'histoire maghrèbine* 33–34 (1984): 127–41.

Kipre, Pierre. "La place des centres urbains dans l'économie de la Côte d'Ivoire de 1920 à 1930." *Annales universitaires d'Abidjan*, I ser. (Histoire), 3 (1975): 93–120.

Klarsfeld, Serge. *Vichy-Auschwitz*. 2 vols. Paris: Fayard, 1983–85.

Konaté, Abdourahmane. *Le cri du mange-mil: Mémoires d'un prêfet sénégalais*. Paris: L'Harmattan, 1990.

Kouamé, Aka. "Mobilité du travail et formation d'une économie capitaliste périphérique relais: Les migrations de main-d'oeuvre en Côte-d'Ivoire de 1900 à 1960." In *Population, reproduction, sociétés, perspectives et enjeux de démographie sociale*, ed. Dennis D. Cordell et al., 311–27. Montreal: P u De Montreal, 1993.

Kouanda, Assimi. "Marabouts et missionnaires catholiques au Burkina à l'époque coloniale (1900–1947)." In *Le temps des marabouts*, ed. Robinson and Triaud, 33–52.

Kuisel, Richard F. *Capitalism and the State in Modern France*. Cambridge: Cambridge University Press, 1981.

Laborie, Pierre. "1940–1944: Double-Think in France." In *France at War: Vichy and the Historians*, ed. Fishman et al., 181–90.

———. *L'opinion française sous Vichy*. Paris: Seuil, 1990.

Lambert, Michael C. "Elite Ideologies in Francophone West Africa." *Comparative Studies in Society and History* 35, no. 2 (1993): 239–62.

Lanne, Bernard. "Chad, the Chadians and the Second World War, 1939–1945." *Africana Journal* 16 (1991): 311–25.

Lawler, E. Nancy. "The Crossing of the Gyaman to the Cross of Lorraine: Wartime Politics in West Africa, 1941–1942." *African Affairs* (London) 96, no. 382 (1997): 53–72.

———. "Reform and Repression under the Free French: Economic and Political Transformation in the Côte d'Ivoire, 1942–1945." *Africa* (London) 60, no. 1 (1990): 88–110.

———. *Soldats d'infortune: Les tirailleurs ivoiriens de la deuxième guerre mondiale*. Trans. François Manchuelle. Paris: L'Harmattan, 1996.

———. *Soldiers, Airmen, Spies and Whisperers: The Gold Coast in World War II*. Athens: Ohio University Press, 2002.

Layish, Aharon. *Divorce in the Libyan Family*. New York and London: New York University Press, 1991.

Leblond, Marius. "La littérature coloniale et l'avenir de la France." *La mer et l'empire: Série de douze conférences*. ed. Institut maritime et colonial. Paris: 1942.

———. "Notre oeuvre d'outre-mer: La race de Japhet à destin de Prométhée." In *L'évolution de la colonisation*, 6–8. N.p.: n.d.

Le Bon, Gustave. *Lois psychologiques de l'évolution des peuples*. Paris: F. Alcan, 1911.

Lebovics, Herman. *True France: The Wars over Cultural Identity, 1900–1945*. Ithaca and London: Cornell University Press, 1992.

Lemoine, Lucien. *Douta Seck ou la tragédie du roi Christophe*. Paris: Présence africaine, 1993.

Leroy, Olivier. *Raisons et bases de l'union des Français de l'empire*. Tananarive, Madagascar: Imprimerie officielle, 1941.

Levisse-Touzé, Christine. *L'Afrique du nord dans la guerre*. Paris: Albin Michel, 1998.

Levtzion, Nechemia. "Accommodation and Tension between the 'Ulama' and the Political Authorities." *Cahiers d'études africaines* 18, no. 3 (1978): 333–45.

———. *Ancient Ghana and Mali*. London: Methuen, 1973.

———. "Rural and Urban Islam in West Africa: An Introductory Essay." *Asian and African Studies* 20, no. 1 (1986): 7–26.

Levtzion, Nechemia, and Randall L. Pouwels, eds. *The History of Islam in Africa*. Athens: Ohio University Press, 2000.

Loucou, J.-N. "La deuxième guerre mondiale et ses effets en Côte d'Ivoire." *Annales de l'Université d'Abidjan*, I ser., 8 (1980): 183–207.

Lyautey, Pierre. *Pour l'empire français: Action et doctrine.* Vichy: Sequama, 1940.

Lydon, Ghislaine. "Women, Children, and the Popular Front's Missions of Inquiry in French West Africa." In *French Colonial Empire and the Popular Front: Hope and Disillusion,* ed. Chafer and Sackur, 170–87.

Ly-Tall, Madina. *Un Islam militant en Afrique de l'Ouest au 19 siècle: La Tijaniyya de saïku Umar Futiyu contre les pouvoirs traditionnels et la puissance coloniale.* Paris: L'Harmattan, 1991.

Manue, George R. "L'empire, garant de l'avenir français." In *Les empires en marche,* ed. Henri Mathieu, 78–91. Lyon: Editions du comité France-Empire, 1943.

Margairaz, Michel. "L'état et la décision économique: Contraintes, convergences, résistances." In *Le régime de Vichy et les Français,* ed. Azéma and Bédarida, 329–44.

Marrus, Michael R. "French Churches and the Persecution of Jews in France, 1940–1944." In *Judaism and Christianity under the Impact of National Socialism,* ed. Dov Kulka and Paul Mendes-Flohr, 305–26. Jerusalem: The Historical Society of Israel, 1987.

Marrus, Michael R., and Robert O. Paxton. *Vichy France and the Jews.* New York: Basic Books, 1981.

Marseille, Jacques. *Empire colonial et capitalisme français: Histoire d'un divorce.* Paris: Albin Michel, 1984.

Marty, Paul. "La politique indigène du Gouverneur Général Ponty en Afrique occidentale française." *Revue du monde musulman* 31 (1915–16): 1–22.

Maunier, René. "Une citoyenneté d'empire." In *L'évolution de la colonisation,* 5–6.

———. "L'empire français et l'idée de l'empire." *L'empire français et ses ressources: Conférences d'information organisés en février–mars 1942.* L'école supérieure d'organisation professionnelle, Paris, 1942.

———. *L'empire français, propos et projets.* Paris: Ernest Flammarion, 1943.

———. "La politique coloniale positive." *L'empire français et ses ressources: Conférences d'information organisés en février–mars 1942.* L'école supérieure d'organisation professionnelle, Paris, 1942.

Mayeur, Jean-Marie. "Les églises devant la persécution des juifs en France." In *La France et la question juive,* ed. Wellers, Kaspi, and Klarsteld, 147–70.

M'Bokolo, Elikia. "French Colonial Policy in Equatorial Africa in the 1940s and 1950s." In *The Transfer of Power in Africa: Decolonization, 1940–1960,* ed. Gifford and Louis, 173–210.

Meillassoux, Claude. *Urbanization of an African Community.* Seattle and London: University of Washington Press, 1968.

Mercier, Paul. "La vie politique dans les centres urbains du Sénégal: Etude d'une période de transition." *Cahiers internationaux de sociologie* 27 (1959): 55–83.

Michel, Henri. *Vichy: Année 40*. Paris: Laffont, 1966.

Michel, Marc. *L'appel à l'Afrique: Contributions et réactions à l'effort de guerre en A.O.F., 1914–1949*. Paris: Edition de la Sorbonne, 1982.

Monod, Théodore. *L'hippopotame et le philosophe*. Paris: Babel, 2004.

Moody, Joseph N. *French Education since Napoleon*. Syracuse: Syracuse University Press, 1978.

Morgenthau, Ruth S. *Political Parties in French-Speaking Africa*. Oxford: Clarendon, 1964.

Mouralis, Bernard, and Anne Piriou, eds. *Robert Delavignette, savant et politique (1897–1976)*. Paris: Karthala, 2003.

Muel-Dreyfus, Francine. *Vichy et l'éternel féminin*. Paris: Seuil, 1996.

Mumford, W. Bryant. *Africans Learn to Be French*. London: Evans Brothers, 1937.

Ndiaye, Mamadou. *L'enseignement arabo-islamiques au Sénégal*. Istanbul: Centre de recherches sur l'histoire, l'art et la culture islamique, 1985.

Oloruntimehin, Olatunji B. "The Economy of French West Africa between the Two World Wars." *Journal of African Studies* 4, no. 1 (1977): 51–76.

Pacque, Viviana. *Les Bambara*. Paris: PUF, 1954.

Paillard, Jean. *L'empire français de demain*. Paris: IECS, 1943.

Palermo, Lynn E. "Identity under Construction: Representing the Colonies at the Paris *Exposition Universelle* of 1889." In *The Color of Liberty: Histories of Race in France*, ed. Peabody and Stovall, 285–301.

Panter-Brick, Keith. "Independence, French Style." In *Decolonization and African Independence*, ed. Prosser Gifford and Roger Louis, 73–104. New Haven: Yale University Press, 1988.

Paxton, Robert O. *Vichy France: Old Guard and New Order, 1940–1944*. New York: Columbia University Press, 1975.

Peabody, Sue, and Tyler Stovall, eds. *The Color of Liberty: Histories of Race in France*. Durham NC and London: Duke University Press, 2003.

Person, Yves. "French West Africa and Decolonization." In *The Transfer of Power in Africa*, ed. Gifford and Louis, 141–72.

———. "Le Front populaire au Sénégal (Mai 1936–Octobre 1938)." *Mouvement social* 107 (1979): 77–102.

Pétain, Philippe. *Discours aux français, 17 juin 1940–20 août 1944*. Edition établie par Jean-Charles Barbas. Paris: A. Michel, 1989.

Pinardel, François. *La France: Métropole et outre-mer*. Paris: Beauchesne, 1941.

Popovic, Alexandre, and Gilles Veinstein, eds. *Les voies d'Allah: Les ordres mystiques dans l'Islam des origines à aujourd'hui*. Paris: Fayard, 1996.

Quinzaine Impériale. *L'empire, notre meilleure chance*. Lyon: M. Audin, 1942.

Ramognino, Pierre. "Le pétainisme sans Pétain: Révolution nationale et contrôle social en AOF, 1940–1943." *Outre-mers* 91, nos. 342–43 (2004): 65–82.

Ranger, Terence. "The Invention of Tradition in Colonial Africa." In *The Invention of Tradition*, ed. Eric Hobsbaum and Terence Ranger, 211–62. Cambridge: Cambridge University Press, 1983.

Rapley, John. *Ivoirien Capitalism*. Boulder and London: Lynne Rienner Publishers, 1993.

Rasson, Luc. "Vichy and French Fascism: On a Recent Controversy." *Contemporary French Civilization* 11, no. 1 (1987): 53–65.

Raulin, G. de. "L'utilisation des colonies." *La mer et l'empire*. Institut maritime et colonial, Paris, 1942.

René Leclerc, Charles. "L'empire et la France." In *L'évolution de la colonisation*. N.p.: n.d.

Reyss, Nathalie. "L'enseignement au Sénégal au début du XIXe siècle." *La revue des français d'Afrique* (1983–1984): 9–12.

Ricord, Maurice. *Au service de l'empire*. Paris: SECM, 1946.

Rivière, P.-Louis. *A travers l'empire français*. Caen: Imprimerie d'Ozanne, 1943.

Robinson, David. "Beyond Resistance and Collaboration: Amadu Bamba and the Murids of Senegal." *Journal of Religion in Africa* 21, no. 2 (1991): 155–67.

———. *Chiefs and Clerics*. Oxford: Clarendon, 1975.

———. "French 'Islamic' Policy and Practice in Late Nineteenth-Century Senegal." *Journal of African History* 29, no. 3 (1988): 415–35.

———. "Malik Sy: Un intellectuel dans l'ordre colonial au Sénégal." *Islam et sociétés au sud du Sahara* 7 (1993): 183–92.

———. *Paths of Accommodation: Muslim Societies and French Colonial Authorities in Senegal and Mauritania, 1880–1920*. Athens: Ohio University Press, 2000.

Robinson, David, and Louis Triaud, eds. *Le temps des marabouts*. Paris: Karthala, 1997.

Rossignol, Dominique. *Histoire de la propagande en France de 1940 à 1944*. Paris: PUF, 1991.

Rousso, Henri. *Le syndrome de Vichy: De 1944 à nos jours*. Paris: Seuil, 1990.

Rouveroy, E. A. B. van. "Chef coutumier: Un métier difficile." *Politique africaine* 27 (1987): 19–29.

Sabatier, Peggy R. "Did Africans Really Learn to Be French? The Francophone Elite of the Ecole William Ponty." In *Double Impact*, ed. G. Wesley Johnson, 179–87. Westport CT: Greenwood Press, 1985.

———. "'Elite' Education in French West Africa: The Era of Limits, 1903–1945." *International Journal of African Historical Studies* 11, no. 2 (1978): 247–66.

Saint-Exupéry, Antoine de. *Le petit prince*. Paris: Gallimard, 1946.

Samb, Amar. "L'éducation islamique au Sénégal." *Notes africaines* (1972): 97–103.

Saussure, Léopold de. *Psychologie de la colonisation française dans ses rapports avec les sociétés indigènes*. Paris: F. Alcan, 1899.

Savadogo, Boukary. "La communauté 'Yacouba Sylla' et ses rapports avec la Tijâniyya hamawiyy." In *La Tijâniyya: Une confrérie musulmane à la conquête de l'Afrique*, ed. Jean-Louis Triaud and David Robinson, 269–87. Paris: Karthala, 2000.

Senghor, Léopold Sédar. O*Euvre poétique*. Paris: Seuil, 1990.

———. *Poémes*. Paris: Seuil, 1964.

Shaka, Femi Okiremuete. "Vichy Dakar and the Other Story of French Colonial Stewardship in Africa: Ousmane Sembène and Thierno Faty Sow's Camp de Thiaroye." *Research in African Literatures* 26, no. 3 (1995): 67–77.

Siegfried, André. *De la IIIe à la IVe République*. Paris: B. Grasset, 1956.

Singer, Claude. *Vichy, l'université et les juifs*. Paris: Les belles lettres, 1992.

Skinner, Elliott P. "The Changing Status of the 'Emperor of the Mossi' under Colonial Rule and since Independence." In *West African Chiefs*, ed. Crowder and Ikime, 98–123.

Smyth, Rosaleen. "Britain's African Colonies and the British Propaganda during the Second World War." *Journal of Imperial and Commonwealth History* 14, no. 1 (1985): 65–82.

Soyinka, Wole. *The Burden of Memory, the Muse of Forgiveness*. Oxford: Oxford University Press, 1999.

Sternhell, Zeev. *Ni droite, ni gauche: L'idéologie fasciste en France*. Paris: Seuil, 1983.

Stoler, Ann Laura, and Frederick Cooper. "Between Metropole and Colony: Rethinking a Research Agenda." In *Tensions of Empire: Colonial Cultures in a Bourgeois World*, ed. Ann Laura Stoler and Frederick Cooper, 4–56. Berkeley: University of California Press, 1997.

Strebel, Elizabeth. "Vichy Cinema and Propaganda." In *Film and Radio Propaganda in World War II*, ed. K. R. M. Short, 271–89. London and Canberra: Croom Helm, 1983.

Suret-Canale, Jean. *Afrique noire*. Vol. 2, *L'ère coloniale 1900–1945*. Paris: Editions sociales, 1964.

———. "The French West African Railway Workers' Strike, 1947–1948." In *African Labor History*, ed. Gutkind, Cohen, and Copans, 129–51.

Sweets, John F. *Choices in Vichy France: The French under Nazi Occupation*. Oxford: Oxford University Press, 1986.

Taylor, Richard. *Film Propaganda: Soviet Russia and Nazi Germany*. 2d ed. London: Palgrave Macmillan, 1998.

Thomas, Martin, "The Anglo-French Divorce over West Africa and the Limitations of Strategic Planning, June–December 1940." *Diplomacy and Statecraft* 6, no. 1 (1995): 252–78.

———. *The French Empire at War, 1940–1945*. Manchester: Manchester University Press, 1998.

———. "The Vichy Government and French Colonial Prisoners of War, 1940–1944." *French Historical Studies* 25, no. 4 (2002): 657–92.

Thompson, Virginia, and Richard Adloff. "French Economic Policy in Tropical Africa." In *Colonialism in Africa, 1870–1960*, ed. Peter Duignan and Lewis Henry Gann, 4: 127–64. Cambridge: Cambridge University Press, 1969.

———. *French West Africa*. London: G. Allen, 1958.

Tobie, Jacques, Catherine Coquery-Vidrovitch, and Charles-Robert Ageron. *Histoire de la France coloniale*. Vol. 2. Paris: A. Colin, 1990.

Traoré, Alioune. *Islam et colonisation en Afrique: Cheikh Hamahoulla, homme de foi et résistant*. Paris: Maisonneuve et Larose, 1983.

Triaud, Jean-Louis. "L'Afrique occidentale et centrale." In *Les voies d'Allah*, ed. Popovic and Veinstein, 417–27.

Trimingham, Spencer. *The Sufi Orders in Islam*. Oxford: Oxford University Press, 1971.

Vaillant, Janet G. *Black, French and African: A Life of Léopold Sédar Senghor*. Cambridge and London: Harvard University Press, 1990.

van Beusekom, Monica M. "Disjuncture in Theory and Practice: Making Sense of Change in Agricultural Development at the Office du Niger, 1920–1960." *Journal of African History* 41, no. 1 (2000): 79–99.

Vaugan, Megan. "Colonial Discourse and African History; or, Has Postmodernism Passed Us By?" *Social Dynamics* 20, no. 2 (1994): 1–23.

Veillon, Dominique. "The Resistance and Vichy." In *France at War: Vichy and the Historians*, ed. Fishman et al., 161–77.

Viard, René. *L'empire et nos destins*. Paris: Sorlot, 1942.

Vidal-Naquet, Pierre. *Les juifs, la mémoire et le présent*. Paris: Points essais, 1981.

Wallerstein, Immanuel. *Africa: The Politics of Independence*. New York: Vintage Books, 1961.

———. "Elites in French-Speaking West Africa: The Social Basis of Ideas." *Journal of Modern African Studies* 3, no. 1 (1965): 1–33.

———. *The Road to Independence: Ghana and the Ivory Coast*. Paris: Mouton and Co., 1964.

Warner, Marina. *Joan of Arc: The Image of Female Heroism*. London: Weidenfeld and Nicolson, 1981.

Weisberg, Richard H. *Vichy Law and the Holocaust in France*. New York: New York University Press, 1996.

Wellers, Georges, André Kaspi, and Serge Klarsteld, eds. *La France et la question juive*. Actes de colloque du centre de documentation juive contemporaine. Paris: S. Messinger, 1981.

Wells, Paul. "Dustbins, Democracy and Defence: Halas and Batchelor and the Animated Film in Britain, 1940–1947." In *War Culture: Social Change and Changing Experience in World War II*, ed. Pat Kirkham and David Thoms, 64–72. London: Lawrence and Wishart, 1995.

Wright, Gordon. *France in Modern Times*. Chicago and London: Rand McNally, 1960.

Yao, Kouassi. "La Côte d'Ivoire pendant la seconde guerre mondiale: Entre fidélité et rupture (1939–1945)." *Africa* (Rome) 48, no. 4 (1993): 549–76.

Zarcone, T. "La Qadiriyya." In *Les voies d'Allah*, ed. Popovic and Veinstein, 461–67.

Zolberg, Aristide R. *One-Party Government in the Ivory Coast*. Princeton: Princeton University Press, 1969.

Zucarelli, François. *La vie politique sénégalaise, 1940–1988*. Paris: Publications de Cheam, 1988.

IN THE FRANCE OVERSEAS SERIES

The French Navy and the Seven Years' War
By Jonathan R. Dull

French Colonialism Unmasked
The Vichy Years in French West Africa
By Ruth Ginio

Praise for *The EarthKeeper*

"What makes Adam's story so compelling is not only the skill with which it is told, or the details of his many daring (and often amusing) adventures—or even his willingness to bare his naked psyche to the judgment of his readers. The biggest reason why his story is so important is that it serves as a perfect mirror for our times...There are many guides and resources to assist those who are now stepping onto the path. This book is such a guide, and a brilliant one!"

—Alberto Villoldo, Ph.D., founder, The Four Winds Society, and author of *Shaman, Healer, Sage*

"*The Earthkeeper* is an authentic revealing story about the inner world of the human psyche. Adam C. Hall illustrates how intention, fearlessness and love can awaken the heart to the joy of being."

—Deborah Rozman, Ph.D., President and CEO, HeartMath Inc.

"*The Earthkeeper* is honest and beautifully written. It is truly insightful and touching. This is a remarkable testament to the power and creativity of Spirit and how we are called toward truth and freedom."

—Rick Jarow, Ph.D., Professor, Vassar University, and author of *The Alchemy of Abundance*

"Adam C. Hall puts forth a microcosmic model of how our overly materialistic world, with its destructive blindness, really could turn itself around and become spiritually and emotionally aware, with a civilization to match. True to his name, Adam is like an archetypal 'first man' of the Age of Aquarius, with all the ups and downs, clarity and confusion, humor and humanness, that such a dawning engenders."

—Lyn Birkbeck, astrologer and author of *Understanding the Future*

"Adam C. Hall was living a life that made no sense. When he finally realized his true purpose on earth, it was almost too late. This is an entertaining and exciting read. Sometimes it is hard to believe that it is all true, but it is."

—Victor Villasenor, *New York Times* best-selling author of *Rain of Gold*

" *The EarthKeeper* is a rite of passage that turns a contemporary businessman's life, otherwise headed towards self-ruin and oblivion, into that of a gentle, wise guardian of the Earth. This courageously-conveyed tale should give every would-be Gordon Gekko ample pause, if not sufficient motivation to turn greed into selfless service, hedonism into a love of nature. Adam C Hall has written a tale of environmental redemption in a world more accustomed to sleep-walking and indifference."

—Michael Tobias, Ph.D., ecologist, filmmaker, and author of *Voice of the Planet*

"In a time of rampant, materialistic consumption, Adam C. Hall's honest tale inspires the possibility of a different world. His encounters with ancient truths and reconnection with the sacred provide medicine for what ails our earth and human family."

—John Quigley, producer, artist, activist

"I am a long-time witness to the evolution of Adam C. Hall's true primal nature. *The EarthKeeper* is an outstanding testament to how each of us can survive and thrive in dire circumstances. Our remote ancestors—original EarthKeepers—were able to cultivate their primal power harmoniously with the environment. Today, many have lost this vital connection. This book offers renewed hope to all."

—Mark Sisson, best-selling author of *Primal Blueprint* and publisher of *Marksdailyapple.com*